THE PERFECT CHRISTIAN

THE PERFECT CHRISTIAN

How Sinners Like Us Can Be More Like Jesus

TONY EVANS

WORD PUBLISHING

NASHVILLE

A Thomas Nelson Company

THE PERFECT CHRISTIAN

Unless otherwise indicated, Scripture quotations are from *The New American Standard Bible*, copyright 1960, 1962, 1963, 1968, 1971, 1972, 1973, 1975, by The Lockman Foundation and used by permission.

Published in association with Sealy M. Yates, Literary Agent, Orange, California.

Library of Congress Cataloging-in-Publication Data

Evans, Anthony T.
    The perfect Christian: how sinners like us can be more like Jesus / by
Tony Evans.
        p. cm.
    Includes index.
    ISBN 0-8499-1505-8 (HC)
    1. Christian life. I. Title.
BV4501.2.E8585 1998
248.4—dc21

98-31358
CIP

Printed in the United States of America.
98 99 00 01 02 03 04 05 BVG 9 8 7 6 5 4 3 2 1

This book is gratefully dedicated to
my good friend
Dr. Joseph M. Stowell, III,
president of the Moody Bible Institute,
whose passionate and faithful pursuit of God
has greatly encouraged and inspired me.

Contents

With Gratitude

I want to express my gratitude to the people who helped shape this book and bring it into being. Mr. Joey Paul and the staff at Word Publishing provided counsel, encouragement, and helpful suggestions at each stage; and my editor and good friend Philip Rawley put my ideas and words into clear literary style.

Introduction

A pastor once asked his congregation, "Does anyone here know any perfect people?"

A short man in the rear of the auditorium stood up and shouted, "Yes, my wife's first husband!" This man had learned from experience how hard it is to measure up to a perfect standard.

Obviously, his situation was more a matter of a selective memory than objective perfection. But that's not the case with our God. When He measures us against the standard of His perfection, our imperfections are glaring—and yet God does not reduce His standard or lower His expectations.

Jesus made this quite clear when He said, "You are to be perfect, as your heavenly Father is perfect" (Matt. 5:48). Clearly, God's holiness is nonnegotiable. He calls us to live up to His standard; He never lowers Himself to ours.

This setup is a far cry from the spirit of the present age. You and I are witnessing firsthand the "dumbing down" of righteousness. Not only has the secular society lost its moral compass due to the erosion of any sense of absolute truth, but we Christians are rapidly descending the ladder of holiness rather than ascending the mountain of godliness to be near to and be like our perfect God.

Day in and day out we are bombarded by the standards of this ungodly age, which dupe us into thinking that being a tad better than the world somehow makes us acceptable to God.

The reality, however, is that God in His absolute holiness is our standard, not the world in its fallenness. Yet we, along with our mates, children, relatives, friends, and other fellow Christians, are falling prey to this softer, easier, and reduced definition of perfection.

That's why I have written this book. I want to call believers back to God's demand for perfection, a demand based on His standard alone. Leaning heavily on the no-nonsense, in-your-face teaching of the apostle James, the half brother of Jesus, I will join him in calling God's people to respond to His demand for perfection.

James makes God's goal plain: "That you may be perfect and complete, lacking in nothing" (1:4). He wants us to grow up, to become mature, to be sanctified, to become more like Jesus. My goal in this book is to prick the conscience of dull, defeated, or delinquent Christians who want to get their spiritual lives back on the right road. But this book is also designed to help those who are already seeking the Lord to know where they stand spiritually and to encourage them to keep on keepin' on in their pursuit of godly perfection.

God's call to perfection, however, creates a dilemma for His children, for the Bible clearly teaches that perfection is not possible in this life (see 1 John 1:8, 10). Why would God give us a standard we can never meet?

But that is precisely the point. God calls us to pursue His perfect standard of righteousness. As we do so, He inches us toward God-like-ness (godliness) day by day, week by week, month by month, and year by year. Furthermore, as we pursue godly perfection, we find ourselves exposed to our own imperfections and needing to turn to God for cleansing. Also, when we live in the light of God's perfection, we begin climbing to a new spiritual level, hating how unlike Him we are and finding an ever-greater passion for being conformed to His perfect image.

In these pages I want to confront you with the reality of your imperfections and then challenge you to march in a new direction in keeping with the perfect demands of our loving heavenly Father.

This is a book not only about facts but about function; evidence, not esoterics; walk, not just talk; production, not just profession; demonstration, not just declaration; duty, not just doctrine; and commitment, not just conversation.

It is my hope that, by the time you finish reading this book and working through the after-chapter applications, you will be ready to do whatever it takes to become a perfect Christian and, in the process, discover a new level of spiritual life, power, and victory.

Although the pursuit of perfection won't produce absolute perfection in your life, you will grow tremendously in your faith when you make perfection your goal. So have a seat and fasten your seat belt. It's time to get busy.

Tony Evans
Dallas, Texas

Chapter 1

How to Withstand Trials

So you want to be more like Jesus? That's great, because that's what Jesus Christ wants for you! "Be perfect," He commands, "as your heavenly Father is perfect" (Matt. 5:48). Let's get started on the process!

I clearly remember, as a boy, listening to the radio. From time to time the normal programming would be interrupted by the announcement that the station was going to test the emergency broadcasting system. Then I would hear a loud, annoying noise for thirty or sixty seconds.

I used to hate those tests because they always seemed to come at the worst time, just when you didn't want the programming interrupted. And since there was never any advance warning that the test was coming, there wasn't any way you could avoid it. The station just broke in and did its test.

The troubles of life are like that. They often come with no warning—just the announcement, "This is a test." There's nothing to warn you that the doctor is going to come back with a bad report or that it's layoff time. Life's tests just show up at the most inopportune times.

In this chapter I want us to see why God puts trials in the path of His children. The first thing we need to recognize is the reality of trials.

The Reality of Trials

We see throughout Scripture that trials are an inevitable reality in life, and we read imperatives like "Consider it all joy, my brethren, when you encounter various trials" (James 1:2).

The Inevitability of Trials

Notice the Bible does not say *if* you encounter trials; it talks instead about *when* they come. Trials are inescapable. Job said, "Man is born for trouble, as sparks fly upward" (5:7). The only way to exit trouble is to exit life. Jesus said, "In the world you have tribulation" (John 16:33). You can bank on it.

Anyone who tells you, "Come to Christ and leave all your troubles behind" is either intentionally lying to you or has not read the Bible very thoroughly.

But notice something else here. Trials are those difficulties we run into as an inevitable part of life, not necessarily the problems we create for ourselves. Those kinds of problems are called sin, and we'll deal with those in a later chapter.

So if you are going through a tough time right now, don't be surprised. If you have just exited a trial, don't be shocked when the next one arrives. They come with living in an imperfect world.

Multicolored Trials

The Greek word used for *trials* here has to do with trouble, tribulation, and difficulties. It's a fairly broad word that can be applied to any number of things. The word literally means "multicolored"—as in blue Monday or pink slip.

We all know the trials that come in the "color" called physical. It may be the bad news from the doctor alluded to above or a nagging physical problem that colors our days—something wrong with the body that just won't go away.

Trials also come in the "color" called emotional. An emotional trial may be something that plagues the mind and heart, a past event you can't forget. Emotional trials also come in the form of discouragement or depression, a darkness of the mind that can color your days gray.

Then there are the financial trials—things like the pink slip that signals the end of a job or red ink that shows you have more bills to pay than resources to pay them. If you have ever been passed over for a promotion you had hoped to get or denied a pay raise you felt you deserved, you know how financially related trials can press in on a life.

Family trials also fit under this heading. The death of a loved one or a child who is causing you grief can certainly darken your days. Marital misunderstandings and parental pain are high on most people's lists of painful family trials.

This is hardly a catalog of every possible trial you and I can face, but you get the idea. Trials come in a multitude of colors, shapes, and sizes. So since we can't avoid them, what should we do with them?

The Reason for Trials

The Bible doesn't shy away from answering that question. God is very open about why He puts trials in our path. In fact, He says you can know why He puts trials in your life.

Why is knowing something about the reason for our trials critical? Because if you are facing a trial and don't know what's going on—if you cannot connect your experience with biblical data—you will be discouraged and overwhelmed by your trial rather than "consider[ing] it all joy" (James 1:2). That joy comes when, in the midst of trials, you realize God is up to something with you! And that realization is the key to overcoming trials.

See, the problem is not so much that we undergo trials. The problem is that we undergo trials and don't know why. Now I'm not suggesting that you can know everything God knows about why your problem has come. But you can know that your trials come for a purpose, which can make the difference between you being on top of your trials and your trials being on top of you.

The knowledge about the purpose that God has for us is crucial because what you know impacts how you feel. When you know what God wants you to know, you can react differently from the way you would if you were totally in the dark.

So what can we know about life's trials? God wants us to have three important pieces of knowledge.

To Test Your Testimony

The first thing God wants you to know is that He places trials in your path to test your faith. When you go through hard times, God is putting your faith on the witness stand.

Untested faith is no better than untested love. Anyone can say, "I love you" on a moonlit night with soft music playing in a fine restaurant. But the test of that love comes in the daylight when things don't look so rosy.

Remember, God could have stopped that trial from getting to you. He could have taken it out of your path so you wouldn't encounter it. God does block an awful lot, in fact. We won't know until heaven how often God protected us from the junk Satan tried to throw in our path.

The point is that when God allows a trial to reach us, He does so for a specific purpose. He wants us to know by firsthand experience something He knows—that faith is strengthened by testing.

Trials also test our heart and reveal what is there. We wouldn't know where we are weak and need to fortify ourselves if our faith were never tested. We wouldn't know what impurities need to be removed from our lives if the fire of trials didn't reveal them.

Trials are designed to call your faith to the witness stand to validate in experience what you declare that you believe. Trials bring you to the point where your faith stands the test, no matter how hot the fire.

The apostle Peter wrote that you and I are "protected by the power of God" in terms of our eternal salvation. But in the meantime, we are "distressed by various trials, that the proof of [our] faith . . . may be found to result in praise and glory and honor at the revelation of Jesus Christ" (1 Pet. 1:6–7).

Now let me tell you something about God's testing. I'm sure you remember what it was like to be tested in school. A good teacher only tests students on information that has already been taught. A good teacher also wants the students to pass the test.

So if you are going through a trial, God has already supplied you with the data necessary to pass the test. And His desire is that you pass the test of this trial so you can graduate to the next level of spiritual maturity.

You may protest, "But I can't remember everything I've been taught." Then you need to do what you did in school and review what God has been teaching you. That's where the spiritual disciplines of prayer, Bible study, and fellowship with the body of Christ come into play.

As God's students, we are responsible for passing the tests He gives us. The reason some of us are still at our desks taking the test, while the other students have already finished and left the room, is that we haven't passed yet. If God has you in a test, He will not let you out of it until you score a passing grade. The test will end when your faith has been tried and proven.

Want a good example of someone passing the test? In the midst of his painful mess, Job declared of God, "Though He slay me, I will hope in Him" (13:15). Job's faith was tested by severe fire, and he passed the test.

Now don't get me wrong. This doesn't mean you have to pretend that a trial doesn't hurt. Job was suffering extreme emotional, spiritual, and physical pain. He didn't just apply the power of positive thinking and say, "This doesn't hurt." He admitted his pain, but he still passed the test of faith.

To Increase Your Endurance

A second reason for trials is to increase our endurance (James 1:3). Again, it's an issue of maturing our faith.

The word *endurance* here is made up of two Greek words that mean "to remain under," to stay put in a trial until its purpose has been accomplished.

We are to submit to God's trials the way a patient submits to a surgeon. As you may know, facing surgery can be pretty scary. A nurse comes into your hospital room to prep you and take your vital signs. Then the orderlies roll you onto another bed to wheel you down to the operating room.

There you are, staring up at the lights, knowing you are about to be knocked out by an anesthetic. Next to you are all these instruments designed to cut you open. People are whispering around you.

Despite all of this, you don't jump off the table and run from the operating room. Why? Because you know you must stay put through this trial if the desired result—your restored health—is to be accomplished.

So the Bible says that we should not run from trials. Instead, we are to run *in* them to develop our endurance. Let me add here that you don't need to run *to* trials either. Some people actually seem to enjoy suffering. They look for trouble. But you don't need to run toward trials. They'll come running to you.

Recently, I got a painful, firsthand lesson in the importance of hanging in there during trials. I decided to start getting up early and going to the gym again.

So I began a weightlifting program that first day—curls, bench presses, the whole bit. Twenty-four hours later, I was in a trial! I couldn't walk. I was in so much pain that my wife, Lois, had to button my shirt.

Now I can assure you, I wanted to run from that trial. I remember thinking, *I don't have to go through all this pain and work. I need the extra hour of sleep anyway.* I rejected the thought of going back to the gym.

But through the encouragement of a friend who was working out with me, I went back and lifted more weights. I struggled as I felt the pain. But my friend reminded me, "Keep lifting because, as you work your way through the pain, it will subside and you'll start to develop your muscles. But if you quit now and then ever decide to start again, you'll have to go through the pain all over again."

Weight training relies on resistance to help muscles grow. In the trials of life, God puts weights on you and says, "Keep lifting. Don't quit even though it will hurt for a while." If you keep on pumping the weight, pretty soon you're going to see spiritual muscle appear where flab had been before.

To Achieve Your Spiritual Maturity

Why does God test our faith in order to increase our endurance? So that "endurance [can] have its perfect result, that you may be perfect and complete, lacking in nothing" (James 1:4).

God's goal for your trials is your growth into spiritual adulthood. That won't happen without some pain, sweat, and effort. Imagine a young person announcing, "I want to be a physician, but I don't want to spend all those years in medical school!"

You and I may chuckle at a comment like that. But we do something similar in the spiritual realm when all we can think of is getting out from under our trials as quickly as possible and avoiding future trials. God wants to mature us, not just make us comfortable.

When a butterfly is ready to leave the cocoon, it has to fight its way out. If you open the cocoon to help the butterfly get out, you have doomed that butterfly because it needs that struggle to strengthen its wings so it can fly.

See, God is too kind and too wise to allow us to remain in spiritual immaturity, whining whenever things don't go our way and demanding what we want when we want it. His goal is that we might "become conformed to the image of His Son" (Rom. 8:29)—and He will not be satisfied until we get there.

I'm told that when a goldsmith in biblical times tested and refined gold, he would keep purifying it until he could see his face in the gold. In the same way, God Almighty will test you until He sees Jesus Christ in you when He looks at you. When you look like Christ, God knows you have come through the fire.

The Bible says that we are to hang in there with God, whatever the trial, "until we all attain . . . to a mature man, to the measure of the stature which belongs to the fulness of Christ" (Eph. 4:13).

I have a good illustration of this verse from the Evans house. My son Jonathan, the youngest of our four children, spent years wanting to be the tallest person in the family. When he got close to Anthony, our oldest son, Jonathan wanted to measure himself against Anthony every day.

Then the day came when Jonathan was taller than Anthony. He

was bragging all over the house, so I told him, "Don't brag. You may be taller than Anthony, but I'm still the tallest one in this family."

So every week he'd come and say, "Let's stand back-to-back, Dad." We would stand back-to-back, and I would say, "You're not there yet."

But then the day came when Jonathan hit six-foot, one-and-a-half inches. He had outgrown me. He would pass me in the hall at home and say with a smile, "Hey, Shorty."

God says, "I want to make you as tall as Christ, not as tall as your neighbor or your spouse." So don't go around measuring yourself against other people or putting your trials back-to-back against theirs, because other people are not the measure. Jesus Christ is. When you can start measuring up to Him—comparatively speaking—then you know you are getting there.

The Response to Trials

So God is testing our faith to build up our spiritual endurance in order that we might become mature in Christ. This means our spiritual resources—not our natural resources—take us through trials. Since that's true, what should be our response? James has three "how-to" tips for us.

Display Some Joy

How should we respond to trials? James first says, "With joy!" (see 1:2). When trials come, instead of getting mad, get glad because you know that God is up to something good in your life.

Now let me repeat the caution I shared earlier. This command does not mean you have to hide the pain of a trial or pretend the pain feels good. The Bible does not say we need to *feel* joyful during the trial, but to *consider* that trial all joy.

The Greek word for *consider* is an accounting term that means "to evaluate." Accountants add up the numbers to make the balance sheet come out right. Well, sometimes our trials don't add up from a human standpoint. They don't seem to make sense; the balance sheet seems to be off.

God tells us to put away our human calculator and use His. He wants us to evaluate our trials from the standpoint of joy. That means you say, "God, I know You're at work here. I don't know all that You want to do in this trial, but I know You allowed it for my good. So rather than complaining, I'm going to praise You in this situation for what You are going to accomplish in me."

That's using God's accounting system. This is so important because your outlook determines your outcome. Your attitude determines your actions. This is not about feeling; it's about accounting. We're talking about a joy that's a decision of the will.

When you are in the middle of a trial, you don't want your emotions to dictate your actions for the same reason a truck driver on the highway doesn't want his cargo to dictate the ride. When that cargo starts shifting and sliding back and forth, the driver soon has a truck that is out of control, swerving back and forth.

A lot of us are like that truck in our Christian lives. Our feelings swing us back and forth and take us where they want to go, instead of where we need to go. So even though you may not be particularly happy about the circumstances you're in at the moment, you can make a decision that you will be joyful because of what you know.

Remember, happiness is circumstantially driven. It depends on what happens. But joy is not related to circumstances; it is a decision.

Why is it important to be joyful in trials? Because if you aren't, then a "root of bitterness" (Heb. 12:15) can spring up and spoil your walk with Christ.

When that happens, you lose the provision of grace, which is God's fuel supply to take you through anything He may give you. God gives greater grace in trials, but you nullify that grace when you react with anger or bitterness to your trial.

Jesus is our great example here. The Bible says He endured the cross because He foresaw the joy of redeeming mankind (Heb. 12:2). Jesus wasn't happy about going to the cross. He prayed for His cup of suffering to pass if there was any way it could.

But Jesus was joyful because He was accomplishing His Father's will by redeeming us from sin. He was joyful because He knew that the Resurrection was coming and that He was going to be enthroned as King of kings and Lord of lords. Jesus was joyful about Easter Sunday morning, not Good Friday afternoon.

"But that's Jesus," you say. "I'm just a human being." OK, let's find out what a human being thought about a severe trial. I'm thinking of Paul's thorn in the flesh (2 Cor. 12:7).

Three times Paul asked God to remove his trial, and three times God said no because He had a greater purpose for Paul. He wanted Paul to learn the sufficiency of His grace, to realize that God's power is perfected in human weakness (v. 9).

So Paul counted his trial as joy. He was able to say, "Most gladly, therefore, I will rather boast about my weaknesses, that the power of Christ may dwell in me. Therefore I am well content with weaknesses" (vv. 9–10). Paul wasn't glad for the pain but for the power of God he knew as he experienced that pain.

Please notice the word *all*. "Consider it all joy," the Word says— not *some* joy or *partial* joy, but *all* joy.

Think of a mother-to-be in labor. She is experiencing plenty of pain, but hers is a joyful pain because she is anticipating a joyful result, the birth of her baby. God is using our trials to bring about the joyful result of Christlike maturity, so we can be joyful in the meantime.

Ask for Wisdom

How are we to overcome trials? The second thing God urges us to do in the face of trials is ask for His help. James tells us to go to God for wisdom, and He will freely and generously give us His wisdom (1:5).

What is the wisdom we need to ask God for? Wisdom to know how to handle the paradox of trials.

In case you didn't notice earlier, there is a real paradox in the Bible's advice about trials. There you are in a situation that is stressful and perhaps even physically painful, yet you're supposed to be joyful in the middle of it all. That seems like a contradiction. How can you "consider it all joy" when you're hurting?

You can't—on your own. So you go to God and pray, "Lord, make sense of this for me. I know You have something good in this for me. Help me to see Your plan and Your hand in this trial. Show me how to respond to get the most out of what You want for me right now." That's seeking God's wisdom.

If you do this, will everything suddenly become perfectly clear and will you see exactly why God has you in this position? No, the Bible never promises that.

But the Bible does promise something better—a generous supply of God's wisdom in answer to your prayer. You also have the blessing of knowing that God is bigger than your problems, and He knows how to deliver you.

One more thing. While you're praying, don't forget the wisdom for trials God has already given you in His Word. Look, for instance, at something Paul says:

> No temptation has overtaken you but such as is common to man; and God is faithful, who will not allow you to be tempted beyond what you are able, but with the temptation will provide the way of escape also, that you may be able to endure it (1 Cor. 10:13).

Here's a great word of encouragement and help. Whatever you are facing right now, you are not the only one who has ever faced it. Other people in the body of Christ have been there and have seen God bring them through. You need to find those people and stay close to them—the second "how-to" element for overcoming trials.

You and I can't afford to be "Lone Ranger" Christians. When you hide out and try to handle your trials alone, you can start feeling that God is picking on you, singling out you alone for hard trials.

But when you fellowship in the body of Christ, you realize God isn't picking on you. A lot of His people have a lot of hard-earned wisdom to share with you.

Aren't you glad God limits your load to what you can bear and then gives you other people to help you bear it? One thing I like about weightlifting is that I don't do it by myself. As I'm straining to do those final repetitions, I start grunting and groaning as the weight starts to become more than I can bear.

If I were alone at that point, I would probably let the weight drop and crush me. But because my friend is standing over me, he can grab that bar in the nick of time and lighten the load by helping me make my last repetition. Then, when I can't hold the weights any longer, he takes them out of my hands and puts them back on the rack.

That's grace. That's what God does for us in trials. When your arms are trembling, when you're grunting and groaning and straining, when you feel like the weight is going to crush you, God steps in and lifts it off of you.

So pray for God's wisdom. But don't pray halfheartedly, James says:

> But let him ask in faith without any doubting, for the one who doubts is like the surf of the sea driven and tossed by the wind. For let not that man expect that he will receive anything from the Lord, being a double-minded man, unstable in all his ways. (1:6–8)

The double-minded person is the split-personality Christian, the one who can't make up his mind. He is like the bumper sticker that says, "I'm not indecisive, am I?"

There are three ways to approach trials. Faith says yes; unbelief says no; doubt says yes and no at the same time. Double-minded Christians want to do it their way, yet they still want God to do it His way. They want some of God and some of themselves.

But God isn't going to play that game. He wants the whole ball of wax. He is saying, "If you are going to bring your need to Me, then you have to turn it all over to Me. You can't have it both ways."

Many times people who come to me for counseling will say, "Pray that I'll do what God wants me to do." Then after we pray and I show them from the Word what God wants in their situation, they still go out and do what they want to do anyway.

God has a strong word for people like that: "Don't expect anything from Me."

Now you see why more of us aren't getting more answers to our prayers. That mate who is messing you over may just be God's test in your life to take you to the next level of spiritual maturity. But if you can't make up your mind whether your marriage is worth the struggle any longer, then you short-circuit God's purpose.

Every time I read about being "driven and tossed by the wind," I remember a cruise Lois and I took to Alaska with some friends from our national ministry. We ran into a horrific storm with waves thirty-five feet high.

This huge cruise ship was tossing back and forth. Food was flying off the table. The stewards were crouching in a corner. People were getting sick all over the place. It was total pandemonium.

In the middle of all this, Lois got a little upset. She was wondering why the captain would take us into this storm since the ship had all this fancy technology on board to detect and avoid bad weather.

So Lois picked up the phone and said, "I want to speak to the captain." She wanted to find out what was going on. The person who answered said the captain wasn't available. But he sent back a message to Lois in which he said basically two things.

His first message was, "You can go back to your cabin and go to sleep because I'm going to be at the helm while you're sleeping, and there is no use for both of us to stay up." And his second message was, "This ship was built with these kinds of storms in mind. It's seaworthy, so you don't have to worry."

We went on to bed that night, and sure enough, the next morning the sea was calm, and we were still afloat.

God says, "You go to sleep, and I'll stay awake. I planned your life with this storm in mind. You will get through it because I'm at the helm." That kind of comfort and reassurance comes when you seek wisdom from God for your trial. Remember, God is bigger than your trial.

Give God Praise

What else can we do to overcome trials? The third piece of sound "how-to" advice James has for us in our trials is to give God praise:

> But let the brother of humble circumstances glory in his high position; and let the rich man glory in his humiliation, because like flowering grass he will pass away. For the sun rises with a scorching wind, and withers the grass; and its flower falls off, and the

beauty of its appearance is destroyed; so too the rich man in the midst of his pursuits will fade away. (1:9–11)

You are to give glory to God in the midst of your trial. Then the Bible names two very common kinds of trials: the poor person who doesn't have the money he needs to meet his trial and the rich person who runs into something that money can't buy his way out of.

Most of us fall into one of these two categories. If you're in the first category, you can praise God because in Him, you have a resource far beyond what money can buy. I've been there, and I suspect you have, too.

The poor person can still say, "Lord, right now I've run out of money, but I want to thank You anyway. I thank You for my health. I thank You for the way You have already taken care of me. Thank You for food on the table and a roof over my head. Thank You that I have clothes on my back. Even in my poverty, I want to praise You."

What about the rich person who has a health problem money can't cure or a wayward child whom money can't bring back home? God says to this person, "Glory in your humility."

In other words, the rich person can say, "Lord, I praise You that this trial is teaching me I can't just pull out the MasterCard or Visa to fix everything. I praise You that You are teaching me to lean on Jesus alone."

So whether you are poor or rich, when the trial comes, give glory to God. He will lift you to a high position at the right time, and He will humble you when you need humbling. Give Him praise either way because He knows exactly what you need.

God causes us to come into conflict with earthly things that we might see eternal things more clearly. And He will keep the trial there until we cry, "Uncle!"

The Reward for Trials

Here's the good part, the spiritual payoff for handling your trials the way God wants you to handle them.

When you hang in there and bear the trial, you get the reward. The Bible teaches, "Blessed is a man who perseveres under trial; for once he has been approved, he will receive the crown of life, which the Lord has promised to those who love Him" (James 1:12).

This is sweet. When the trial is finished and the lesson has been learned, then God's approval comes. In school, when you have finished all the classes and passed all the tests, you get to wear a special hat on your head and walk across the stage to receive your prize—your diploma—from the president of the school.

God's reward for the person who endures his trials is the crown of life, the reward of kingly glory and recognition. This reward involves a change in your circumstances. You move into the realm of spiritual victory. It took Abraham twenty-five years to see God's promised son come along, but Abraham graduated from his trial.

It took Joseph thirteen years of slavery and prison in Egypt to finish his trial and graduate to the throne next to Pharaoh. And Moses spent the first eighty years of his life in God's "School for Liberators," but he finally passed all the tests and led Israel out of Egypt.

How long will your trial last? Only God knows. But I do know this: Once you have overcome the trial, you'll see a reward greater than anything you could have thought of on your own. But as long as you're refusing to pass the test, God is going to keep you in the classroom.

Now don't miss an important point here. God wants you to pass the test—to overcome the trial—not only so that He can give you the reward, but so that you will learn to love Him more, to love Him with Christlike passion and devotion. The crown is promised to those who love God, and He wants you to fall in love with Him more. He wants to draw you very close to Himself.

When I was dating Lois, I wanted her to fall more in love with me. I wanted to draw her very close to me, so I had a plan. I took her to the amusement park and put us on a ride called the "Wild Mouse."

You may remember this particular ride. The car would swing way out to the edge before it would turn and go back the other way. Now I loved this ride, but I knew it would be a trial for Lois because of her temperament.

I didn't tell her about that, however. I just said, "Let's go for a nice ride on the Wild Mouse." So we got on, and that thing shot way out to the edge. Lois screamed and came closer to me. Then that car turned and shot back the other way. Lois screamed again and came a little closer.

By the time that car made its third turn, Lois wasn't sitting on her side anymore. She was very close, clinging to me for dear life.

See, the trial I planned for Lois worked! I wanted to draw her closer to me, and by the time that ride ended, she wasn't just close. She was *real* close.

That's what God wants from you. He puts you in trials to draw you close, to teach you to cling to Him, to grow you into spiritual adulthood, and to bring you along in your journey toward being a perfect Christian. Let Him finish His work, and you'll have His reward.

Test Your Perfection I.Q.

- What do you now understand about God's reasons for putting trials in our lives? Give yourself four points for each of the three reasons discussed that you can list here.

    1.

    2.

    3.

- Consider your most recent trial and rate how well you're doing on the following points on a scale of 1 to 10. On this scale, "1" is "Just one step out of the starting block" and "10" is "Nearing the finish line of full-fledged sainthood!"

—*Choosing joy*
Using God's accounting system and resting in the fact that He is at work

        1 2 3 4 5 6 7 8 9 10

—*Asking for wisdom*
Praying, seeking out Christian fellowship, and opening God's Word

        1 2 3 4 5 6 7 8 9 10

—*Praising God*
Finding reasons to be thankful in the midst of the fire

        1 2 3 4 5 6 7 8 9 10

Total Points _____

Chapter 2

How to Resist Temptation

God is concerned with practical Christianity. He wants us to live out our faith, not just discuss our doctrine. He wants His people on a journey toward Christlikeness, not stuck on the side of the road, talking about truth.

We have already seen how we can withstand trials along that journey toward spiritual maturity. Now we'll consider how to resist the spiritual-death-dealing process of temptation.

As we said earlier, when you are tested by the Lord and pass the test, then you receive the spiritual blessing and maturity that go along with passing the test. It's important to respond properly to your trials because God's purpose in trials is to bring you into spiritual adulthood. He also wants to develop an intimate love relationship between you and Himself.

In light of what you've learned about trials, it's important to note that, in the Greek, *trial* and *temptation* are the same word. That Greek word can be translated either way, depending on the context. So now let's talk about the problem of temptation, the other side of trials.

The Substance of Temptation

I want to begin this chapter by briefly introducing what I call the substance of temptation. What constitutes a temptation?

The simplest definition of *temptation* is "a solicitation, or invitation, to do evil." As such, it is the direct opposite of a God-sent trial. Just as painful trials are designed by God for your growth, temptation is designed by Satan for your destruction.

The connection between trials and temptation is even stronger than simply the fact that they come from the same Greek word. When you are in the midst of a painful trial, Satan is there with temptation, trying to get you to do something wrong to alleviate the trial or to get out of it.

So temptation is an opportunity presented to you to do something wrong. It can even involve taking a good thing and using it in a bad way. For example, it's good to pass a test, but it's wrong to cheat on the test you're trying to pass. The test may be a trial, but your decision to cheat is a sin.

Satan seeks to take the trials God sends to grow you up and turn them into temptations—opportunities for sin that, if acted on, will tear you down.

Job is a good example. Job was definitely being tested by God, but at the same time he was being tempted by Satan to curse God. Sometimes the same event may either be a cause of trial or a cause of temptation for you.

It's like a car manufacturer measuring its cars against its competitors' cars. When a car manufacturer tests its own model, the idea is to show how well that car performs, how roomy it is, how affordable, etc.

But when that same car manufacturer tests a competitor's model, the goal is to expose the weaknesses and shortcomings of that car. A car manufacturer tests its own cars to show their "glory" and tests competitors' cars to expose their unworthiness and cause consumers to reject them.

God tests you to show His glory in you. Satan tempts you to expose weakness in you and bring you down to defeat.

If you do not learn to love and trust God during trials, then you will become angry at God, and that anger will lead to sin. You may even find yourself wanting to blame God for your problem.

That's what the nation of Israel did. God tested them in the wilderness, and they grumbled. Instead of using the wilderness testing as an opportunity to grow, they turned it into an occasion for sin. So the substance of temptation is the attempt to produce evil in your life.

The Source of Temptation

What is the source of the temptations we face? The Bible answers that without a stutter: "Let no one say when he is tempted, 'I am being tempted by God'; for God cannot be tempted by evil, and He Himself does not tempt anyone" (James 1:13).

God Does Not Tempt

If you are caught in sin, don't blame God for it. Don't say, "Well, if God didn't want me to have sexual relationships, He wouldn't have made me with these desires" or "If God didn't want me to eat all this food, He wouldn't have made it taste so good." People make excuses like these all the time.

But God does not lead anyone into sin. That is impossible, given His perfect nature. There is nothing in God that can accommodate or receive sin. So there is nothing in God that can initiate sin. He is totally and utterly separate from sin.

The reason Jesus was able to defeat Satan in the wilderness temptation is that even though Satan gave Jesus his best shots, there was nothing inside of Jesus to receive the appeal. There was nothing on the other end of the line to pick up the signal. It was impossible for Jesus to sin.

Since God has nothing at all to do with sin, when you sin, you need to blame someone other than God.

By the way, we can be thankful that neither God the Father nor God the Son is capable of sin. The Bible says that in Christ, God holds this universe together. God holds everything together by virtue of His character. If God were ever to sin and violate His character, everything He is holding together would come flying apart.

It is because God cannot sin that today, tomorrow, and even one hundred million years from now in heaven we won't have to worry about something going wrong.

Temptation Arises from Within

The Bible identifies the true source of temptation: "Each one is tempted when he is carried away and enticed by his own lust" (James 1:14).

That's about as clear as it gets. You and I sin because we choose to sin. So we can't blame God. But that's not all this verse means. It also means we can't blame our sin on Satan. Satan cannot make you and me sin.

Now you may already know that, but a lot of people don't. They think the devil drags people into sin against their will, making them do things they don't want to do. God says no to that idea.

Of course, the devil has a part to play in temptation. He can place things in front of you that he knows you'll respond to. He can't make you sin, but he can make you like the sin enough that you want to do it.

So what is the source of sin? Sin is born out of our desires because, unlike God, we human beings have something in our makeup that responds to sin. The Bible calls it our flesh. Our flesh was trained in sin. You and I were born in sin, and even when we get saved we do not immediately or completely eradicate the sinful flesh.

Let me illustrate the interplay of Satan and the flesh in this process of temptation. We know that professional football teams spend a lot of time studying their opponents' game films, looking for weaknesses and tendencies they can exploit. Players will study films of their individual opponents, looking for that little advantage they can use on Sunday.

Let me tell you something. Satan has "game film" on you and me! He is aware of our weaknesses. He knows our tendencies to sin.

Satan's job, then, is to set up situations like those in the film so he can trip us up again. He knows that if he can re-create the temptation that led us into sin before, there is a great chance we will fall again. Satan knows us well. That's the bad news. But the good news is, we have some game film on Satan, too! The Bible is our game film on the devil. It shows us his weak spots and his wiles so we can stand strong against him, rather than being used or deceived by him.

Trust me, I know about temptation. I was driving by a local fried chicken restaurant recently, and I heard that place calling my name! I recognized it because I've heard that call many a day.

But if I turn into the parking lot and get a box of chicken, I can't blame the restaurant for being there. Nobody made me turn in there.

Temptation gets a lot more serious than that. I've had men tell me, "My wife made me hit her."

What? Do you mean she formed your fist into a ball, cocked your arm, and then whacked your elbow into her face? No, when we sin we can't point the finger at anyone else. All Satan did was study our game film and set up the right "play" to bring out the tendency we already had.

So if you are sinning today, it is your own fault. But what does Satan want you to do? He wants you to blame somebody or something else.

Passing the Blame Along

Blaming others for sin started in the Garden of Eden. Eve blamed the serpent, and Adam blamed Eve—even implying that God was partially at fault for giving Eve to him (see Gen. 3:12).

But until you take full responsibility for your sin (see 1 John 1:9), the problem can't be fixed. It's like the little boy whose mother caught him eating the cookies she had told him not to eat. "I thought I told you not to eat the cookies," Mama said.

The boy replied, "Mama, I just got up on the chair to smell the cookies, and my teeth got caught." That is the way a lot of us are about sin. We give excuses rather than owning up to it and seeking Christ's forgiveness. The source of sin is within us. It's our problem. Satan can only arrange the temptation.

The Steps of Temptation

The Bible is helpful in this matter of temptation and sin because the Word shows how it works.

We learn that sinning is never just an event. It is a process, a series of steps set into motion to produce sin. The process starts with desire or lust.

From Desire to Enticement

Sin starts with a desire. The Word calls it "lust," an evil desire that tempts us to sin. The various words for *desire* in the Bible are not always used in a negative way because our God-given desires are not evil in and of themselves.

For example, God has given us the desires for food, sexual fulfillment, and sleep. These are good desires. Without them, something would be lost. You can't live unless you eat. Without sexual relationships, there would be no procreation of the race. And without sleep, you could not function properly.

These desires only become evil when you seek to satisfy them in illegitimate ways. Desire only becomes temptation when you allow yourself to be carried away and enticed to fulfill that desire sinfully.

God's Word uses very picturesque language to describe this enticement. One picture is that of hunters or fishermen luring their prey into the trap or onto the hook.

Bears don't go looking for bear traps. They get caught in the trap when they go for the bait. Likewise, fish don't go looking for hooks. They get snagged by the hook and dragged to the surface when they bite down on the bait.

Satan baits his trap so he can ensnare us and drag us into sin. The purpose of Satan's bait is not only to lure us to the sin, but also to hide from us the consequences of our sin.

A fisherman hides the hook in the bait so the fish thinks all it's getting is a free meal. The fisherman is nowhere in sight, so that's not a problem. The bait is either alive and moving, or the fisherman is moving the hook so his fishing lure will catch the fish's attention. When it's done right, the only thing the fish sees is the enticement of the bait.

But when the fish gives in to the enticement and bites the bait, it gets a lot more than it bargained for. The fish bites into the consequences of its action. It bites into the intention of the fisherman— which is not good for the fish because the fisherman plans to clean, fry, and eat it.

That fish is biting into its death. Instead of getting a juicy worm, the fish gets the fisherman, who doesn't care about anything except reeling in that fish. In the same way, Satan doesn't care about anything except enticing you into sin and getting you hooked.

So we get dragged into sin when we allow our desires to lead us straight into Satan's deception. We don't see the consequences of our sin, but Satan does.

You may not do any fishing, so let me change the imagery to something that most of us know too much about. A lot of us bit on the hook that MasterCard, American Express, or Visa threw us.

They baited the line: "Charge now, pay later. Your exceptional credit record entitles you to this card." Folks don't worry too much about the consequences of out-of-control spending with credit cards because the consequences come later.

Now don't misunderstand. I'm not saying that credit cards are evil in and of themselves. I'm saying that companies know how to frame an offer that looks awfully good. They know how to entice the potential buyer.

It's Satan's enticement that turns normal desires into lust. The normal desire of hunger only becomes evil when it turns into gluttony. Our desire for sex becomes evil when it leads to immorality. The desire for sleep becomes evil when it's transformed into laziness.

Let me say it again. Satan entices us into sin by hiding from us the consequences of our sin. He invited Adam and Eve to eat some delicious-looking fruit. He didn't say anything about God's judgment, being kicked out of the garden, pain in childbirth, hard labor, or one son killing the other son.

Satan simply said, "Doesn't this fruit look good?" But the desire turned evil, and Satan used that evil desire to entice and deceive our first parents. From deception, the process of temptation degenerates into disobedience.

From Deception to Disobedience

Sin starts with desire that is fueled by Satan's deception. When you follow through on an enticement and your desire leads you to disobey God, a conception takes place. Your act of disobedience gives birth to a child called sin—and the child is definitely illegitimate (James 1:15).

We already know that our desires in themselves are not sinful. Sin does not automatically come to birth even when you've been deceived about your desire. Sin only happens when you act in disobedience to God's law according to your desire. When your will connects with your desire, and you choose to fulfill that desire illegitimately, that desire leads to sin.

Jesus said that any man who looks at a woman "to lust for her" has committed the sin of adultery in his heart (Matt. 5:28). The sin is not in a man looking at a woman. The sin is in allowing that look to become a lustful stare in which the man commits in his heart what he may not do with his body.

Lust is an act of the will. You have to engage your will in order to pass from looking to lusting. You can't say, "I couldn't help it." When Satan places a temptation in front of you, it takes effort to conceive of a way to take the bait. And in that moment, your act gives birth to a grotesque-looking child called sin.

Some people say, "It was only a little sin." Well, committing a little sin is like being a little pregnant. It will show up after a while.

Let me give you a fundamental fact about the Christian life. This thing we call Christian living is a matter of the *will*, not of the emotions. Emotions are very important, but they are not to guide our decisions. They must be the result of our decisions.

There are times in your Christian life when, in order to please God and grow in your faith, you must say no because no is the right thing to say, not because you feel like saying no.

When the drug addict says, "No, I will not take that drug today," all the emotions in his body rebel against that decision. His emotions and his body scream, "But you've been taking that drug for five years. You have to have it!"

But to get that drug monkey off his back, that addict has to be able to stand there and say no. And he can do it because that decision—like the Christian life—is a matter of the will.

Too many Christians say, "I felt like doing it." But God is not dealing with your feelings; He is dealing with your willful choices. Suppose you told your child to wash the dishes, and the answer came back, "I don't feel like washing the dishes." Your response would be, "I didn't ask you what you felt like doing. I told you to go into the kitchen and wash those dishes."

"But Mama, you don't understand what it will do to me emotionally to wash the dishes. You don't know what I'm going through inside just thinking about washing the dishes!"

At this point, I suspect your child's conversation will become irrelevant to you. Why? Because that child has a responsibility to carry out, and the child's will needs to be activated to produce obedience rather than merely an emotional response.

All of us have battled with our emotions when it comes to obeying God. We have won some and lost some. But we need to understand where disobedience is heading: It always leads to death.

From Disobedience to Death

When sin is finished, it produces death. Carrying through the Bible's analogy of birth, we might say that we now have a grandchild on our hands.

The grandmother is called lust, which gives birth to a baby called sin. Then this baby called sin brings forth a child of its own called spiritual death. This is the genealogy of evil.

Sin has the power of reproduction—and Satan is the father of this whole mess.

God told Adam that the day he ate from the forbidden tree, he would surely die (Gen. 2:17). He and Eve did die the day they ate the fruit because they were driven from Eden and found themselves separated from God.

Separation from God (not the cessation of existence) is the biblical definition of *death*. In the Bible, separation from God constitutes spiritual death, and eternal death is separation from God forever. Sin breaks fellowship with God and causes us to be separated from Him.

That's why when you sin, you must confess your sin. That's why receiving God's forgiveness is important, to reestablish your fellowship with God. Sin always leads to spiritual death, and, if continued long enough, it may lead to physical death, too.

If sin causes death, why do people sin? Because it feels good temporarily. I don't know of any sin that doesn't feel good or taste good, or else people wouldn't want to do it.

The problem with sin is that you usually don't get the real deal—death—until the end of the process. Sin starts you off saying, "Ahhh!" but you end up saying, "Ohhh!" That's because sin produces death.

God may start you off saying, "Ohhh!" but you end up saying, "Ahhh!" Remember, sin's advertised price is always lower than its actual cost. Jut like those super deals you hear about on TV that are gone by the time you get to the store, sin lures you in with a bargain rate. But you end up paying the full price—spiritual death immediately, and physical and eternal death eventually.

The Solution to Temptation

Now let's talk about the good part, the solution to temptation. Scripture gives us three things to remember on our journey to Christlikeness, three things that will help us stand strong in the problem of temptation as Jesus did.

Whatever temptation you may be facing right now, these three steps will help get you back on track with God. Then you'll be growing and maturing spiritually through your testing, rather than dying through your temptation.

Remember God's Character

The first solution to temptation the Bible offers is rooted in some good theology: "Do not be deceived, my beloved brethren. Every good thing bestowed and every perfect gift is from above, coming down from the Father of lights, with whom there is no variation, or shifting shadow" (James 1:16–17).

One of the basic truths of theology is that God is good—so completely good that everything He gives is good, and anything that is not good does not come from Him. God is good, and He is good all the time.

God is called "the Father of lights." That is, God is Creator of the sun, moon, and stars—the lights in the heavens.

Is the sun good? Do we benefit from the sun's light? Do we see during the day because of the sun and have some light at night because the moon reflects the sun and the stars shine? The answer to these questions is yes.

And how consistent is the sun in giving us light? Very consistent. The sun has been giving light for countless ages, and no one worries whether the sun is going to shine tomorrow. The heavenly lights are also so consistent you can bank on them. The Bible picks these dependable things in nature—each one created by God—to illustrate His good character.

So God is the Father of the lights that are so consistent and provide us with so many benefits. You may say, "That's great, but what does that have to do with temptation?"

Everything! This God who is the source of everything good, and who is the Father of the lights that make life possible, does not change, vary, or move.

This fact is important because it means that if you aren't experiencing God's goodness, it's not because He has moved. You are the one who keeps turning and moving, going from the sunshine into the shadows.

We all know what produces shadows and why it gets dark at night. When the sun is no longer streaming in your window, it isn't because the sun has quit shining or has moved. It's because the ground you are sitting on is moving.

As the earth rotates on its axis, it turns you away from the sun for part of the day. Shadows and darkness will come, but don't blame the sun. As powerful as the sun is, it can't keep shadows from falling over you as long as you are on a planet that turns away from the sun every night.

Do you get the point? Let me say it again. If you and I are not experiencing God's goodness, it's not because His totally good nature has moved or changed or shifted. The problem is that we keep turning in circles, moving away from Him.

So if there is a shadow in your life, stop turning away from God. Remember His goodness, His perfect character, and come into His sunlight. Keep facing the Son, and you'll keep enjoying the sunshine of the goodness of God.

But what do we so often do? We love God on Sunday and bask in His light. But a shadow falls across our lives on Monday, and we wonder what happened. It could be that we just turned away from the Father of lights.

So one solution to the problem of temptation and the sin it conceives is to stay focused on God's character. Keep your life turned toward Him and His goodness, live in His light, and He'll enable you to make the right decisions when you are tempted. He'll use those times of temptation to make you more like Christ.

Let me give you a positive and negative illustration of this principle from Scripture.

The positive example is Joseph, a slave in the house of the Egyptian official Potiphar. You may know Joseph's story, found in Genesis 39:1–9.

Joseph was handsome and well built, and Potiphar's wife wanted him. She kept trying to seduce him, but Joseph wouldn't yield because God had been good to him. So he said to Potiphar's wife, "How then could I do this great evil, and sin against God?" (v. 9). Joseph could not sin in the face of God's goodness.

In sharp contrast is David after his sin with Bathsheba. David sinned against a God who had given him everything, so the prophet Nathan came to David with this message from the Lord:

> Thus says the LORD God of Israel, "It is I who anointed you king over Israel and it is I who delivered you from the hand of Saul. I also gave you your master's house and your master's wives into your care, and I gave you the house of Israel and Judah; and if that had been too little, I would have added to you many more things like these!" (2 Sam. 12:7–8)

God was saying, "David, look at all of My good gifts to you, and look what you did in light of My gifts!" David forgot the good character of God, and he fell into temptation and sin. And his sin meant death for a lot of people.

So, like Joseph, remember the goodness of God. Start every morning by saying, "Lord, You have been good to me. I just want to praise You." Praise is important because it reminds us of the goodness of God. Because He has been good to us we want to be good and obey Him.

Remember God's Word

Sin has reproductive power, but so does the Word of God. After all, the Word is what brought us to new birth. You are not saved because of your relatives, because of any resolutions you have made, or because of any religion you may practice. You are saved because the Word of God was placed in your heart by the supernatural work of the Holy Spirit.

God uses His Word to give birth to new life. It is the Word that the Holy Spirit uses to convict us of our sin and our need of a Savior, and it is the Word that shows us our Savior and how we can be made new in Him. It is in this sense that the Word gives us new life. And this new life is perfect in every detail (see 1 John 3:9 and 2 Cor. 5:17–18).

Satan, on the other hand, uses temptation to give birth to death. Now the link between the Word and overcoming temptation is strong: The Word defeats the devil.

We have the perfect example of this in the Lord Jesus Christ Himself (see Matt. 4:1–11). What did Jesus say when He was tempted? "It is written." And what did the devil do? He had to flee from Jesus, because the devil is allergic to the Word. He can't handle the spiritual pollen in the air. He starts jerking and twitching all over.

Now let me ask you this. When was the last time you used the Word of God against the devil when you were being tempted? Sin can make you forget the Word, but if you can remember to use the Word when you face temptation, the same Word that gave you spiritual life can produce life instead of death.

The devil has to flee before the Scriptures. So if you can't quote its powerful truth, pick up the Book and read it. God in His goodness will always make a way of escape (1 Cor. 10:13).

Jesus said that His people are to live by "every word that proceeds out of the mouth of God" (Matt. 4:4). God's truth gives you life.

This is why you need to study the Bible. You may not need what you're learning right now—but one day you will need it. If you learn the Word now, you'll have it when you need it.

See, sin is like the creature in those old B-grade monster movies. The monster always had to feed on something to survive and keep growing.

Sin is like that. It must have something to feed on in order to live and grow. So when you feed your sin, you give it more life no matter how much you think you are not ever going to commit that sin again.

But when you feed your heart and mind on the Scriptures, you starve sin and nurture your growth in the Lord. The Word of God is so powerful within you that, if you will live it and use it, it will help dry up sin and cause it to shrivel like a prune.

Remember God's Plan

The third and final solution to temptation involves remembering God's plan for you, His chosen one.

The Bible says we Christians are God's first fruits. "First fruits" means the first part. In the Old Testament, when the people gave offerings to God, they gave Him the first fruits, the first part of what came out of the ground. The idea is that, in His eternal plan, God has placed us at the top of His list in all of creation. He has chosen us for redemption and made us His special people.

What does that have to do with beating temptation? If we are this special to God, it is beneath our dignity to fall for Satan's bait. A higher birth means a higher life. If God made you His first fruits, then live like the person you are. Remember His great plan for you.

Some of us have forgotten who we are in Christ. And when you forget that you are somebody special, that royal blood is flowing through your veins, you start living and acting like a pauper. God says, "I have made you My first fruits. I have made you someone special, so lift up your head."

God's plan for you is victory over Satan, not enslavement to sin. God's plan for you is to keep your eyes on Jesus and grow into His image.

I'm told that when dog trainers are training a dog to be obedient to its master, they teach the dog to look at its master and let nothing distract it until the master says, "Move."

One way a trainer tests a dog's obedience is by putting a fresh piece of meat beside the dog while it is supposed to be looking at its master. At first, the untrained dog allows itself to be tempted by the meat and breaks concentration.

But the trainer keeps going through the exercise, teaching the dog to look at its master even with a juicy piece of meat lying nearby. Finally, the well-trained dog is able to ignore this huge temptation and keep its focus on the master.

That's the way it is with temptation. We need to keep looking at Jesus Christ. Yes, the red meat of sin looks good at first. But the more you look at Jesus, the less power temptation has over you, because you know that what He has for you is infinitely better.

The solution to temptation is a steady focus on the character, the Word, and the plan of God. Put these to work in your life, and you will see moments of temptation turned into opportunities for triumph and further growth toward spiritual maturity. Also, remember that sin's advertised price is always lower than its actual cost—and the Christian who is growing toward the perfection God calls us to refuses to pay sin's inflated price.

Test Your Perfection I.Q.

• What are God's goals in testing you and Satan's goals in tempting you? Give yourself four points for each answer.

1.

2.

3.

• Even though Satan has a game film on you, you can resist temptation! Think back to a recent temptation you faced and rate how well you did on a scale of 1 to 10. On this scale, "1" is "Tried to overcome on my own—and failed mightily" and "10" is "Graduated with honors from Jesus' class in standing up to Satan!"

—*Stayed focused on God's character*
   Lived in His light and remembered His goodness to you
          1 2 3 4 5 6 7 8 9 10

—*Remembered God's Word*
   Followed Jesus' example and knew what "is written"
          1 2 3 4 5 6 7 8 9 10

—*Remembered God's plan*
   Lived up to the high calling as God's "first fruits"
          1 2 3 4 5 6 7 8 9 10

Total Points _____

Chapter 3

How to Respond to God's Life-Changing Word

If there is one thing we ought to have no doubt about at all, it is the power of God's Word. We have learned that it has life-giving power. We were brought to spiritual birth by God's Word. It can take root in our souls and give us a new life, a new nature.

God's Word also has the power to shape our character and guide our behavior if we give it the opportunity to work deep within us. The Word has the ability to go deep and divide "soul and spirit" and "joints and marrow" and is "able to judge the thoughts and intentions of the heart" (Heb. 4:12). In other words, God's Word has the power to transform us and grow us into the image of Christ, our model of the perfection God demands of us.

God's powerful Word can also keep us faithful when we face a faith-building trial and keep us from sin when we encounter a faith-threatening temptation. The key is in how we respond to the Word. You need to know how to respond to God's Word so the Holy Spirit can use the Word to do His sanctifying work in your life.

Resign Yourself to the Word

The first response is what I call resignation to the Word. By this I mean that God wants you to shut yourself up with the Bible and not to look anywhere else for your life's direction.

After all, God's Word gave us spiritual birth. So, already transformed by its power, we should "be quick to hear, slow to speak and slow to anger" (James 1:19). Let's look at each of these three commands.

"Be quick to hear." Quick to hear what? To hear what God says about the situation you're facing. When you are up against a trial or temptation, be quick to find out what God has to say to you and to consider what He is doing to grow your faith through those circumstances.

Where can we find out what God has to say to us? In His Word. But we must have spiritual ears that are open and listening if we are to hear God speak through His Word. The Bible is the first place we should go when we face trials or temptations. Don't wait to go to the Word until after you have tried everything else. Don't start listening to God only after you have listened to everyone else.

Many of us are not passing our spiritual tests or overcoming temptation because God's Word is the last place we go. We don't check with God until we have gotten an opinion from everybody else. Maybe if we went to God first we wouldn't have to live in defeat or confusion so long.

Being quick to hear also applies to the everyday kind of trials we all face. Recently, Lois lost track of the checkbook. She began to panic, trying to remember where she had left it.

But then she stopped and told herself it wouldn't do any good to get frantic. She decided to get on with her day, listen to God, and see what He would show her.

Later on, a location suddenly flashed into her mind, a place she hadn't thought to look for the checkbook. She went to this place and found the checkbook. As Lois did that day, we need to listen with our ears and our hearts.

The Bible's second exhortation is a natural corollary to the first: "Be slow to speak." When you find out what God is saying, don't be so quick to argue with it or to suggest another approach.

You may not like what God is saying. It may not fit your preferences. Even so, be slow to open your mouth, because most of us get ourselves in trouble if we talk long enough.

Certainly there is a time for talk. But when you are dealing with a situation for which you need God's wisdom, it's the time to be silent and let your spirit pick up on what the Holy Spirit wants to say to you.

When Job was enduring his great trials, a painful ordeal most of us can't even imagine, he spent a lot of time early on talking about it and defending his innocence in the face of his friends' accusations and assumptions.

One of the men would say, "This is what I think, Job."

And Job would come back, "No, I don't think it's that."

Another would say, "Job, I think you're going through this because you sinned."

Job would answer, "No, I haven't sinned. It can't be that."

They went back and forth for most of the book—until God showed up. Then it dawned on Job that perhaps he had been talking too much. How did he figure that out?

Because God asked Job a question: "Will the faultfinder contend with the Almighty? Let him who reproves God answer it" (Job 40:2).

Job only had one response: "Behold, I am insignificant; what can I reply to Thee? I lay my hand on my mouth" (v. 4).

In today's language, Job said, "Lord, since I really don't know what's going on here, I am just going to chill. I am going to listen to what You have to say about what is happening to me and how I should respond." Then God gave Job a magnificent revelation of His power.

Job didn't get a direct answer to his question "Why me?" He got something better: a panoramic picture of the nature and character of God. But it only came with Job's willingness to pause and listen.

Now you may have a dimmer switch in your house. Dimmer switches are designed to turn up the lights progressively. The Holy Spirit is your divine dimmer switch. He turns up the light of the Word so you can see things you couldn't see before.

But you have to allow the Spirit to do that. You have to be more ready to hear from God than to try to answer Him or argue with Him. The light doesn't always come on all at once, like throwing on a light switch. Oftentimes it comes on gradually, like bringing up a dimmer switch.

So we're talking about responding to Scripture and then shutting up rather than arguing with God's Word. Third, you are to "be slow to anger." Why? "For the anger of man does not achieve the righteousness of God" (James 1:20).

Most of us tend to get mad when things get tough or seem to go wrong: "Lord, why do I have to go through this?" But if God is doing something in your life and you get mad about it, you're getting mad at the wrong Person.

See, if God is the One sending your trial or helping you in temptation, He's trying to perfect and mature you spiritually.

So don't get ticked off too fast. Something good is about to happen because God is in the situation. Besides, your anger won't help accomplish God's purposes.

You and I have to understand that God is not impressed by our temper tantrums. Do your kids ever throw a fit when they don't get their way? Are you impressed by their tantrums? I hope not. My father wasn't. He used to tell me, "I'll give you something to cry about." Dad wasn't moved by my anger, and neither is God.

So be slow to anger, because anger is not going to get you where you want to go. Instead, listen to the Word, hold your words, and respond correctly to the Word of God.

You say, "Tony, how do I do that?" Let's go back to the Book.

Receive the Word

Having talked about your resignation to the Word, let's consider how you are to receive the Word. James tells us to "[put] aside all filthiness and all that remains of wickedness, [and] in humility receive the word implanted, which is able to save your souls" (1:21). In order to receive the Word, you have to get rid of one thing and welcome another. You need to deal with sin and humbly open yourself to the Word, which has the power to save.

Get the Wax Out

The Greek word used here for *filthiness* was also used to refer to wax in the ear. We need to get the excess wax out of our ears if we are going to hear and receive God's Word.

Excess wax in the ear has to be dealt with because it interferes with the way your ear was designed to work. Leave excess wax in your ear, and pretty soon you'll start having trouble hearing.

We can have wax in our spiritual ears, too. The writer of Hebrews was having trouble getting through to his readers because they had become "dull of hearing" (Heb. 5:11).

The Greek word for *dull* suggests another interesting image. It means "mule-headed." You know how stubborn a mule is when it comes to obeying what its master wants it to do. A mule-headed person is one who refuses to hear and obey what God has to say.

Pull the Weeds

Once we have put aside the "filthiness" that keeps us from hearing and obeying God, James tells us to "receive the word implanted" (1:21). This farming analogy relates a critical truth.

If you are a believer, the Word of God has already been planted within you. It is a past act, a done deal. As a believer, you do not receive the Word as something that comes into you from somewhere outside of you but as something that is already resident within you.

Let me explain the idea here. The Bible is picturing the soul as a garden in which a seed has been planted. But that seed may not grow and produce the fruit it was designed to if weeds have sprung up around it.

And that's exactly the strategy of Satan. He wants to sow the weeds of sin and spiritual dullness in your life to keep the implanted Word from producing to its maximum ability. Satan knows his weeds will stifle our spiritual growth if we don't get them out of our life.

There are two reasons you need to pull these weeds of sin. The first and obvious reason is that sin is wrong. Second, sin also stifles the growth into Christlikeness God wants to see in your life.

Knowing that God wants you to grow into fruitful spiritual maturity and that Satan is trying to choke off that growth ought to be motivation enough to pull the weeds. So when God shows you your sin, don't treat it lightly. You can't just say, "Oh, well. I got weeds; you got weeds; all God's children got weeds."

No, when God shows up and shows you your sin, your reaction

needs to be the same reaction that godly people have always had to God's holiness and to their sin—humble and immediate repentance.

Isaiah saw God, realized his sinfulness, and said, "Woe is me, for I am ruined!" (6:5). Job saw God and said, "I repent in dust and ashes" (42:6). Peter said to Jesus, "Depart from me, for I am a sinful man, O Lord!" (Luke 5:8).

When these men saw God in His glory, they saw the ugliness of their sin. One reason too many of us are not pulling Satan's weeds from our lives is that we are not seeing God for who He is. Therefore, we feel pretty good about ourselves. But the more spiritually mature you become, the more sensitive to sin you become.

So God says to get rid of anything that will block the growth of the Word, "which is able to save your souls" (James 1:21). This is not referring to the moment of salvation, but to the power of God's Word to preserve your spiritual and even your physical life.

Preserve Your Life

Receiving God's Word preserves your life in two ways. First, you preserve your life spiritually. Too many believers are dying spiritually. Their spirits are shriveling up; their souls are shrinking. The implanted seed of the Word isn't growing in them. People in this condition need to stimulate the growth of the Word so their spiritual lives will not continue to wither.

Second, receiving the Word can also preserve a believer's life physically. This is a more extreme case in which a Christian gets so far off the mark that God has to take him or her home. It happened in the New Testament (see Acts 5:1–11; 1 Cor. 11:30), and it happens today. Getting serious about spiritual growth can keep us from heading in that dead-end direction.

We're talking about receiving the Word with open ears and an open heart, ready to hear and heed what God says to us. Peter urged the same kind of attitude toward sin and the Word when he wrote: "Therefore, putting aside all malice and all guile and hypocrisy and envy and all slander, like newborn babes, long for the pure milk of the word, that by it you may grow in respect to salvation" (1 Peter 2:1–2).

Peter is talking about the Word that comes to you from outside, that you either hear in a sermon or read yourself and take into your heart. There is a connection between the Word from without and the Word that is implanted within you.

When you have been given new spiritual birth by the Word of God, the Word that comes to you makes a connection with your new nature. Something inside of you resonates with what you are hearing or reading. That's one way you know you are saved.

So we need to receive the Word that can preserve our lives. This doesn't mean the process is always pleasant. I had to take a medical test recently that required me to drink the nastiest stuff I have ever tasted in my life. I had to drink a lot of it, too!

I was trying every way I knew to get this stuff down without getting sick. And getting that stuff down was necessary because without drinking that nasty liquid I could not have taken the test. And when I had finished the test and the results were in, I will never forget the exact words the doctor said to me: "You are clean."

This is what it's all about. God is saying, "Welcome the Word, even though sometimes it may not taste very good. It may not be what you wanted to hear. But welcome it because it is necessary for your spiritual growth."

Your new nature has been so constructed that it needs to drink in the Word the way a seed drinks water from the earth. And because the Word of God is alive and your new spiritual nature is alive in Christ, when these two connect there is growth.

Reflect on the Word

After we have received God's Word, we must properly reflect on it so that its truth can shape and guide our life. As James puts it, we are to "prove [ourselves] doers of the word, and not merely hearers who delude themselves" (1:22).

Either Progress or Regress

To hear the Word and not do anything about it is to regress spiritually. Many people mark their Bibles but never let their Bibles mark them.

I hope you know there is no such thing as neutrality in the Christian life. You are either progressing or regressing, going forward or going backward. In fact, to think you can just coast for a while by going to church and hearing sermons is self-deception.

Let me tell you, it is better to do more with less knowledge than to do less with more knowledge. Some Christians would be better off if they did something with what they knew rather than always trying to stuff more spiritual knowledge in their heads.

Don't get me wrong. I'm a pastor and Bible teacher, so I have nothing against God's people learning more. What I'm talking about are people who run from this conference to that conference, collecting notebooks full of truth but never doing anything with what they have already learned. There is little real value in that. To hear the Word and not *do* the Word is to delude yourself.

Using the Mirror

God's Word offers an illustration all of us can identify with. You don't even have to be spiritual to understand this one: "For if anyone is a hearer of the word and not a doer, he is like a man who looks at his natural face in a mirror; for once he has looked at himself and gone away, he has immediately forgotten what kind of person he was" (James 1:23–24).

Now this is very interesting. The word for "man" in verse 23 is the specific term *male,* not the more general word for mankind.

This passage is dealing with men and mirrors. The Bible says a person who looks into the Word and does nothing about it is like a man who glances at himself in a mirror and goes on. The reason the Word specifies males here is because women don't look into a mirror and move on. Men glance at mirrors, but women gaze into mirrors. A woman is not about to step in front of a mirror and then do nothing!

One Sunday in church, I asked all the women in the congregation who had mirrors in their purses to stand. A sea of women stood up. Then I asked all the men who had mirrors in their wallets to stand. Nothing happened—which was my point.

My wife has to have a minimum of one hour to get ready when we go someplace. If I give her fifty-five minutes, she says, "Don't rush me." Men are satisfied with a glance in the mirror, but most women aren't.

Well, God doesn't want you just glancing into the mirror of His Word for a few minutes. He doesn't want you reading the Bible simply because you heard that a verse a day keeps the devil away.

Instead, God wants you to gaze into the Word—to reflect on it, roll it over in your mind and soul until you begin to see yourself as you really are and God as He really is. That's when the Word will begin to take hold of your soul.

Let me point out something very interesting here. The phrase "natural face" means literally "the face of his birth." That makes sense, because when you look in a mirror you see the face you were born with.

The same thing happens spiritually when you look in the Bible. You see your "spiritual face," the face of your new birth in Christ.

And just as a mirror shows you exactly what you look like at any given moment, the Bible is totally accurate in reflecting your spiritual condition back to you. When you look into the Word, God shows you what He sees in you. You see the good and the not-so-good so that you can correct the flaws.

This is why Satan wants to keep you away from the Word. He wants to get you looking into his trick mirror. When you use the devil's mirror, everything always looks fine because he doesn't tell you the real story. The devil's mirror will make you think you're OK when you're not.

One way Satan tricks us is by getting us to reflect not on the Word but on other Christians. We look at the person next to us and say, "I'm doing better than he is," or "I sure don't have the problems she has. I must be OK."

Wrong mirror. God says we need to look into the mirror of His Word and reflect deeply, not forgetting what we see but doing what God calls us to do and get rid of the sin that His Word reveals.

Respond to the Word

Looking into the mirror of God's Word and choosing by the power of God's Spirit to abide by what you see there can result in great blessing. James says, "Not having become a forgetful hearer but an effectual doer, this man shall be blessed in what he does" (1:25). God's blessing depends on how we respond to His Word.

A Sufficient Response

In His famous parable of the soils (Luke 8:4–15), Jesus talks about four kinds of responses to the seed of His Word. The first is actually a lack of response: The soil does not receive the seed at all.

Then there is the shallow response, those people who receive the Word but do not water and care for it, so that it soon withers away.

The third response Jesus talked about is what I call the inadequate response. These people are too much into the cares and worries of this world to give God the time and attention He deserves. As a result, their spiritual lives fall into a state of neglect.

The fourth response is the sufficient response: The good soil absorbs the Word and produces fruit. It takes a lot of time and attention and care to respond to God's Word and know that kind of growth.

Some people say, "But you don't know how busy I am." Really? Suppose you were suffering from pain or an illness and went to your physician. Chances are you're not going to say, "Listen, Doctor, I'm way too busy for you to do a thorough examination. Just put the stethoscope on me for a few seconds and tell me I'm all right."

Your doctor isn't going to buy that approach to your treatment. A good physician isn't looking to hustle you out the door as quickly as possible. Instead, that doctor will give you the time necessary to diagnose the problem and then tell you the truth about your illness.

Jesus is the Great Physician who is ready to give you the time you need and tell you the truth about your spiritual condition. But you have to come to His "office," the Word of God, prepared to be diagnosed and treated.

A Transforming Response

When you come to the Word of God, you are not looking only at a Book, you are coming before a divine Person. The question is "What are you going to do about what this Person has told you?"

Many Christians treat the Word like they do chewing gum. They come to the Word for something new, something sweet they can enjoy for a while. Then when the newness has worn off, they discard that piece and look for a fresh one. Rather than allowing the Word to transform them, they want something that will leave a nice taste in their mouths.

According to 2 Corinthians 3:18, we who are "beholding as in a mirror the glory of the Lord, are being transformed into the same image." God wants us to see His glory and become more like Jesus as a result of gazing intently into the mirror of His Word.

David prayed, "Search me, O God, and know my heart; try me and know my anxious thoughts; and see if there be any hurtful way in me, and lead me in the everlasting way" (Ps. 139:23–24).

That's the prayer of someone who is coming face-to-face with God, willing to be transformed. David wanted to see God, and he wanted God to show him in the mirror what he looked like so he could be changed. The Word is transforming if we will respond to it.

The Perfect, Liberating Law

James also points out that God's Word is "the perfect law, the law of liberty" (1:25). No wonder we need to "look intently" at it! That kind of response allows the Word to do its work. The Greek word for "look intently" means to stoop down and look closely at, the way Peter and John stooped down to look into Jesus' empty tomb. Clearly, God is telling us once again not to treat His Word lightly.

The Bible calls itself a law that liberates us when we respond to it correctly. That seems like a contradiction to a lot of us because we think of law as something that hinders and restricts, not liberates.

Not so in the Bible. David said, "I will walk at liberty, for I seek Thy precepts" (Ps. 119:45). He was saying, "I'll be a free man when I follow God's rules. Jesus Himself said, "You shall know the truth, and the truth shall make you free" (John 8:32).

You may say, "I know the truth, but I'm not free." That could be because you know it in your head, but you're not doing it in your heart. It's obedience to the truth that brings true freedom, not just the information.

So let's talk about the seeming contradiction of a law that makes you free. How can you have law and freedom at the same time?

The key is the new nature we received when we first trusted Christ. Your new spiritual nature has been programmed to respond to God's Word, to the demands of Christlikeness. When you obey God's Word—His law—you are doing what you were redeemed to do, and a tremendous sense of freedom comes in doing that.

But most people misdefine freedom. They think freedom is the absence of any rules, doing whatever they want whenever they want. But such "freedom" is actually the worst form of slavery. Jesus said, "Everyone who commits sin is the slave of sin" (John 8:34). Therefore, the only true freedom comes when we are set free from sin and made slaves to Christ. That kind of slavery liberates us!

This feeling of freedom that comes with obeying God's law is also accompanied by a great sense of delight. That's why Paul was able to say, "I joyfully concur with the law of God in the inner man" (Rom. 7:22). The law freed Paul to be the person God had saved him to be. God's Word *obeyed* is the road to freedom.

If this is true, why aren't more Christians experiencing freedom? Because their response to God's Word is flawed. Let me explain this by changing the metaphor and comparing the Christian life to a course in college.

The problem with too many Christians is they want to audit the Christian life the way a student may audit a course in college.

You know what happens when you audit a course. You get the information, but you don't do any of the work or take the tests. You don't get credit for the course. It doesn't show up on your transcript, so it doesn't help you progress to the next level. It is of no benefit toward graduation.

Likewise, if you audit the Word of God, you will gain no credit toward your graduation to the next spiritual level. You and I must respond to God's Word by doing what it says. It's not enough just to sit in church and hear the Word.

But some Christians are just sitting in the back of the class, trying to take a few notes here and there and catch most of the content.

They nod off every now and then, but they don't worry about it because they think they aren't going to have to take the test.

But in reality, the Christian life cannot be audited. It has to be lived, and everyone is being tested by God. All of us are being measured by the perfect standard of His Word.

That's why you need to take the Bible seriously. You need to take hold of it and look into it until you hear from God, until the truth of God jumps off the page and grabs your soul. When that happens, you'll be experiencing its transforming power, living according to its truth, and moving ahead on your journey toward becoming more like Christ, more like the perfect Christian God calls you to be.

Test Your Perfection I.Q.

- In order to become a mature Christian, you need to submit to God's Word. James gives a three-part rule of thumb for doing just that. Complete each command. Then give yourself four points each time you explain why that particular instruction is important.

  1. "Be quick to _____."

  2. "Be slow to _____."

  3. "And be slow to _____."

- Resigning yourself to God's Word, receiving His Word, reflecting on it, and responding to it are four aspects of responding to Scripture. Evaluate how well you're doing on some of these counts on a scale of 1 to 10. "1" is "Auditing Scripture 101—and not even paying much attention in class" and "10" is "A doer of the Word on every single count!"

—*Receiving God's Word*
Getting the wax out of your spiritual ears and pulling weeds
    1 2 3 4 5 6 7 8 9 10

—*Reflecting on God's Word*
Using the mirror to see God's holiness and your sin—and doing what God calls you to do to get rid of that sin
    1 2 3 4 5 6 7 8 9 10

—*Responding to God's Word*
On this scale, "1" is a lack of response (not receiving the Word at all), "4" is a shallow response (watering the Word but not caring

for it), "7" is an inadequate response (letting the cares and worries of this world choke out the Word), and "10" is a sufficient response (absorbing the Word and producing fruit).

1 2 3 4 5 6 7 8 9 10

Total Points _____

Chapter 4

How to Make Your Faith Pure and Valuable to God

To get the maximum enjoyment from your television, you need two things: sound and picture.

One without the other just doesn't work. It's not enough to see the picture with no sound or to hear something but have no picture. Television was designed to deliver both sound and picture.

The Christian life is a lot like television. It's not enough for people just to hear what we say. They need to see a picture, too. They need to see our faith in action. Our Christianity must deliver both sound and picture as we grow to spiritual maturity and Christlikeness.

The Bible gives us a great way to determine the genuineness of our faith along our journey to be more like Jesus:

> If anyone thinks himself to be religious, and yet does not bridle his tongue but deceives his own heart, this man's religion is worthless. This is pure and undefiled religion in the sight of our God and Father, to visit orphans and widows in their distress, and to keep oneself unstained by the world (James 1:26–27).

Here we have it, the contrast between worthless and worthwhile faith.

The former is what we might call futile religion. It's the kind of religion that doesn't take us where we need to go. Like a fruit tree that is bad at the root, this religion doesn't produce anything.

But true faith is first "pure," meaning unmixed, clean. It is also "undefiled," not polluted or stained.

The term *religion* here is being used as something of a synonym for genuine faith. The outward evidence (or lack of it) reveals the inward faith we possess (or don't possess!).

So how can we determine the purity of our religion—and how can we make our walk of faith more valuable to God and more fruitful for His kingdom? By the time the Word of God gets through with us, some answers should be clear. We may not like what we find, but we won't be left in doubt about the answers.

First, it's important to note up front that the contrast here is not between those who never darken the door of a church and have nothing to do with God and those who go to church regularly and say they are Christians. That kind of contrast would be too easy, too obvious.

Instead, these verses were written to Christians who were in church all the time. They practiced plenty of religious rites and had plenty of religious observances, just as most of us who call ourselves Christians do today.

These people had a lot of religion. What they needed to find out was whether it was worth anything—that is, whether it had value to God. That's important to know: Is our faith genuine in God's eyes? We just saw that the person whom God blesses is the person who *does* the Word, not the person who just hears the Word (James 1:25). That's the first "how-to" clue for determining the purity of your religion.

See, God is not interested simply in which version of the Bible you carry under your arm when you go to church on Sunday. His main concern is not how many Bible verses you have memorized or how many perfect-attendance pins you have collected in Sunday school. God wants to know what you are doing with what you have learned.

A lot of Christians consider themselves religious because they do the things religious people are supposed to do. They pray and go to church. They participate in the church's rituals and liturgy. They observe special days—giving thanks at Thanksgiving, paying homage to the Baby in the manger at Christmas, and celebrating the Resurrection on Easter Sunday.

There is certainly nothing wrong with these things. But what God wants to tell us is that vertical religion by itself is not enough. Unless your vertical worship (your relationship with God) also produces horizontal action (your relationships with people), your religion is less than "pure and undefiled."

We're talking about the difference between what a person thinks and what he really is.

If anyone thinks he is religious, yet cannot point to evidence of his faith in everyday life, that person is self-deceived. Vertical religion must find horizontal expression. Religious ritual must result in right living. Vibrant faith must actualize itself in a righteous life. This is the heart of the contrast between worthless and worthwhile religion.

So how do you know when you have the genuine article? How can you be sure your religion is worthwhile?

Three specific aspects of your life will be affected when you take the Word of God seriously and begin to act on it. Worthwhile faith will show up in your conversation, your compassion, and your conduct. Let's take each of these in turn.

Your Conversation

One of the first places pure religion should manifest itself is in that piece of flesh attached to the back of your throat. You need to bridle your tongue if your religion is going to be worthwhile.

The Bible has a lot to say about people who can't discipline their tongues, suggesting that this has been a major problem among believers since the earliest days of the church.

The Deception of the Tongue

What's the problem with a person who can't bring his tongue under control? That person is deceiving himself if he thinks his religion has any value to God's kingdom. Religion characterized by a loose tongue is worthless.

An out-of-control tongue is like an out-of-control horse, which is what you have when a horse isn't bridled. We need to put a bridle on our tongues and rein them in. Too many Christians have galloping tongues, as uncontrollable as the horses on a runaway stagecoach in those old Western films.

Too many of us have tongues that keep on moving when they ought to stop. Don't talk about how you said "Amen!" on Sunday if your mouth isn't bridled Monday through Saturday. Don't talk about how you sang and shouted praises to God on Sunday if your tongue rips and tears people to shreds during the week.

If your weekday tongue is loose or hurtful, your activity on Sunday was basically a waste of time. Your religion didn't change your speech, so that religion is worthless.

The Destruction by the Tongue

James tells of another problem with having an "unconverted" tongue. He explains that, when we speak against a fellow believer without any warrant, we place ourselves above the Word of God and show our contempt for God's law (4:11). When we attack a brother or sister, God views that as an attack on Him.

Some Christians can shred a fellow believer with their tongues during the day and then get on their knees that night to ask God to bless them. But we've read that if we want God's blessing, we have to be doers of the Word, not just people who hear and then forget what they heard (see 1:25).

I'm convinced that many of us are forfeiting God's blessing because our speech is out of control in one way or another. If the Word has taken root in our souls, one of the first places it ought to bear fruit is in our tongues.

You know how some Christians spiritualize the way they talk. They say, "Now I'm not gossiping when I tell you this. This is for your information only," or "Let me share something with you as a prayer request."

It's fine to be concerned about others, but the difference between a gossip and a concerned friend is the difference between a butcher and a surgeon. Both cut flesh, but for totally different reasons.

The Motivation of the Tongue

Your motivation is everything when it comes to your conversation. Are you speaking to help or to hurt others? Is what you say going to build people up or tear them down?

God commands, "Let no unwholesome word proceed from your mouth, but only such a word as is good for edification" (Eph. 4:29). This doesn't mean you never say anything negative. But if you do say something negative, it needs to be for the purpose of helping, not hurting. One of the worst things that can happen in the body of Christ is for believers to cut up one another through their conversation.

Improper speech can show up in lying, slander, profanity, and a host of other forms. But all such valueless talk reveals a valueless religion.

When one Christian tears another Christian down, and when the speaker is not willing to go to the other person to try to fix the problem, God says the person doing the wrong kind of talking has become an evil judge of His Word. And that person has just signaled God to withhold His blessing.

Some believers are going to see heaven before they see God's blessing because they are the "kings" and "queens" of the telephone—and maybe the e-mail, too! They use their mouths to tear other people down instead of to build them up.

It's no surprise, then, that many sins are committed with the tongue. Paul, for instance, put gossip and slander in the same camp as the sin of homosexuality. Then he said that those who commit such things are worthy of death (Rom. 1:32).

Someone may say, "You can't compare gossip with homosexuality." I didn't; God did.

Taming the Tongue

When the Word of God and the Spirit of God take hold of your life, you will find the ability to take hold of your tongue and control it rather than letting it control you. You won't say, "I couldn't help myself" because God's Spirit is more powerful than the tongue.

Now I realize that none of us is perfect here. We're all going to blow it now and then. Someone is going to tick us off and we are going to say something we will later regret. Scripture warns that "the anger of man does not achieve the righteousness of God" (James 1:20). Still, anger comes. But we should be getting better at holding our tongues as we mature in our faith, not worse.

The tragedy is that some Christians are getting worse in this area. They are "backward Christian soldiers." We are immersed in a trash-talking society, but God can give us the power to control what we say.

And what we need in the body of Christ are husbands who say, "I'm going to bless my wife today, not dump on her." We need wives who say, "I am going to lift my husband up today, not put him down." We need parents who say, "I am going to encourage my children with my tongue, not exasperate them."

When that happens, we'll see some real faith in action. After all, the worth of your religion is revealed in part by the way you use your tongue.

Your Compassion

How else can you determine the reality of your faith? Authentic religion shows itself in compassion. This is compassion in action. It's visiting "orphans and widows in their distress" (James 1:27)—and the Greek word for *visit* in this verse doesn't mean to drop by once in a while to see how things are. That word means to care for people, to meet their needs.

Helping the Helpless

True religion is not selfish. It helps those who can do nothing for us in return for what we do for them. False religion says, "I do for you; you do for me." That's a business deal, not faith in action.

In the economy of the first-century world, orphans and widows were the most helpless people in society. They were the poorest of the poor. They often needed help, but they could offer their helpers nothing material in return. And because widows and orphans were basically powerless, they were often the victims of injustice. So God warns His people to make sure they defend the helpless. Let me tell you, this is where our faith gets down to the nitty-gritty.

In Isaiah 1:11–17, God has some biting words for Israel. He begins by asking:

"What are your multiplied sacrifices to Me?" says the LORD. "I have had enough of burnt offerings of rams, and the fat of fed cattle. And I take no pleasure in the blood of bulls, lambs, or goats. . . . Yes, even though you multiply prayers, I will not listen." (vv. 11, 15)

What had Israel done to cause God to despise their sacrifices and prayers? Scripture goes on to tell the story: "Your hands are covered with blood" (v. 15).

In other words, Israel was a place where injustice and treachery flourished. The helpless were mistreated by the powerful. Things were so bad that the people's hypocritical acts of religious observance made God sick. Look at His remedy: "Wash yourselves, make yourselves clean; remove the evil of your deeds from My sight. Cease to do evil, learn to do good; seek justice, reprove the ruthless; defend the orphan, plead for the widow" (vv. 16–17). James 1:27 is a one-verse summary of Isaiah 1:11–17!

To live out a faith that is valuable to God, we must reach out to those who cannot help themselves. Why? Because that's what our heavenly Father did for us. When we were sinners and could do nothing for God in return, God in Christ became sin for us that we might become the righteousness of God in Him. God wants His kids to act like their Father.

Accepting Our Responsibility

How can we be sure our walk of faith pleases God? Our God-given compassion will move us not only to help the helpless but also to take ongoing responsibility for doing so. This is one place where we believers have really dropped the ball. We have turned over to the government our spiritual responsibility to care for the needy among us. Scripture asks the question, "What use is it, my brethren, if a man says he has faith, but he has no works? Can that faith save him?" (James 2:14).

What good is your faith when you have the wherewithal to

help a person in crisis, but you don't? What good is a religion that's all talk?

This call to show compassion to the helpless and needy is a strong thread in the New Testament. The apostle John writes:

> We know love by this, that He laid down His life for us; and we ought to lay down our lives for the brethren. But whoever has the world's goods, and beholds his brother in need and closes his heart against him, how does the love of God abide in him? Little children, let us not love with word or with tongue, but in deed and truth. (1 John 3:16–18)

John says our faith must include both conviction and action. It's not a matter of one or the other; it's both.

Now we in the evangelical church are strong on truth. We've got that down. But we need to match our commitment to truth with a commitment to put that truth into action—especially with action on behalf of those who are unable to do anything for us in return.

In Matthew 25:31–46, Jesus talked about the judgment of Gentile nations that will occur at the end of the Tribulation. His teaching illustrates the principle we're talking about because Jesus will judge these nations based on their actions.

Jesus said the sheep saw Him hungry and thirsty and naked and a stranger and in prison—and met His needs. The goats saw Jesus in need but did nothing. The sheep will ask, "Lord, when did we see You in need and serve You?" Jesus will answer, "To the extent that you did it to one of these brothers of Mine, even the least of them, you did it to Me" (v. 40).

In other words, Jesus credits your account in heaven when you help people in need. And in His day, widows and orphans were at the top of the "least of these" list. When you obey the command to help the helpless, you are in line for God's blessing.

So let me say it again. One of the great crimes of our day is that we as Christians have let everybody else take care of our spiritual responsibilities. We've turned the care of the needy over to government and social service agencies who turn it into a big administrative program. But if Christians would simply act as Christians, we would see the blessing of God in the lives of others and in our own families.

Sharing the Blessing

How can we be sure to receive God's blessing for our heartfelt acts of compassion? Let's get personal here.

We have been blessed by God. A lot of us have left our one- and two-bedroom apartments far behind and are now living in three- and four-bedroom homes. We have as many garage spaces now as we used to have bedrooms.

That's not all. We've gone from walking or taking the bus to driving a nice car. Some of us have come a long way from an impoverished background. Our salary is comfortable now.

To us God asks the pointed question, "Is anyone else benefiting from My grace to you? Are you helping those who cannot pay you back? That's what I want you to do because, trust Me, you can never pay Me back for what I have done for you."

Now I realize that some people try to justify their lack of action by claiming they don't know anyone in real need. People like the ones Jesus was talking about don't live in their neighborhoods, so these folks who are looking for an excuse think they can escape on a technicality. If you know the story Jesus told in Luke 10:25–37, you know there's nothing new about this kind of effort. An expert in the Jewish law came to Jesus one day and asked, "Teacher, what shall I do to inherit eternal life?" (v. 25).

Jesus turned the question back to the man, and he answered correctly: "You shall love the Lord your God with all your heart, and with all your soul, and with all your strength, and with all your mind; and your neighbor as yourself" (v. 27).

Jesus replied, "Yes! You have it right. Now go live it!"

But the lawyer was looking for a loophole. The Bible says he was trying to justify himself, so he asked, "Just exactly who is this neighbor I'm supposed to love?" As lawyers are prone to do, this man wanted to get technical. He wanted to discuss the fine print of the command to love his neighbor as himself to see if there was some way he could get out of his duty.

The lawyer wanted Jesus to say who qualified as a neighbor. Was it the guy next door, the people three doors down, the family around the corner? Did Jesus mean the people on the "other side of the tracks"? Who was this lawyer's neighbor?

The answer Jesus gave him was the familiar story of the Good Samaritan. I won't try to retell the whole story here, but you will recall that a man traveling the narrow highway from Jerusalem to Jericho was robbed, beaten, and left for dead by thieves.

Three people walked by the man. Now this hurts because the first one was a priest, the preacher of that day. He saw the wounded man, but passed by on the other side. So did a Levite, the Jewish equivalent of an assistant pastor. To them, this man bleeding by the side of the road did not qualify as a neighbor.

But a Samaritan, who was the enemy of the Jews and considered pretty worthless, saw the wounded man and did everything necessary to help him. The Samaritan bandaged the man's wounds and paid for his further care. Now you can't bandage someone's wounds without getting blood on your clothes and your hands. You have to mix it with a person to fix his injuries, lift him onto your own donkey (or into your own car), and take him to a place where he can recover.

But the Samaritan didn't stop there. The next day he paid for any care the wounded man might need. He must have spent the night at the inn himself so he could watch over the injured man. So in every way possible, this Samaritan lived out God's command to love his neighbor as himself.

So, Jesus asked the lawyer, "Who was the injured man's neighbor— the priest, the Levite, or the Samaritan?"

Whereas the lawyer wanted a technical definition of *neighbor,* Jesus said the real question is whether a person is going to be neighborly to the needy people God has already placed in his path.

Do you see the difference? The lawyer wanted to look at the bleeding man and ask, "Does he qualify as my neighbor? If so, I'll help him. If not, forget it."

But Jesus was saying, "Don't ask if a person in need qualifies as your neighbor. He does. So, what are you going to do to help him?"

Being a Neighbor

So don't go around saying, "I can't find anybody to serve. I can't locate a neighbor." Jesus is saying that misses the point. You don't have to locate your neighbor. What you have to do is *be* a neighbor. Somebody in need will locate you. And when that happens, real faith doesn't stand around arguing about who qualifies as a neighbor. Faith that is pure and pleasing to God bends down and starts bandaging the wounds.

Your Conduct

How else can you determine if your religion is worthwhile? It will be obvious not only in your conversation and your compassion, but also in your conduct. You will keep yourself "unstained by the world" (James 1:27).

Let's not get confused about this. God doesn't mind you being *in* the world. He just doesn't want you to be *of* the world (see John 17:15–26). God doesn't mind you enjoying the benefits of the world as long as you're not falling in love with the world and becoming a friend of the world (see James 4:4).

The Problem with the World

What's wrong with the world? Why does God expect a Christian who wants to be more like Jesus to avoid being stained by the world? Because the world system wants to leave God out of the picture.

The Greek word for "world" here is *kosmos,* a word that means "to arrange." This world has an arrangement, a system, an order that wants to exclude God.

Therefore, the definition of *worldliness* is to leave God out and oppose God. When the Bible talks about the world in the sense we are using it here, it is not talking about the created order. It is referring to a society apart from God.

So whenever we believers allow the world system to crowd God out of our lives in some way, we have become worldly. That's not what God wants us to be. We are supposed to be "spotless and blameless" (2 Pet. 3:14).

See, Satan's agenda for us is simple. He wants us to become friends with the unsaved world so that we might be led to love the world.

But God says, "Do not love the world, nor the things in the world" (1 John 2:15). If we start loving the world and its godless way of life, we will soon find ourselves being "conformed to this world" (Rom. 12:2). Then God will have to discipline us so we won't be "condemned along with the world" (1 Cor. 11:32).

Avoiding the Stains

But how can we be in the world and stay pure? The only way to avoid being stained by the world's sin and keep ourselves clean is to stay close to the Lord.

You know what it's like to have a stain. When you have a big spot on the front of your dress or shirt, what do people focus on? The stain.

You could be dressed to kill but, if the outfit is stained, people aren't going to say, "She sure looked nice today." They are going to say, "Did you see that big stain on her dress?" When believers get stained by the world, all the world can see is the stain.

A good illustration of a believer becoming stained by the world is Abraham's nephew, Lot. According to Genesis 13:10, Lot looked toward Sodom and liked what he saw. He eventually moved into Sodom. It was the happening place to be. Lot wanted to hang out in Sodom, but Abraham kept his focus on God and kept himself away from Sodom.

Lot became contaminated by Sodom, and even though he did not lose his faith, he lost his family and everything he owned when God set the place on fire.

Now, it's not that God minds us enjoying the good things He has created. He wants us to enjoy the many blessings He showers on us (1 Tim. 6:17). We can possess material things if we acquire them legitimately. The secret, however, is not to let those things possess *us*.

To keep that from happening, we have to keep an eternal perspective on our possessions. If we lose that, our value system starts getting all out of whack.

It's like a wedding ring. The ring Lois gave me on our wedding day is an important symbol of our commitment. But God never meant for me to love my wedding ring more than I love the person who gave it to me.

Imagine a groom during his wedding, saying, "Stop the ceremony. I want to look at the ring. My, this is a pretty ring! I've never seen a stone this big in my life."

The preacher says, "Do you take this woman to be your wife?"

"I take this ring! That's what I take."

"Do you promise to love and honor this woman?"

"I promise to love and honor this ring."

That will probably never happen in a wedding. We don't get hung up on the ring. It's only symbolic of something much better. God did not give us the things around us so that we might love the world, but that we might love Him who gave us all things.

The great tragedy of Christianity today is that so many Christians have been stained by the world. A man once told me, "I'm going to worship God on the golf course this Sunday."

To which I replied, "No, you are going to worship golf on God's course." An authentic faith is one in which we keep our values in the right order.

Cleansing the Stains

How can we remove the stains that we don't avoid in the world? First, let me say that all stains are not created equal.

People get small stains on their clothes by accident even when they are being careful and watchful. But the big stains come when a person is being careless and indulgent and doesn't care how much of a mess he makes.

Having the real item when it comes to faith doesn't mean you never get a stain. Believers still sin, but genuine faith means you deal with the stain as soon as it appears, cleansing your life by confession and forgiveness. Genuine faith also means you try to keep as far away from sin as possible so you don't get stained.

But sometimes I forget to put the cap back on my pen after I've used it. Then when I put the pen in my shirt or pants pocket, I wind up with an ugly stain.

This happened to one of my favorite pairs of pants. There was a big blue stain at the bottom of the pants pocket. So every time I wanted to wear those pants, I had to wear a jacket to hide the stain. But then I found a dry cleaning store that specializes in removing ink stains. I was back in business.

If you want to be a Christian who lives a pure and undefiled faith, you will need to keep yourself unstained by the world. The good news is that, no matter how deep the stain, I know a Cleaner in glory who can take care of the worst possible stain you and I will ever have.

God specializes in stain removal! When He does His work, you and I won't need to worry about trying to hide our stains. We can walk through this world clean, and the devil won't have any basis for accusing us.

Doctors wash their hands before performing surgery so they will be free of contamination and not pass any more germs on to the patient. Only the doctor who is free from stain can do something for the desperately sick person who needs help so badly.

Christians are God's surgeons to help fix this sin-stained world. But we can't help the patient if we ourselves have dirty hands that need disinfecting. So God wants us to keep ourselves spiritually clean.

Chasing Mice

When I think about our need to live out our faith, I recall the children's nursery rhyme about the pussycat who went to London to see the queen. When asked what he did on his visit to Great Britain, the cat replies, "I frightened a little mouse under her chair."

Now think about that for a minute. I want to ask that cat, "Cat, why go all the way to London to scare a mouse when you can do that anywhere? Why waste a trip to London by scaring a mouse when you had Westminster Abbey and Big Ben and all of that to see? Why waste your time with a mouse when you were in the queen's palace and could have enjoyed the environment of royalty?"

The answer to those questions is simple. The cat did that because it's a cat. It thinks like a cat and reacts like a cat—and cats are into mice. So even though you show a cat all the wonders of London, that feline is going to go for the mouse every time. That's the nature of a cat.

There's a lesson here for us because, unless we let the Word and the Spirit of God change us, we can become satisfied with chasing mice, even though we're in the presence of royalty. God has made us kingdom people to reign with Him, but unless we're careful we can find ourselves playing with mice under the throne.

That may sound ridiculous, and it is. But it's possible. It's possible for Christians to talk like people whose tongues have not been transformed by the grace of God. It's possible for Christians to speak like the most insensitive unbeliever and have little or no compassion for the needy. And it's possible for Christians to become so stained by the world that the spots seem impossible to get out.

The challenge for us is to have a pure religion, a perfect Christianity as modeled by Christ, a genuine faith that goes beyond attending church on Sunday and Wednesday and reading a verse a day to keep the devil away. We need a genuine faith that reflects Jesus and glorifies God.

Test Your Perfection I.Q.

- If you were on trial for being a Christian, what evidence from your life would support your claim to be a believer whose faith is pure and undefiled? Is there any visible evidence that you are a Christian whose righteous life goes far beyond proper observance of church rituals? Give yourself four points for each item.

1.

2.

3.

- Every aspect of your life will be affected when you take the Word of God seriously and begin to act on it. Worthwhile faith will show up, for instance, in your conversation, your compassion, and your conduct. Take some time to evaluate how your faith is impacting each of these areas of your life.

—*Conversation*

Is gossip a problem for you? What motivates your words? Do you edify others with your tongue rather than tear them down? On this scale, "1" means that your tongue is a wild stallion whose strength is destructive and "10" means your tongue is a trained thoroughbred whose power is used to build up others.

1 2 3 4 5 6 7 8 9 10

—*Compassion*

Do you give to folks who can give nothing to you in return? Are you actively involved in ongoing relief efforts through the church rather than the government or social services? Rate your compassion on a scale of 1 to 10. "1" is "Who is my neighbor?" and "10" is "Mother Teresa would be proud!"

1 2 3 4 5 6 7 8 9 10

—*Conduct*

Are you staying close to the Lord, avoiding sin as much as possible, confessing sin as soon as you recognize it, and loving the Giver more than the material gifts He has given you? On this scale of 1 to 10, "1" means that you are a "friend of the world" and "10" means that you are "in the world but not of it."

1 2 3 4 5 6 7 8 9 10

Total Points _____

Chapter 5

How to Avoid the Sin of Partiality

This sanctification stuff—this process of becoming more like Jesus—is getting pretty gritty, isn't it? Well, hang on, because it gets even grittier when we start dealing with the way we talk about and treat other people.

In the previous chapter we began to get a good idea of how God expects us to treat people. Now we are going to get a more complete picture of how a Christian who is growing in Christ should relate to all kinds of people—especially those who are different.

The setting for this discussion is a sin that was frequently committed in the early church. That's not hard to imagine because this sin has been committed ever since, both inside and outside the church.

The Bible calls this sin "personal favoritism" (James 2:1). It can go by other names, such as racism, classism, or culturalism.

Racism is prejudice against someone whose skin color is different from yours. Classism is prejudice against a person whose economic status does not match yours. And culturalism is prejudice against someone whose way of life, manner of dress, or personal preferences are different from yours.

The problem comes when we start making judgments about a person's worth based on such external criteria. The sin of partiality occurs when I decide how I am going to treat other people based on the color of their skin, their economic status, or their accent.

This does not mean we all have to have the same likes and dislikes. Different personal preferences in nonessential areas are fine, as long as we don't use these things to determine how we are going to think, feel, or act toward somebody else.

The sin of prejudice was prevalent in the first century because the Jews and Gentiles couldn't stand one another. Then there was the class issue between the rich and the poor, the free and the slaves. And all of these problems were imported into the church when Jews, Gentiles, slaves, and slave owners got saved and came together in the body of Christ.

God's Word goes right to the core of the problem without any sugarcoating or corner-cutting. That's what I want to do, too, because nothing less than the truth on this issue will get us where we need to go.

Before considering what Scripture says about partiality, think about the way Jesus Christ treated the people He met. His ministry gives us the standard we need to strive for on our journey toward spiritual maturity.

When we look at how Jesus dealt with the people He encountered during His time here on earth, one fact jumps out at us. Jesus did not relate to people based on how they looked or spoke or how much money they had.

On the contrary, Jesus often turned the world's standard on its head by the way He related to poor people and the outcasts of society.

Remember what He said about the poor widow's offering? Widows were at the bottom rung of society's ladder, but Jesus said this woman gave a better offering than all the rich folk because she gave all she had. Jesus made a value judgment on the widow and her offering based on her heart attitude, not the amount she contributed.

And what about the woman at the well? She was a Samaritan half-breed and an immoral person, making her a two-time loser in the eyes of the Jews. Based on the criteria of race and culture alone, Jesus should not even have been talking to her.

Who would have thought that this despised Samaritan prostitute would become one of the leading evangelists in the New Testament, leading a whole city full of men to the Savior? Jesus looked past this woman's obvious problems and dealt with her as a person who was worth His time.

I suspect that in a similar situation, many of us would have said, "I'm not going to sit next to any prostitute and try to talk to her! What would people think?"

But Jesus Christ was more concerned about the individual than the opinion of onlookers. He related to people based on what they could become on the inside, not what they were on the outside. That's why the people called Jesus "a friend of sinners." He was their friend, and He related to them without compromising His holiness or sharing in their sin.

In fact, when we consider the earthly family of Jesus Himself, it becomes obvious that He was not from the "upper crust" either economically or socially.

Jesus was a blue-collar person, a poor carpenter from a nowhere village called Nazareth. Jesus did not own a home. He had no social status, or, as the prophet Isaiah wrote, no "stately form or majesty" (53:2) that would cause heads to turn when He walked into a room. Jesus looked quite ordinary.

So Jesus lived on the earth He created, but He made no claims of wealth or worldly greatness. Anyone who judged Jesus by the world's standards (wealth, status, appearance, etc.) was sadly off the mark. And all the time He was the Son of God, or, as James says, "our glorious Lord Jesus Christ" (2:1). James uses the Lord's full title and refers to His glory because he wants us to remember that Jesus is no longer the despised, rejected carpenter from a dead-end town in Galilee. He is now the risen, ascended, exalted Lord of heaven who has all authority over heaven and earth.

The point is that, in Jesus' presence, all of us look shabby. The richest, most powerful, and most well-bred among us have nothing to brag about before Jesus. And the poorest and least well-connected have nothing to be ashamed of in His presence. None of the world's standards of accomplishment, status, or greatness count anymore.

So how are we relating to other people? We need to see them the way Jesus saw them. We also need to get a proper view of Jesus, as well as a proper view of ourselves in light of who Jesus is.

When we have all of that in focus, we will see the sin of partiality for what it is. Let's talk about the problem and what we can do about it.

The Sin of Partiality

The Bible puts the cookies right down on the lower shelf for us when it addresses the sin of partiality. Scripture plainly states, "My brethren, do not hold your faith in our glorious Lord Jesus Christ with an attitude of personal favoritism" (James 2:1).

There it is. Faith in Jesus Christ and prejudice against others are incompatible. Do you believe in Jesus Christ? Have you come to the correct conclusion that He is your personal Savior, and have you put your faith in Him for salvation? The answer is either yes or no. There are no other options.

If you answered yes, then prejudice and favoritism have no place in your life. But they crept into the church in the first century, and they still exist among believers today.

The Situation
Two visitors show up at church one Sunday. The first guy looks like he stepped from the pages of *GQ* or *Ebony*. He has a tailored suit, French cuffs, and rings on his fingers. He looks like a man of influence and wealth. It's obvious that he has been somewhere and done something. He has made a mark, and it is clear when this man walks in that he deserves attention.

Then another man steps into church from right off the street. It's obvious from the way he's dressed that he doesn't have a lot going for himself, materially speaking. He doesn't even have a good suit to wear to church. It's not that he is deliberately trying to be dirty. It's just that the best he has is shabby.

The Separation
Two men from very different economic groups coming to church—there's nothing wrong with that. The problem is what happens next.

The ushers get into the act. Guess who gets the preferential treatment? The man in fine clothes gets a good seat; the poor man is told to stand in the back.

Fifty years ago in this country, it would have been, "Hey, colored man, you can't come in here," or "Go as far toward the back as possible so we don't have to know you're here."

Now please notice who makes the value judgment here. It's not the rich man. The Bible doesn't condemn successful people just because they are successful. God is not saying a person needs to apologize for being blessed. Neither should a poor person feel bad because he hasn't climbed the ladder of success.

But the people at church separated the rich man and the poor man, making one feel welcome and the other unwelcome.

The Sin

The sin was the faulty value judgment God's people made and the motive that prompted them to make it. The Bible says when you treat people differently based on their wealth (or skin color or ethnic origin), "Have you not made distinctions among yourselves, and become judges with evil motives?" (James 2:4).

The church made a sinful value judgment about its two visitors because that judgment was based solely on external criteria—in this case, the men's economic status. And the motive that prompted the church to show this personal favoritism was also evil.

Although the motive is not stated, it's pretty obvious. Those who show partiality to the rich usually do so because they know a rich person can offer them something a poor person can't. The rich have clout. The poor are left out.

Now notice the phrase "among yourselves." See, it's bad enough that the rich man was honored and the poor man discriminated against simply because of their economic class. But the sin was worse than that because of the message it sent to the rest of the church.

If you were sitting in church and saw this happen, you might conclude several things. First, you might conclude that the rich man must be a better person than the poor man. Maybe God likes this guy better because He made him rich. Maybe God doesn't like poor people that much. Maybe poor people have a character flaw.

You might also conclude that when it comes to the kingdom of God, money talks. The church obviously treats rich people better than it treats poor people, so maybe you'll get further if you're rich. Maybe money opens doors to you in God's kingdom.

Now you might not have thought any of that before you went to church. But witnessing a situation like the one described here could cause you to think differently. That's one reason why the sin of partiality or prejudice is so insidious: It spreads and infects so many people.

A Personal Example

Back in 1970, I went to an all-Anglo church one Sunday in a major Southern city where I was attending college. It was a well-known church, one of the most bustling in that area. I went with one of my professors, who was a church member.

That particular Sunday, the man preaching was being considered for the position of pastor. He was preaching his candidating sermon, as some call it.

This man preached a wonderful message on the importance of rededicating ourselves to the Lord. Then he called those forward who wanted to do that. I went forward to reaffirm my commitment to the Lordship of Jesus Christ in my life.

And when I did, all hell broke loose. I know because I was there. The deacons went into a tizzy. I knew what they were thinking:

What are we going to do about this black man? Maybe he'll want to join the church. Then maybe he'll get married and his wife will want to join the church. Then maybe they'll have children who will mix with our children. And then maybe his kids will like our kids, and they'll want to start dating or—God forbid!—get married!

The deacons made it clear that I could not be part of that church. When the man who preached that day found out about the deacons' reaction to my presence, he wrote the church an open letter saying he was sorry, but he could not accept a call to a church that judged people by external criteria like race.

The motivation behind the deacons' behavior was evil. Years later that church called me and offered me a public apology. They said God had judged the church because it never dealt with that sin.

The issue in prejudice is sin, not simply skin. It's not just a social problem or a matter of how you were raised. It's not just culture. The Bible calls it sin, and it's very real.

The Ignorance of Partiality

Partiality or prejudice is not only sinful, but it's ignorant as well. The person who practices this sin is displaying a form of spiritual stupidity or dullness. Let me show you what I mean.

Partiality Ignores Spiritual Reality

Now that we have seen the problem acted out before us, let's see how the Bible deals with the sin and sets the record straight. James boldly writes, "Did not God choose the poor of this world to be rich in faith and heirs of the kingdom which He promised to those who love Him? But you have dishonored the poor man" (2:5–6).

One reason that partiality reveals spiritual ignorance is because it ignores the reality of what God is doing in the world. If you want to know where God is hanging out, you'll often find Him hanging out with the poor, the outcast, the discriminated against, those despised by this world. God is doing His greatest work among such people.

Now I need to say up front that there's nothing inherently spiritual about being part of a particular racial, economic, or ethnic class. Just being poor or outcast doesn't make you a saint.

But the fact remains that God often chooses to do His work among the poor and despised. God uses the poverty of the poor to give them a richness of faith that a lot of affluent people may never know.

A person who doesn't have much materially often understands better than others the kind of spiritual poverty and dependency that God demands if we are going to follow Him. A lot of rich people in this world are too busy being rich and self-sufficient to sense their spiritual poverty and need for God, which results in a more shallow spiritual experience.

We can see this process at work in our lives. Remember when you were starting out and had nothing? Chances are that when you had nothing, God had more of you.

When you were eking out a living and trying to survive, you never missed church and had lots of time for devotions. God was important. He was a priority.

But then you moved uptown or out to the 'burbs. You acquired the nice house and the cars and the clothes, and suddenly your time was eaten up by efforts to maintain your lifestyle.

Now I'm not pointing a finger at you. It happens to all of us if we're not careful. And when we get like this, our spiritual vision becomes blurred. We begin measuring people by their possessions or other physical or material criteria because that's what has become important to us.

This blurred vision breeds spiritual ignorance, because the people the world values least are highly valued by God. And at His judgment, things are going to be reversed and we'll find out who the real millionaires are. People's true wealth and status will show up on that day.

At the judgment bar of Jesus Christ, the poor folk and nobodies of this world will rise to the top. But the sin of prejudice and discrimination lets this spiritual reality get all out of focus.

So if your success in the marketplace, the color of your skin, or some other factor has produced prideful insensitivity toward those you consider beneath you or even less valuable to God, it's time to wise up.

Partiality Ignores the Place of Faith

Here's another aspect of the sin of partiality: It ignores and denigrates the great faith of people who are the victims of mistreatment and discrimination. Believers who are so easily looked down on due to lack of status or wealth are often rich in faith. Let me offer one reason why.

Jesus taught us to pray each day for our daily bread. Most of us don't pray with that kind of intensity because we not only have today's bread in the house, we have tomorrow's and next week's and next month's food in the refrigerator and freezer.

But many people in this world have to get on their knees every day and say, "Lord, if we are going to eat today, You will have to supply our food." They are trusting God literally day by day. In some parts of the world, people are trusting God meal by meal. These folks are rich in faith, and God says these are the wealthy people.

Since that's true, it is an act of spiritual ignorance to practice prejudice against materially poor or outcast people. It tells them (and even onlookers) that they and their faith aren't worth much in God's sight.

Let me pause and add a word of warning about a popular form of teaching known as prosperity theology. This is an evil teaching not only because it's bad theology, but because it inadvertently helps feed prejudice against those who have little.

Prosperity theology teaches people to gauge their spirituality by the level of their prosperity. To be in need, therefore, means your faith is deficient.

That idea is evil, because it implies that someone who has great, unmet material needs is somehow weak in faith. It is also evil because it implies that Third World people are carnal because they don't have all the stuff we have here in the West.

So the "name it and claim it" crowd can invite us to look askance at those who are poor, but some of God's choicest servants in the Bible had nothing. Many heroes of the faith went around "in sheepskins [and] goatskins" because they were "destitute" (Heb. 11:37).

People who are poor by the world's standards will be great in the kingdom. God says He is going to make them His heirs. So how can you and I discriminate against somebody who is going to wind up at the top of the heap?

In fact, if you are in a crisis, the poor saint is the person you want to have pray for you. Such saints know how to trust God and rely on Him in an emergency.

Partiality Ignores God's Priorities

You may have noticed that God delights in reversing the world's idea of things. Paul spells this out:

> Consider your calling, brethren, that there were not many wise according to the flesh, not many mighty, not many noble; but God has chosen the foolish things of the world to shame the wise, and God has chosen the weak things of the world to shame the things which are

> strong, and the base things of the world and the despised, God has
> chosen, the things that are not, that He might nullify the things that
> are, that no man should boast before God. (1 Cor. 1:26–29)

Now don't misunderstand. God is not saying we should treat rich
people badly in favor of the poor. That's reverse discrimination.

But Jesus did say it's easier for a camel to go through the eye of
a needle than for a rich person to enter the kingdom of God! According to the Bible, there aren't going to be a lot of rich people in
heaven. God's priority is what's on the inside of a person.

But the sin of partiality causes us to ignore that priority. Since
wealth, skin color, or ethnic origin say nothing about a person's real
value, we ought not judge and treat people on the basis of these
external criteria.

We also need to remember that God's judgment in the last day
will address how the "least" of His people were treated (see Matt.
25:31–46). At the judgment, we'll be glad we treated people with justice. It's the way a Christian who seeks to glorify God in this life
should live.

Partiality Ignores Spiritual Warfare

A soldier who is supposed to be at war yet can't tell who the enemy
is, is dangerously ignorant! So are we believers when we practice
prejudice.

Scripture asks, "Is it not the rich who oppress you and personally drag you into court? Do they not blaspheme the fair name by
which you have been called?" (James 2:6–7). That's definitely a
description of the way the world works. The world's "Golden Rule"
is, "He who has the gold, gets to rule." And usually the highly affluent
and highly educated people are the most resistant and opposed to the
Christian faith.

Now we can't generalize too much on this. But, by and large, the
story of mankind has been the oppression of the poor and weak by
the wealthy and powerful. It is the rich and powerful who often
lobby for laws that go against our Christian faith and values.

This principle carries over to the spiritual realm. The Bible is saying that if you favor the rich over the poor, you may be favoring your oppressors.

People are not the real enemy, of course. But the devil uses people to accomplish his agenda, and he often finds his most useful recruits among those who think they have reason to feel superior to others. So prejudice gives the devil another weapon to use against us.

The Solution to Partiality

Now the good news! You who are growing into the image of Christ need to know that there is an answer to prejudice, a cure for discrimination. The solution to the sin of partiality is conformity to the objective standard of God's Word. Even Peter, the once-bigoted Jew, came to understand that "God is not one to show partiality" (Acts 10:34). Neither should His kids show partiality.

Now let me emphasize again the problem is not that people are different. God designed us with differences, whether the differences are in superficial things like clothing, musical taste, and food preferences, or more deep-seated characteristics like our race or ethnic background.

Differences are legitimate. The problem arises when we let those differences keep us from treating people justly and biblically. When we say we can't relate to each other because one of us is black or white, you have the beginnings of prejudice. The only solution is a biblical one.

Obey the Royal Law

So how can you avoid the sin of partiality? James sets forth the standard: First, by obeying the royal law. "If . . . you are fulfilling the royal law, according to the Scripture, 'You shall love your neighbor as yourself,' you are doing well" (2:8).

The more complete statement of what James calls the "royal law" is found in Matthew 22:37–40. There Jesus said that the greatest commandment is to love God with all of our being and to love our neighbor as ourselves. The royal law is the law of love.

The royal law has two dimensions to it: the vertical and the horizontal. We need both. Love of God and love for your neighbor are intimately related. The Bible declares, "The one who does not love his brother whom he has seen, cannot love God whom he has not seen" (1 John 4:20).

The royal law is to love others as you love yourself. That covers the sin of partiality. This law is royal because it was originally given by the Ruler of heaven back in the Law of Moses (see Lev. 19:18). Then it was reiterated by Jesus, the King of kings.

But the ultimate reason the law of love is called the royal law is that it rules over all the other laws.

The Bible says, "Love does no wrong to a neighbor; love therefore is the fulfillment of the law" (Rom. 13:10). Love is the fulfillment of the law because when you act in love, you don't need the other laws.

You see, we need all kinds of laws because of our sinful lack of love. If people lived by the royal law of love, they wouldn't steal from others because they wouldn't want others to steal from them. They wouldn't hurt others because they wouldn't want to be hurt by others.

The royal law demands that we love God with everything that is in us. But the Bible says we can't love God unless we love one another. This is not just an emotional love, the feeling of love we may have for someone. When the Bible talks about love, it is talking about a decision of the will.

This is why God can command us to obey His royal law. Biblical love is not necessarily related to how you feel about someone at any given moment. Biblical love can say to a person of another race, class, or culture, "I am going to treat you right even if I have to work through how I was raised."

This is why I say that obeying God's royal law of love offers a solution to the problem and sin of partiality.

Now I realize that putting this love to work is not always easy. Each one of us has ingrained emotions and prejudices and ideas to work through because each one of us is a flawed human being. But biblical love says, "Although I still have some stuff to deal with emotionally, I am going to obey God and show biblical love toward you." That's love. Love is righteousness in action.

Someone may say, "That sounds good, but I'm just not there

yet." You're telling me how you *feel,* but that's not what God is after. He wants to know how you are going to *act.* He wants you to make a decision of your will to show biblical love.

And when you obey, God will respond and reward you for your love. But He wants nothing less from us than obedience to His royal law—and we will be judged by it.

Call Partiality What It Is

What else can you do to avoid discriminatory attitudes and actions? James is very direct: Simply call partiality what it really is. "If you show partiality, you are committing sin and are convicted by the law as transgressors" (2:9). Partiality is sin, pure and simple. And it's as heinous in God's sight as any other sin.

We won't get anywhere in our growth toward Christlikeness until we label sin correctly. A person who shows prejudice against those of a different race is a racist—and racism is sin. The same is true for any other kind of prejudice or discrimination.

Now it's getting heavy. When we commit this sin, God puts us in a category called "transgressor."

You say, "Wait a minute, Tony. You mean God puts the prejudiced person in the same category as a murderer or thief?"

Yes, that's what this means. God's standard is so absolute that "whoever keeps the whole law and yet stumbles in one point, he has become guilty of all" (James 2:10).

James goes on to explain what that guilt means by using the example of murder and adultery. He argues that a murderer can't expect to get off by pleading his innocence on the charge of adultery.

Imagine a person standing before the judge and confessing, "Yes, Your Honor, I committed this murder. But before you sentence me, I just want to let you know that I have never committed adultery."

That point of innocence won't get the murderer anywhere because it is irrelevant to the issue at hand. Not committing one sin doesn't cancel out the penalty for the sin the guilty party did commit.

Now in the Old Testament, murder and adultery were both punishable by death. They were serious, capital offenses. And here God puts the sin of prejudice and discrimination in the same category.

In other words, don't call partiality a minor sin. Don't say, "This is a 'social' thing. It isn't as serious as murder. I may be a little prejudiced against people of a different color, but I certainly haven't killed anybody."

The Bible says the same God who tells us not to murder or commit adultery also tells us not to show partiality toward people based on evil motives.

If you are hanging over the side of a cliff by a chain with ten links, it doesn't matter if nine of the links hold. If just one link breaks, you are going down, because all the links are interconnected.

The reason the church of Jesus Christ has not been able to solve its race or class or culture problem is that we have not treated the sin of prejudice with the same seriousness we have applied to other sins.

We have excused it based on how people were raised or what happened in a person's past. But partiality is a sin in God's sight that needs to be eradicated, and He wants us to do so in our hearts and lives.

Show Mercy to All

One more way of avoiding the sin of partiality is a "how-to" found in a word of hope. The Bible says, "Judgment will be merciless to one who has shown no mercy; mercy triumphs over judgment" (James 2:13).

Hang on—this is rich! When we show mercy to others, when we act with love and justice to all regardless of race, class, or culture, God turns that mercy around to our eternal credit.

Let me paint a picture of what the Bible is talking about here. One day you and I are going to stand before the judgment seat of Christ to have our lives evaluated and see kingdom rewards handed out—or denied.

At this judgment Jesus Christ will play back the videotape of your life, so to speak. This tape will provide a comprehensive review of your service for Him (or lack of it) since your salvation.

Let me tell you, our thoughts, words, and actions are going to be revealed and reviewed on that day. We'll have plenty to account for just with that, but the Bible also says the fire of Christ's judgment seat will test our works for the motives behind them. That's going to be tough because we do a lot of good things for the wrong reasons.

Now here's where mercy comes in. As we are being evaluated for possible rewards in heaven—not whether we go to heaven, because that issue was settled when we accepted Christ—many of us are going to be looking for mercy because we failed God on so many occasions.

So Jesus Christ will "fast-forward" the tape and stop at every place where we showed mercy to someone else. The tape stops at a place where you made a nobody in the world's eyes feel like somebody. That counts toward your mercy.

Another time you treated a brother or sister of a different skin color according to the royal law of love. Or you reached out to a person who had nothing and shared your resources. Those acts of love go into your "mercy" account, too.

You get the idea. God is going to figure mercy into His evaluation of your life. With enough mercy, you can still win the day because mercy triumphs over judgment.

So what does the solution to partiality look like when you, growing to be like Christ, put it all together? It begins with naming and confessing partiality as sin. It includes a commitment to obey the royal law of love, and it means looking for opportunities to act with justice and mercy to those who differ from you.

The great Hindu leader Mahatma Gandhi was drawn to the teachings of Christianity early in his life. But when he tried to attend a Christian church in India, he was treated badly. Later he wrote in his memoirs that if Christianity had a caste system, too, he might as well remain a Hindu. Gandhi also said he might have become a Christian if it were not for Christians. Let's make sure no one of any race, economic class, or ethnic group can say that of us. If we are walking in Christ's footsteps toward the goal of perfection and following His example along the way, the sin of partiality will not be a problem.

Test Your Perfection I.Q.

- Partiality (or prejudice) is not only sinful, it's also ignorant. Give yourself three points for each point of ignorance listed below you can explain.

  1. Partiality ignores spiritual reality.
  What can poor and humble people learn about themselves more easily than rich and arrogant people?

  2. Partiality ignores the place of faith.
  What can the impoverished learn about God that others who are blinded by material possessions cannot see?

  3. Partiality ignores God's priorities.
  What does God value more than externals?

  4. Partiality ignores spiritual warfare.
  Why can favoring the rich be ironic as well as self-defeating?

- There is an answer to prejudice, a solution to the sin of partiality. That solution is conformity to God's Word. Before considering how closely you're conforming to the standards of Scripture, take an open-eyed look at your own prejudices and points of discrimination.

—*Obey the royal law.*
  Are you loving God with all your being and your neighbor as yourself? On this scale, "1" is "Help! I'm stuck in upbringing and rationalizing!" and "10" is "Consistently choosing to do loving, kind things in Jesus' name and for His sake."

  1 2 3 4 5 6 7 8 9 10

—*Call partiality what it is.*

How partial am I toward others? Is the sin of prejudice present within my heart? What behaviors do I have that reflect this sin? The person who chooses to avoid this question is at "1" on this scale. The person who reaches out to the Samaritan woman at the well as Jesus did is at "10."

1 2 3 4 5 6 7 8 9 10

—*Show mercy to those who are different from you.*

Do you make the "nobodies" in the world's eyes feel like "somebodies"? Do you treat people of a different skin color according to the royal law of love? The person at number 1 says, "Clothes—skin color, bank accounts, corporate titles, and education—make the man!" The person at number 10 sees people as Jesus sees them: The internals matter more than the externals.

1 2 3 4 5 6 7 8 9 10

Total Points _____

Chapter 6

How to Balance Faith and Works

This may be reaching back a long way for you, but remember when the teacher handed out a test in school that included a question you didn't understand?

That essay question counted for a big part of the grade, but the wording was very confusing. You didn't know exactly what the teacher wanted, but the question was too important to skip. So you had to raise your hand (or hope someone else did) and ask, "What does this mean?"

Sometimes a passage of Scripture can also be confusing, causing controversy as well as misunderstanding. But we can't let confusion turn us away from such a passage or keep us from trying to understand what God wants us to know. He wants us, for instance, to understand the relationship between our faith *in* Christ and our works *for* Christ.

At first glance, the matter of faith *in* Christ and works *for* Christ may sound like just an item for discussion and debate among seminarians. Not at all! This is everyday stuff. Getting this truth under your spiritual belt will make a huge impact on your daily Christian life.

If you want to enrich and maximize your spiritual experience— if you want to be the perfect Christian God calls you to be—it is critical that you understand how God designed faith and works to interact with each other. Let me make two statements that summarize the message of this chapter, and then we'll unfold the Word.

First, faith in Christ—faith alone—is what justifies us and gets us to heaven. The Bible says, "By grace you have been saved through faith . . . not as a result of works" (Eph. 2:8–9). Good works can't save anyone from the consequences of their sin.

Second, while good works can't save people, they do play a vital role in helping saved people experience all that God has for them here on earth. Immediately after reminding us that we are not saved by works, Paul said we are "created in Christ Jesus for good works" (Eph. 2:10). So works are indeed an integral part of a believer's growth toward Christlikeness and perfection. Let's see just how crucial they are.

Faith and Works

I'm assuming you want to grow in your Christian life, or you wouldn't have picked up this book. My guess is also that you don't want a useless kind of faith that doesn't take you anywhere or do anything for the kingdom.

God doesn't want you to have a useless faith, either. That's why He asks this important question: "What use is it, my brethren, if a man says he has faith, but he has no works? Can that faith save him?" (James 2:14).

The key word here is *use*, because this passage is talking about your usefulness while you're on earth, not your future entrance into heaven.

But this verse makes it sound as if faith is not enough to save us. And yet the apostle Paul said again and again that faith apart from works is the only thing that saves us.

My purpose here is not to debate fully the issue of the relationship between faith and works, but that doesn't mean the question is unimportant. In fact, it is so deeply interwoven with the message I want to get across that we need to take a little space and try to resolve the apparent problem.

The great reformer Martin Luther got upset when he read James 2:14 because it seemed to contradict what Paul had written in the book of Romans. For example, Paul wrote:

Abraham believed God, and it was reckoned to him as righteousness. Now to the one who works, his wage is not reckoned as a favor, but as what is due. But to the one who does not work, but believes in Him who justifies the ungodly, his faith is reckoned as righteousness. (Rom. 4:3–5)

That's about as clear as it gets: If you try to add works to faith, you cannot be saved, says Paul. But James seems to say if you *don't* add works to faith, you aren't saved.

That's an apparent contradiction. But since we know God does not contradict Himself, there must be a solution. There is—and the answer is not just academic. The degree to which you understand how faith and works fit together is the degree to which you will be free to go for the gold in terms of what God has waiting for you!

So how do we harmonize these two teachings? Actually, James has already done this with the simple word *brethren*. Whereas Paul was explaining how sinners become saints, James was explaining how believers in Christ progress in their faith. James was dealing with the issue of sanctification or Christian growth; Paul was dealing with the matter of salvation.

Paul is telling us how to get from earth to heaven. James is telling us how to get heaven back down to earth. Paul is explaining how to know where you are going to spend eternity.

James is explaining how you can experience some of eternity while you are waiting to get there.

Here, when James uses the word *saved,* he is referring to the justification of the believer, not the justification of the sinner. Here James is concerned about believers becoming impoverished and losing their spiritual vitality because of carnal living.

In other words, these two apostles were writing about two different groups of people—sinners and saints. Like James, I'm talking to saints here, to people like you who want to know what it takes to live life to the fullest for God. One thing it takes is good works. As a matter of fact, good works are indispensable.

Works Are Indispensable to Spiritual Progress

We've established that faith in the finished work of Jesus Christ is sufficient for our salvation in eternity. But we need to put our faith to work now if we want to experience God's power and presence in history.

My concern is that a lot of Christians who are on their way to heaven won't experience much of heaven until they get there. That's not what God had in mind for us. Eternal life doesn't begin the moment you die but the moment you trust Christ. God wants us to experience more and more of heaven until we arrive and get the whole glorious thing.

To experience heaven in our fallen world requires both faith and works, not just faith. Martin Luther put it this way: "We are justified by faith alone, but not by a faith that is alone." In other words, once your eternity is taken care of in Christ, you should want to serve Him in time because you are so grateful for your salvation.

But many Christians are stumbling downhill when they ought to be climbing higher. They have faith, but they aren't really doing anything significant for Christ, so their faith isn't growing.

A Practical Illustration

To bring this discussion of the importance of works to the world of everyday living, consider this situation:

Suppose your doorbell rings and you open it to find a family from your church that has hit hard times. The father says, "We haven't eaten in several days. Can you help us?"

So you take the family into your living room, get out your Bible, and say, "Let's have a Bible study." You start reading passages that tell how God can make a way where there is no way, how He rained manna on the Israelites when they were in the wilderness, how He miraculously fed five thousand people with a few loaves of bread and a couple of fish.

Then you say, "My Bible says God can feed you when you're hungry. He's a doctor when you are sick, a shepherd when you're lost, and a rock when you're in the midst of storms. My Bible tells me God can do anything. Isn't that encouraging? Let's have a word of prayer." You ask God to meet the needs of this brother and sister and their children, lay your hands on them and say, "Go in peace," show them to the door, and close it behind them.

God's question to you in that situation is, "What good is that kind of faith?" That hungry family didn't need a sermon; they needed supper. They didn't need to sit in your living room but in your kitchen. They needed you to open your refrigerator, not your Bible.

Now don't misunderstand. There's nothing wrong with sharing the Word with people in need. The problem is when you don't heed the Word you're sharing and meet the need God brought to you (see James 2:15–16).

Wasting Your Time?

I'm convinced that a lot of people who go to church on Sunday are wasting their time. In fact, some people are in the process of wasting fifty-two perfectly good Sunday mornings this year.

Why? Because although they go to church and get the right biblical information, it never produces the right action in their lives and so they gain no benefit at all from the Word. They are no further along spiritually this year than they were last year. After all, we cannot grow in our faith if our faith is not married to action. Put differently, "Faith, if it has no works, is dead, being by itself" (James 2:17). Faith that does not grow, dies. It shrinks and shrivels and becomes a mere creedal corpse. Faith must be energized by being put into action—by works—in order to be potent.

You can go to church and "Amen!" the preacher, you can shout and weep over the Word, you can even jump over the pews if you want. But you will be no further along in your spiritual experience unless you put your faith to work.

Now let me clarify again. I am not talking about working to earn or to secure your eternal salvation. That was settled when you first trusted Christ. My concern here is what that faith produces in you while you're on your way to heaven.

To borrow from the marriage analogy again, when genuine faith is married to good works, that union produces a child called spiritual growth. Just as both parents are indispensable in the conception of a child, faith without works will remain infertile.

Works Are Indispensable to Verify Faith

Whenever the subject of faith and works comes up, an objection such as this also arises: "Someone may well say, 'You have faith, and I have works; show me your faith without the works, and I will show you my faith by my works" (v. 18).

The Connection

This hypothetical objector maintains there is no necessary connection between faith and works. The objector argues that a person's works don't necessarily prove anything. After all, isn't faith merely an internal system of belief?

This person might say, "Look, tell me about your doctrine, what you believe. And after you do that, I'll show you what I believe by what I do. You'll be able to read my beliefs in my actions."

Then the objector offers an example to prove his argument that faith and works are not connected: "You believe that God is one. You do well; the demons also believe, and shudder" (v. 19).

The demon world certainly has right doctrine. The devil believes that there is only one God and so do his demons. Remember, Satan and the demons used to live in heaven with God. Their "faith" is correct. But the devil's belief doesn't produce any good works.

So the person objecting to James says, "You believe in God, the demons believe in God. Same faith, but two very different results. So there is no relationship between what a person believes and what he does. The demons believe and do wrong; you believe and do right. You can't try to marry faith to works because they're unrelated."

This argument may sound good for a minute, but the retort takes care of that. "But are you willing to recognize, you foolish fellow, that faith without works is useless?" (v. 20). The answer to the hypothetical objector is that a person's faith and works have everything to do with each other. In the eyes of those around us, our works verify the reality of our faith. Without such a visible verification, our faith appears to have no usefulness. And in fact, faith without the works that flow from it is of little use.

There's that key concept again: uselessness or usefulness. The issue we are dealing with is how to make sure our Christian lives are of benefit to God and others while we're here on earth.

A Useless Faith

My guess is that you have some useless stuff sitting in your garage and lying around in your attic. We all accumulate things like that: half-cans of paint, gadgets we haven't used in years, the exercise bicycle covered with dust. Such items no longer make any positive contribution to your life. They don't add anything to your existence. They offer no benefit to anyone. All they do is take up space.

Likewise, many believers fail to make significant contributions to the world around them; theirs is a useless faith. Oh, they believe in Jesus, but their faith hasn't been joined to good works, so it hasn't become useful to themselves or to others. As we've seen, the Bible says works are not only beneficial, they are indispensable because, without them, our Christianity becomes useless.

A useless faith doesn't sustain you in trials or help you break the hold of addictions. It doesn't produce joy when things are tough; it doesn't give you victory over circumstances or patience and self-control when your life is spinning. And a useless faith doesn't allow your life to overflow to the benefit and blessing of others.

Works Have Always Been Indispensable

Just as the reference to demons illustrated that the same belief can lead to different actions, James refers to Abraham and Rahab to illustrate and to prove his thesis that our faith needs to be a working faith.

Abraham's Sacrifice

Abraham is the embodiment of faith, the "father of the faithful," the classic example of what a life of faith looks like. It's no wonder, then, that James refers to him to argue his point: "Was not Abraham our father justified by works, when he offered up Isaac his son on the altar? You see that faith was working with his works, and as a result of the works, faith was perfected" (2:21–22). Clearly, the life of Abraham proves that works have always been indispensable to spiritual maturity. This vital connection between faith and works was not some new idea being imported into the Scriptures.

James points specifically to Abraham's willingness to offer Isaac on an altar to the Lord (Gen. 22:1–18), arguably the greatest act of faith ever by a human being. The Bible says that when Abraham laid Isaac on that altar and raised the knife, he was justified by his works. His faith was perfected, raised to a higher spiritual level.

Now we need to understand that this sacrifice had nothing to do with Abraham being justified before God. Years before Isaac was even born, he had been declared righteous by virtue of his faith in God (see Gen. 15:6). Since Isaac was probably in his late teenage years at the time of the sacrifice, many years have passed between these two events.

The sacrifice of Isaac was not about Abraham's salvation for eternity but instead was about his sanctification, his experience of God in history. God sent Abraham the greatest test of his life in order to take him to a level of faith he had never before reached.

But when God told Abraham to take Isaac to Mount Moriah and sacrifice him as a burnt offering, Abraham faced a huge dilemma. First, Isaac was his long-awaited and beloved son. Second, Isaac was the son who fulfilled God's long standing promise to Abraham to give him innumerable descendants and bless all the nations through him. Isaac was Abraham's covenant son, and now God was telling Abraham to kill him.

As we continue, remember the context. James is using Abraham to illustrate the way faith *and* works bring us to spiritual maturity and perfection (James 2:22).

Now Abraham was already a man of faith when this hard command came from God. But put yourself in Abraham's place, and you can imagine the tremendous test this would be to your faith. You might even be saying, "This can't be from God. He wouldn't ask me to do anything this difficult."

We don't know what went through Abraham's mind the night before the sacrifice. But we do know that he got up, went to Mount Moriah, and told his servants, "Stay here with the donkey, and I and the lad will go yonder; and we will worship and return to you" (Gen. 22:5).

So Abraham and Isaac went up the mountain, and Isaac asked where the sacrificial lamb was. Abraham answered, "God will provide for Himself the lamb for the burnt offering, my son" (v. 8). That was the last word either one spoke until Abraham tied Isaac up, laid him on the altar, and raised his knife.

As a father, I can easily imagine Abraham wondering at each stage where God was and when He was going to intervene. Abraham had obeyed by getting up, going to Mount Moriah, building an altar, and laying Isaac on the wood. He had even reached for his knife. And still God had not shown up.

Why? Because God's command was not just to get up, travel to the mountain, and lay Isaac on an altar. The command was to kill Isaac and offer him as a burnt offering to God—the ultimate act or work of faith.

It wasn't until Abraham took that ultimate step by starting to plunge the knife into Isaac that the angel of the Lord stopped him. Only at that point did the pronouncement of Abraham's "justification by works" come. At that point, God said, "Now I know that you fear God" (v. 12), and Abraham looked up and saw the ram caught in the thicket by its horns.

With that act of radical obedience, Abraham's faith was justified; it was demonstrated for all the world to see. The world clearly saw that Abraham's faith was not just a set of beliefs in his head.

Abraham's faith in God caused him to do the works of God. And

God could say, "Now I know that you are serious about Me. Now I know that you love Me more than anything or anyone else. Now I know you are for real."

You see, God had that ram there all the time. But that was the quietest ram in the history of Israel because it didn't budge until Abraham had gone all the way in obedience. In this sense Abraham was "justified by works" (James 2:21): His faith was perfected because it proved to be a working faith.

In terms of salvation, Abraham was justified by faith and faith alone. But in terms of his earthly experience and in the eyes of others, Abraham was justified when his faith went to work and he was able to obey God in the most difficult assignment ever given to a human being.

Now I'm convinced that God has a ram hidden in the thicket for a lot of us. God has the answer to our prayers waiting for us, but we can't see the ram or hear the ram moving because we haven't obeyed God all the way. Our faith is not yet working the way God wants it to work.

Until our faith gets to work and we obey God all the way, we will not see Him enter into our experience and bring about the deliverance we need. We will not see God take our faith to the next level of spiritual growth He desires for us.

Furthermore, a faith that isn't yet working is not a faith that can be vindicated or demonstrated to the world. Now God knows whether you truly believe in Him, but everyone else knows your faith is the real article only when they see your good works.

Imagine how Abraham felt after he had offered Isaac. His trust in God must have soared! He had experienced a huge taste of glory, of heaven on earth. He wasn't any more saved than when he started up Mount Moriah. But when he came back down, his faith was a whole lot more perfect.

James puts it this way: "And the Scripture was fulfilled which says, 'And Abraham believed God, and it was reckoned to him as righteousness,' and he was called the friend of God" (2:23). Now get this: The offering of Isaac fulfilled God's earlier declaration of Abraham's justification by faith because it publicly demonstrated the truth of that declaration (Gen. 15:6).

This principle is important for you to understand. Abraham's life shows that, from the very beginning, God intended that Abraham's faith (and our faith) should be accompanied and verified by good works.

The Development of Faith

Let me point out one other thing about the way God developed Abraham's faith. When God first promised Abraham and Sarah a son, they laughed because they both knew they were too old to have a child. Abraham's body and Sarah's womb were as good as dead. The idea of conceiving a child at their ages made Sarah shake her head and chuckle—but Isaac was born!

Now Abraham hadn't known how God was going to pull off the miracle of a son, but he didn't have to understand it. All he had to do was believe it.

My point is that the promise of Isaac's birth took Abraham's faith to a new level because he had to believe God against all appearances. The lesson of faith that Abraham learned was that God can give life to a dead body.

And do you see how that lesson prepared Abraham for the next level of his faith? How could he say that he and Isaac would return from the mountain? Because Abraham had seen what God could do with a dead body. He believed God could give life to his son's dead body if it came to that.

Now that doesn't mean Abraham didn't struggle with obeying the command to kill Isaac. But his experience shows why our works are so totally indispensable to the perfecting of our faith. If Abraham had not learned the earlier lesson of faith, he would not have been ready for the next one.

Having learned these lessons, though, Abraham was called "the friend of God." What a tremendous statement of intimacy with God, the kind of intimacy most of us would love to have! And Abraham's life shows us what it takes to achieve it. Intimacy with God takes the kind of working faith that will lead us to do whatever God asks us to do, even if it makes no sense to us.

The Example of Rahab

James gives us one more illustration of working faith, the story of Rahab: "In the same way [as Abraham] was not Rahab the harlot also justified by works, when she received the messengers and sent them out by another way?" (2:25).

It's a big step from a patriarch to a prostitute, but Rahab's life proves the same point as Abraham's. Rahab demonstrated her faith when she received and hid the two Israelites who came to check out Jericho for Joshua before Israel attacked the city as part of its conquest of Canaan.

As Rahab was talking with the spies, she declared her faith in the God of Israel when she said, "The LORD your God, He is God in heaven above and on earth beneath" (Josh. 2:11). At this point we can say that Rahab was saved in the New Testament sense of the word. She put her faith in Jehovah for salvation when she took in the spies.

But James goes on to say that Rahab was justified by works when she hid the men in her home and sent them safely on their way. Rahab's reward for her working faith was that her whole family was spared when Israel marched around Jericho and brought the place crashing down.

So like God's friend Abraham, Rahab was justified by her works. Her faith in God transformed her eternity, but her act of faith in protecting the spies preserved her and her family in history. When you go all the way with God, He enters history and transforms your daily life.

So if you want to see things changed on earth, yours needs to be a faith that works. This has always been the case and always will be.

Works Are Indispensable to Vibrant Faith

So far we have encountered some strong statements about the importance of works in a Christian's life. Now we come to the strongest statement of all: "For just as the body without the spirit is dead, so also faith without works is dead" (James 2:26). Faith that produces no works has no life to it.

But a physical body that is dead was once alive. Likewise, a faith that is dead was once alive. True Christians can lose the operative reality of their faith: Their lives can stop reflecting their beliefs.

Now physical death occurs when the spirit leaves the body. The spirit is the life principle of the body. When you accepted Jesus Christ as your Savior and Lord you became spiritually alive. What, then, causes your faith to die?

If your faith is dead, if it isn't making itself apparent in any actions or behaviors, if your spiritual "get-up-and-go" has gotten up and gone, if you are living a defeated life instead of a victorious life, it is not that you never had spiritual life if in fact you have trusted Christ alone for salvation. The problem is that the life principle that keeps faith functioning is no longer operating in you.

If you want the body of your faith to get up out of that spiritual coffin, you have to put the spirit—the life principle—back into it. The life principle for the faith of the believer is the biblical application of truth to life on a daily basis—what the Bible calls works.

Seeing Your Faith at Work

You may be waiting for blessings from God that He is not going to give you until He sees your faith at work. Saying to a needy brother, "Go in peace" is not good enough. Having the right belief system in your head is not enough when the discussion is about putting your faith to work.

I want to close this chapter with two powerful Old Testament stories in which God saw faith at work and rewarded those involved with blessings. The first is the well-known confrontation between David and Goliath.

Do you think it was David's faith or the stone that killed Goliath? It was both. That stone would have done no damage if it had not been thrown in faith by David, trusting in God's power.

But if all David had done was go out, meet Goliath, and say, "Oh yeah? Let me tell you, my God is big! He's so high you can't get over Him. He's so low you can't get under Him. He's so wide you can't get around Him. He's the Rose of Sharon. He's the Balm in Gilead. He's the Bright and Morning Star," that child would have been squashed in the ground by Goliath.

David was victorious over Goliath because he not only believed God, but he picked up some stones to use on that bad boy. David's readiness to use his sling, married to his faith in God, allowed him to bring down Goliath and helped pave his way to the throne of Israel.

The widow of Zarephath is another example of faith and works that I like because she used her last meal to feed the preacher.

The famine was bad in Israel, and the people north of Israel were starving, too. This woman and her son were down to their last handful of flour. She was going to bake some bread for their final meal.

God had told this woman, "A preacher is coming to town named Elijah. I want you to take the last of your bread and feed him."

When Elijah arrived, he asked her for a piece of bread. But the woman said, "This is all my boy and I have. We're going to eat it and then we will die."

Elijah said, "Do what I ask because the God of Israel says your flour bowl will never be empty."

If you know the story, you know what happened next. As the widow fixed her last meal for the preacher, the flour just kept on coming and coming. She trusted God, but He didn't make a way for her until she opened her flour container and poured out what she had left for God's prophet.

Of course, the story doesn't end with an abundant food supply. Later on the woman's son died. But because she had put her faith to work in caring for Elijah, God gave Elijah the power to raise her son from the dead.

What is God asking you to do? Is there an area of your life where your faith is either dead in terms of doing good or only half-alive? What God wants from you is faith that works.

Test Your Perfection I.Q.

- Give yourself four points for each of these three answers. What are the two illustrations James gives of works being evidence of faith?

1.

2.

In this context, how is "justified by works" different from being "saved by works"?

3.

- Faith gets to work and obeys God all the way.

—When God gives you the opportunity, how willingly would you go all the way for God as Abraham did when he was willing to sacrifice Isaac and as Rahab did when she hid the spies? On this scale, "1" is "This can't be from God! He wouldn't ask me to do anything this difficult" and "10" is "Just call me Abraham or Rahab!"

1 2 3 4 5 6 7 8 9 10

—A more significant gauge of your balance between faith and works is how well you apply God's truth to your life on a daily basis. Here "1" means your faith is dead to good works and in a spiritual coffin and "10" means your faith is alive and well; you are continually applying God's truth to every aspect of your life.

1 2 3 4 5 6 7 8 9 10

—In general, evaluate the balance you maintain between being ready to act for God and having faith in Him. On this scale, "1" means you have faith like a stone, inert and lifeless, and "10" means you have faith like David as he faced Goliath, ready to act and trusting God to complete his efforts.

1 2 3 4 5 6 7 8 9 10

Total Points _____

Chapter 7

How to Control Your Tongue

You may remember the case of the Unabomber, the long-sought killer who mailed letter and package bombs to people for about fifteen years.

Several people were killed in these attacks, and others were badly maimed when they opened what they thought was a normal package—only to have it explode in their faces.

Why do I bring this up? Well, I can't help but think there are some spiritual Unabombers running around in the body of Christ today. These are people who use their tongues to destroy others, sending out verbal bombs that explode in people's lives and maim them spiritually and emotionally.

Some husbands and wives are like Unabombers to each other. Husbands beat down their wives emotionally and break their spirits through criticism and the use of destructive language. And wives shred their husbands by attacking them rather than meeting their need for honor, respect, and a sense of significance.

Some parents maim their children with such verbal explosives as "Can't you do *anything* right?," "You're never going to amount to anything," and "Why can't you be more like your sister [or brother]?" And children do their own damage by insulting their parents and refusing to give them the honor and respect they deserve.

You may not have considered the connection, but such damaging words often come in lives devoid of good works. If you don't have a faith that produces works, something has to fill that works vacuum— and more than likely, it will be words. If you don't spend your energy doing, you'll spend your energy talking. In the absence of works, you will usually find an abundance of words.

The Problem of the Tongue

If there is one point you take home from this book, I hope it's this: If you want to reach God's goal for you and be a perfect Christian, you must control your tongue. We noted earlier that one characteristic of faith that is valuable to God is the ability to keep our tongues in check.

Now we are going to see that what we do with our mouths impacts every part of our lives. How can that be? Because the human tongue is powerful, perverse, and polluted—and that makes for a big problem.

That same tongue, however, is also used to speak words of truth, freedom, and encouragement. At this point a word of caution is appropriate: "Let not many of you become teachers, my brethren, knowing that as such we shall incur a stricter judgment" (James 3:1). Some Christians wanted to be in places of leadership in the church, but they didn't understand that when people claim to speak for God, He takes that very seriously.

A Higher Standard
It was often the custom in the Jewish world that visiting rabbis were allowed to speak, so Jesus was welcome to teach in the synagogue at Nazareth.

Jesus had no problem with His speech. But when the rest of us speak on God's behalf, our words do not go unnoticed by heaven. Our speech is recorded, if you will. God takes careful note of what His teachers say.

You may be saying by now, "So what's the problem, Tony? I'm not a teacher or preacher." The problem is that this principle does not apply only to preachers. It applies to anyone and everyone who follows Jesus.

All of us believers are being held to a pretty high standard when it comes to our words. For instance, when you are about to speak a word of judgment or criticism against another believer, you'd better be careful because God will turn that judgment back on you. God will hold your life up to the standard you set for someone else.

If we really believed that truth, we would think more before we spoke. If I knew that what I said about you would come back to me, I would be a lot slower to put you down.

Many of the things going wrong in believers' lives are happening because the damage they did with their tongues has become God's boomerang back to them. And the higher you go on the spiritual leadership level, the faster and harder the boomerang comes back.

A Stricter Judgment

The Bible clearly sets forth the strictness of God's judgment on those who claim to speak for Him. Jude indicates, for instance, that false teachers who lead others astray will incur more severe punishment in hell than others. False teachers are indicted for more severe punishment because they used their mouths to deceive people and lead them away from the truth.

Even legitimate teachers are held strictly accountable for their words. Remember when Moses learned that lesson?

The congregation of Israel was complaining about conditions in the wilderness. Nothing new there. This was a congregation in which every member had a viewpoint and a complaint.

When the people wanted water, God told Moses, "Take the rod; and you and your brother Aaron assemble the congregation and speak to the rock before their eyes, that it may yield its water" (Num. 20:8).

Moses took his rod and assembled the people, just as God had said. But then Moses lost his cool—and control of his tongue. "He said to them, 'Listen now, you rebels; shall we bring forth water for you out of this rock?' Then Moses lifted up his hand and struck the rock twice with his rod; and water came forth abundantly, and the congregation and their beasts drank" (vv. 10–11).

The people got their water, but Moses came under God's judgment for telling the people off and hitting the rock instead of just speaking to it the way God had instructed.

Moses got in trouble not only for his disobedient actions, but also for what he said. His question ("Shall we . . .") in verse 10 implied that he and God were equal partners in this deal. So, as he tongue-lashed the people, Moses lifted himself up and devalued God.

God's judgment was severe: Moses was banned from entering the Promised Land. Prompted by the people's obstinance, Moses spoke rashly. He used his tongue illegitimately to put himself on par with God and incurred God's severe judgment. As he called the people rebels, Moses himself rebelled against God's command.

The Power of the Tongue

The tongue is a problem for us because it's so powerful. It's hard for us to control our tongues, and it's even harder to control the consequences of what we say.

We're talking about what it takes to be a perfect Christian. Well here it is, a clear target for all of us: "If anyone does not stumble in what he says, he is a perfect [completely mature] man, able to bridle the whole body as well" (James 3:2).

You want to be a perfect Christian? Get control of your tongue, because your tongue has the power to control your whole life.

The Power to Control

You have problems; I have problems; all God's children have problems. "We all stumble in many ways," as James says (3:2).

The problems we have can be serious. I'm not minimizing them at all. But the reason some of God's children can't fix some of the things that are wrong in their lives is that they haven't dealt with the root of their problems. God's Word says if we ever get our mouths right, we'll be able to get the other stuff right.

Why? Because the tongue has power to control a person's life. Men and women who can control their tongues can control other things that get out of kilter in their lives. To prove it, James offers two powerful illustrations:

> Now if we put the bits into the horses' mouths so that they may obey us, we direct their entire body as well. Behold, the ships also, though they are so great and are driven by strong winds, are still directed by a very small rudder, wherever the inclination of the pilot desires. (vv. 3–4)

A horse may weigh more than a thousand pounds, but a hundred-pound woman in the saddle can control that horse if she has the reins and controls the bit in the horse's mouth. I know that from personal experience.

I will always remember the day at a Christian camp when Lois and I went riding. We used to go to this camp every year when the children were small, and after years of trying to get Lois on a horse, I finally persuaded her to go horseback riding.

Lois wasn't keen on the idea, but I reassured her, "Just follow me and you'll be all right."

Things went fine for a while, but then the leader of our ride asked me if I wanted to gallop. I'm always up for a challenge, so I took off.

The problem was I forgot Lois was following me. Her horse, taking the cue from my horse, took off right behind me, and we were flying. I was doing my "Lone Ranger" thing. I was really into this gallop.

But then I heard someone screaming behind me and I thought, *Oh no!* I had forgotten Lois was back there. She was screaming and yelling for the horse to stop and saying, "Tony, I'm going to get you!"

I tried to turn around and holler for her to pull back on the reins, but I was too far out in front for her to hear me. Lois's horse wasn't impressed by her screaming. It didn't care that Lois was a pastor's wife. That horse didn't have any respect at all for the Lord's servant.

Besides, that horse was accustomed to responding to one thing only, and that was the bit in its mouth. When Lois finally recovered her senses and pulled back on the reins, the rest of the horse came under control. By pulling on a small piece of metal in the horse's mouth, Lois brought hundreds of pounds of galloping power into conformity with her will.

The example of a ship teaches the same principle: Something very large can be controlled by something very small. I've been on enough cruise ships to appreciate what a rudder means to a ship.

Just as a ship can be maneuvered by its rudder, so we as saints can be guided by our tongues. That's why it is so important that we bring our speech under the control of the Holy Spirit. If you can fix the smaller problem—the tongue—other problems that seem a lot bigger will come under control. For example, if you would stop complaining about your problem and start looking at it from God's perspective, you might discover that your trial may not be so overwhelming after all. Words are so potent that they have the power to control our attitudes and our actions.

The Word on Your Words

I am amazed at how much the Bible says about our speech. If you want to do a study that will challenge and change you, check out God's Word on your words. Let me give you just a few examples from the book of Proverbs.

Proverbs 10:19 says, "When there are many words, transgression is unavoidable, but he who restrains his lips is wise." According to Proverbs 12:22, "Lying lips are an abomination to the LORD." And Proverbs 15:1 tells us, "A gentle answer turns away wrath."

We could go on and on. The Bible's advice about our words can be summed up in the phrase, "Be quick to hear [and] slow to speak" (James 1:19). God wants us to weigh and measure our words and make sure they are aimed in the right direction before we let them fly.

We'd better make sure we know where our words are taking us because the rest of us will follow like a horse obeying its rider or a ship being guided by its rudder. People who have a negative word to say about everything tend to become negative in every area of their personalities. People who are profane in their speech become profane people in every area because the rest of a person follows the tongue.

The Bible is full of real-life examples of the good and the bad that words can do in people's lives. I'm sure you could add your own examples.

So you and I need to hear what the Word says about our words. It takes effort to control our tongue because to do so we must overcome the contrary pull of our sinful nature. A bit must overcome the horse's tendency to go wherever it desires, and the ship's rudder must overcome contrary winds and waves.

In the same way, we feel the contrary pull of our sinful nature when we attempt to control what we say. The tongue is not only powerful; it is, by nature, perverse.

The Perversity of the Tongue

This is a tough subject to deal with, but it's important. After all, before we can talk about purifying our speech, we need to understand how our words cause us problems and why it is so hard to tame the tongue. James gets us started: "The tongue is a small part of the body, and yet it boasts of great things. Behold, how great a forest is set aflame by such a small fire!" (3:5).

A Lot of Brag

There is no limit to the great things people boast about. We get tired of hearing some folks talk about what they are going to do, not going to do, and have already done.

God gets tired of people's bragging, too. Reflecting that, the psalmist prayed that God would cut off "the tongue that speaks great things" (Ps. 12:3). And often the boaster is in fact the person who ends up being hurt.

The story is told of a frog who wanted to escape the coming winter by going south to the warm weather.

So the frog found two birds that were getting ready to fly south for the winter and asked if he could go with them. The birds said, "There's no way we can fly you south with us."

But the frog came up with a clever idea. "Why don't we get a stick? We can put one end of the stick on one bird's back and the other end on the other bird's back. Then I'll hold on to the stick with my mouth and you two can fly me south."

The birds thought about it and replied, "OK, we think we can do that." So they got a stick and laid it across the birds' backs. The frog took hold with his mouth and off they flew, just in time to escape the bad weather.

As they were flying over a farmer's field, the farmer looked up, saw this unusual sight, and remarked, "That is the most ingenious thing I have ever seen in my life. I wonder whose idea it was."

The frog was so flattered he said, "It was miiiiine. . . ." Bragging at the wrong time will cost you!

A Blazing Fire

We all know that a single ember from a fireplace can burn down an entire house. One lone match can take out a huge forest. The Bible uses the powerful imagery of fire to illustrate the perversity of the tongue and its ability to set things aflame.

A lot of married people wish they could take back words spoken in anger or frustration, words that burned their mates with fire that is still smoldering.

Some believers have started gossip fires that consumed someone's reputation. Remember, a person who will gossip *to* you will certainly gossip *about* you.

And when it comes to gossip, it's not the things that go in one ear and out the other that do the harm, but the things that go in one ear, get all mixed up, and then slip out of the mouth. God's Word says, "For lack of wood the fire goes out, and where there is no whisperer, contention quiets down" (Prov. 26:20).

Now we've seen how a tongue can spark a fire. James goes on to say, "The tongue *is* a fire, the very world of iniquity; the tongue is set among our members as that which defiles the entire body, and sets on fire the course of our life, and is set on fire by hell" (3:6, emphasis added). What a sobering statement! The fire of the tongue is lit by hell.

That word *course* here is very interesting. It means "wheel." You may have seen those fireworks wheels that spin fast and shoot off firecrackers when they are lighted. Those wheels go off when the center of the wheel is lighted.

That's the picture we have here. The tongue is at the center of life, so when the tongue is set on fire the rest of life starts spinning and exploding. This is another way of saying our tongues direct our actions. The tongue heats up the rest of life, and it is lighted by Satan.

Untamed and Deadly

Just in case somebody doesn't have the full picture yet, James adds: "Every species of beasts and birds, of reptiles and creatures of the sea, is tamed, and has been tamed by the human race. But no one can tame the tongue; it is a restless evil and full of deadly poison" (3:7–8).

We can train seals to clap and dolphins to speak on cue. We can train dogs to jump through hoops. We have tamed large animals to work for us and perform for our pleasure. But only God can tame a tongue.

And He calls us to work with Him so that taming can happen:

Let no unwholesome word proceed from your mouth, but only such a word as is good for edification according to the need of the moment, that it may give grace to those who hear. And do not grieve the Holy Spirit of God, by whom you were sealed for the day of redemption. (Eph. 4:29–30)

First we read that we are to watch how we use our tongues. Immediately after that we see the warning not to grieve the Holy Spirit. This juxtaposition is significant. When our words are profane or hurting or inappropriate, we sadden the Holy Spirit who lives within us.

This fact is all-important because the Holy Spirit is the One who gives you the power to live the Christian life. Therefore, grieving the Spirit—and thereby rendering His power ineffective in your life—is like allowing corrosion to build up on the battery of your car.

That corrosion can interrupt the charge from the battery that allows your engine to roar to life. Many believers have too much corrosion around their mouths. Thus no power from the Holy Spirit flows to the engine called life.

If you want power in your life, you must remove the corrosion from your mouth. When you do, the Holy Spirit charge will be restored, and you'll have power to live out the victorious Christian life.

Let me ask you a question: If you were given ten dollars for every helpful, edifying word you have ever said and lost five dollars for every hurtful and destructive word you have ever said, would you be rich or poor today?

Some of us need to go to God and confess the profanity, the criticism, the gossip, and the judgmental words that corrode our mouths.

Some of us spend all day dismantling other people with our tongues and then wonder why there is no power in our lives and no life in our relationships. The Bible says the problem is that you have grieved the Holy Spirit, who is your power connection.

When you visit one of those drive-through parks that feature wild animals roaming free, you will always see one sign: "Keep your doors locked and your windows up." That's the only safe way a visitor can make it through the park and enjoy it as it was meant to be enjoyed.

In much the same way, if we want to make it through life as victorious Christians, we need to keep our mouths locked up when it comes to harmful speech.

The Bible compares the damage our tongues can do to the deadly venom of a poisonous snake. When a snake bites you, you now have in your system what is in the snake—his poison.

And when you hang out with "snaky" people, you are going to get what is in them. You may say, "I'm not a gossip." But if you allow another person's gossip to poison your spirit, that person's venom becomes your venom.

So what can you and I do? Recognize the perversity of the tongue and be on guard against it in ourselves and in others.

The Purifying of the Tongue

Our speech is not only perverse, it is polluted. And the only cure for pollution is purification.

Just as something cannot be polluted and pure at the same time, we cannot use our tongues both to praise God and put down others and expect to receive any blessing from God.

We all know how this works. We get dressed in our Sunday clothes, put on our Sunday smiles, and use our Sunday words. We sing and pray and worship God. We say "Amen," "Glory to His name," and "He is worthy to be praised."

But before we have even made it out of the church parking lot, we are tearing down someone. Some husbands can reduce their wives and children to nothing with sharp words even while they're on their way home from church.

Wait a minute! Didn't we just praise God? Didn't we just sing about our love for Him? Something's very wrong with this picture.

Speaking with a Forked Tongue

What is wrong is how we've used that perverse tongue. James knows the pattern: "With [the tongue] we bless our Lord and Father; and with it we curse men, who have been made in the likeness of God; from the same mouth come both blessing and cursing. My brethren, these things ought not to be this way" (3:9–10). The Indians used to call this behavior "speaking with a forked tongue."

The Bible says that when we curse people who are made in the image of their heavenly Father, we are cursing the Father Himself. When married couples or parents or children or fellow church members use their tongues to shred each other, there is an attack against God because the person attacked has the stamp of God on him or her.

I don't know any Christian who would sit in church and say, "God, You are worthless. You are not worthy of my attention." I'm sure none of us would do that to God. But when we curse and devalue His creation, we are in essence doing exactly that. We are saying that God made a big mistake when He created that "worthless" person.

And that kind of statement can happen so fast. A husband and wife can be arguing about a legitimate problem, but soon they lose sight of the issue and begin attacking each other's worth as people. God takes those attacks personally, and the result is that He cuts off His fellowship. God doesn't differentiate between direct attacks on Himself and direct attacks on His kids.

The Potential for Refreshment

Being a perfect Christian—growing in our faith to be more like Jesus—means using our tongue (despite its perversity and with the help of the Holy Spirit) to refresh others rather than rip them apart.

Proverbs 10:11 says, "The mouth of the righteous is a fountain of life." According to Proverbs 13:14, "The teaching of the wise is a fountain of life." The difference between the right word and the wrong word is the difference between a lightning bug and lightning.

Is your tongue offering right words, wrong words, or a mixture of both? Put differently, "Does a fountain send out from the same opening both fresh and bitter water? Can a fig tree, my brethren, produce olives, or a vine produce figs? Neither can salt water produce fresh" (James 3:11–12).

Nothing would be more contradictory than a water fountain that mixed fresh and salt water and sent them out the same opening. It ought not happen. But too many Christians are like that mixed fountain: Their tongues speak forth both sweet and bitter words.

Where does this kind of mouth problem originate? Jesus gave us the answer: "The mouth speaks out of that which fills the heart" (Matt. 12:34). The person who uses profanity or indulges in destructive criticism and gossip does not do so because someone else provoked it. The problem is that this person has a wicked heart. Listeners merely give the speaker the opportunity to reveal the wickedness of his or her heart.

But we can make a difference when we use our mouths to nourish and refresh others. The Bible describes a righteous person as being "like a tree firmly planted by streams of water, which yields its fruit in its season" (Ps. 1:3).

How do we become such people who provide the good fruit of verbal refreshment? We begin by giving God control of our tongues. As we said earlier, until He has that part of us, He won't deal with anything else because this rudder called the tongue controls the whole ship.

We give God that much-needed control of our tongue through prayer. Why not make this prayer from God's Word your own? "Set a guard, O LORD, over my mouth; keep watch over the door of my lips. Do not incline my heart to any evil thing, to practice deeds of wickedness with men who do iniquity; and do not let me eat of their delicacies" (Ps. 141:3–4).

The psalmist is praying that God will help him speak only what he ought to speak. He does not want to misuse his tongue lest it lead him into evil. Amen to that!

One Sunday a woman went to her pastor and said, "Pastor, today I want to lay my tongue on the altar."

The pastor replied, "Madam, our altar is not big enough. It's only fifteen feet long."

If your tongue is out of control, you can change that by praying, "Lord, I give You my tongue that You might guide the rest of my life, that You might steer the rudder on this ship." The Christian who is being sanctified and is growing toward God's standard of perfection keeps his words in check.

Test Your Perfection I.Q.

- The tongue is powerful but perverse in nature, in need of God's purifying touch.

—If you were given ten dollars for every helpful, edifying word you have ever said and lost five dollars for every hurtful and destructive word you have ever said, would you be rich or poor today? On this scale, "1" is "I don't have a cent to my name!" and "10" is "Who needs to win the lottery? I'm set for life!"

1 2 3 4 5 6 7 8 9 10

—Not only is the tongue perverse, it's also quick. The tongue often does its damage long before the mind realizes what has happened. How well do you do on that count? On this scale, "1" is "Get that bit in my mouth! I never think before I babble!" and "10" is "Thought always comes before talk! My tongue has a rudder perfectly controlled by the Holy Spirit."

1 2 3 4 5 6 7 8 9 10

—The tongue has been described as untamed, deadly, and forked. Of all the images, though, the most powerful one is fire. In general, how many sparks fly off your tongue? On this scale, "1" is "I could be arrested for arson any minute!" and "10" is "Smokey Bear and God Himself are pleased!"

1 2 3 4 5 6 7 8 9 10

- Give yourself four points each for three examples of edifying and encouraging words you have spoken in the last twenty-four hours.

1.

2.

3.

Total Points _____

Chapter 8

How to Tap into God's Wisdom

About a week after our youngest son, Jonathan, got his driver's license, he announced that he wanted to drive the family to downtown Dallas. So he escorted me to the passenger seat up front. Lois and our oldest son Anthony sat in the backseat.

Lois was sitting behind Jonathan, and it wasn't long after Jonathan started out that agonizing groans were coming from that area. If you have ever ridden with a new teenage driver, you know exactly what was going on.

Sometimes those groans turned to specific pleas, such as "Tony, you drive!" One of those groans came when Jonathan turned out of a parking lot and ran right over the curb.

This drive—however traumatic for Lois—was a defining moment for Jonathan. He had taken the prescribed driver's training course. He had learned the basics. Now the question was how well he would apply the knowledge he had gained. How would he negotiate the turns in the road, the traffic lights, the expressway ramps, and the traffic conditions he would meet?

Some situations arise that a driver can't control, but a driver also has a lot of choices to make. There are different routes to choose from and wrong turns to avoid.

Needless to say, Jonathan was not a perfect driver that evening, but he did do better on some points than on others.

A lot of people could say this very same thing about their lives. After all, life is a lot like driving. Sadly, many people have not negotiated the turns and twists of life very well. If they could do things over again, they would take a different route in their career or avoid that wrong turn in their marriage.

Since none of us can drive the road of life perfectly, we need divine direction, heavenly help, to negotiate the road ahead. God offers us that help in abundance as He offers us His wisdom in abundance. You and I can't expect to become mature believers without knowing what God's wisdom is and how to tap into it for our lives.

Using our driving analogy, we can say that God's wisdom gives us the ability to steer the car properly, to know when to accelerate and when to apply the brake. Relying on the wisdom God supplies, we gain the ability to use the right gear at the right time and to make the right choices so that we wind up going the right way on the right road.

Wisdom is seeing and interpreting life from God's perspective and then making life's decisions based on that understanding.

We know that wisdom is important because the word itself occurs hundreds of times in the Bible—and more than one hundred times in the book of Proverbs alone. God is deeply concerned that we learn to live wisely according to His definition of wisdom. Let's find out exactly what that involves.

The Concept of Wisdom

I'm sure that if I asked, you would say you want to be a person God considers wise. So let me ask you this biblical question: "Who among you is wise and understanding? Let him show by his good behavior his deeds in the gentleness of wisdom" (James 3:13).

To appreciate this question and its answer, we need to remember our discussion of the tongue and the way some people use it both to bless God and to curse others. This should not be happening, the Bible says, just as a fountain should not, and in fact cannot, send out bitter and sweet water at the same time.

Obviously a person whose mouth is pouring out blessing and cursing has taken a wrong turn in life and is badly off course when it comes to living according to God's wisdom. We know that about a person because godly wisdom produces good and gentle behavior that is the exact opposite of the wicked and disruptive effects of a poisonous tongue.

The Value of Wisdom

We could go many places in the Scriptures to demonstrate the value of God's wisdom. But I've chosen the book of Proverbs, since it was written specifically to tell us what God's wisdom is and how it works. Consider Proverbs 4:7–9:

> The beginning of wisdom is: Acquire wisdom; and with all your acquiring, get understanding. Prize her, and she will exalt you; she will honor you if you embrace her. She will place on your head a garland of grace; she will present you with a crown of beauty.

God says you and I need to get wisdom before we get anything else. We should value wisdom so much that it's our primary goal and paramount task in life.

Why? Because wisdom is the vehicle that will get you to your destination. We have defined that destination as being a Christian who is mature and complete, a Christian who has grown into the image of Jesus, a perfect Christian.

You say, "Tony, I do want God's wisdom even more than anything." That's great. God wants us to have His wisdom more than some of us want it.

Where do we find wisdom? According to the Proverbs:

> Wisdom shouts in the street, she lifts her voice in the square; at the head of the noisy streets she cries out. . . . "Turn to my reproof, behold, I will pour out my spirit on you; I will make my words known to you." (1:20–21, 23)

Even though everybody else has an idea and a viewpoint, wisdom shouts to us not to miss what God has for us. Only simpletons, scoffers, and fools would ignore and even despise God's wisdom.

In fact, Solomon goes on to warn that it would be disastrous to miss wisdom (vv. 24–32). Those who reject God's counsel will fall into calamity one day, and then it will be too late to seek, find, and live by God's wisdom. Those of us wanting God's wisdom can rely on His Spirit to help us hear her voice over the din of our world.

And keep in mind that you and I can't conjure up godly wisdom on the spur of the moment, even though that's the way a lot of people want to do it. They want to pull the rip cord of God's wisdom when they are falling through the air, but that's not the way it works. We need to value wisdom so much that we make it a way of life, not just a parachute to help us escape disaster.

Now what exactly does wisdom—a very valuable commodity—consist of? The Bible makes it clear that wisdom is not a philosophical system that is unrelated to life. At its heart, godly wisdom is the skill of righteous living.

In other words, wisdom is effectively applying God's truth to everyday circumstances. It is taking the data in your head and getting it down to your feet.

With this definition, you can see that wisdom is more than acquiring knowledge. You can go to school and acquire knowledge, but it's possible to have a Ph.D. degree and yet be at the kindergarten level where godly wisdom is concerned.

A Body of Knowledge

Now don't misunderstand. Wisdom does involve a body of knowledge. Certain information is crucial to gaining wisdom, and that information is found in Scripture. You must know and understand the right spiritual facts if you are to mature in your faith and become more like Christ. God's wisdom is founded upon His truth, upon the facts revealed in His Word.

One reason this point is so important is that our culture tells us that no objective, universal truth exists. The message of the culture is "It's only true if it's true for you, and what's true for you may not be true for me."

But—as I've said—there is a body of truth, and it's called the Word of God. Jesus said to God the Father, "Thy word is truth" (John 17:17). God's Word, then, is the source of His wisdom.

A Heart of Understanding

Some people gain knowledge of God's truth but fail to see the relationship between what they know and what they should do about what they know. These people miss out on acquiring wisdom because they lack understanding.

Understanding means taking the body of knowledge you have and doing the right things with it. The Bible refers to this as having the heart to understand what God is saying.

Knowledge tells you, "This is true." Understanding says, "Now that you know what is true, this is what you are supposed to do."

Knowledge gives you the data. Understanding helps you see the relationship between the data and how you should function based on the data. Let me give you a simple illustration.

Imagine a couple who can't pay their bills. In their case, the facts are pretty straightforward. The couple adds up their income and totals their bills and gets a pretty accurate picture of their financial situation. They see exactly how much money they need to pay off their bills.

The couple can set forth the financial facts of the case. The facts—this knowledge—lead the couple to conclude that their problem is simply that they need more money. If they had more money, they could pay off their bills and be debt-free.

But this knowledge alone would not fix the problem, because the facts have not led the couple to the proper understanding of their situation. They need to understand *why* they are in debt so they can avoid falling into debt again.

In this case, the real problem is that the couple is not managing their money wisely. They are spending money they don't have by using credit cards and making unwise purchases. So more money would just lead to more debt until the facts of this couple's financial situation lead them to the proper understanding of the root problem.

So let's say this couple one day gets the real picture. They begin to understand why they are so deeply in debt. They come to recognize that they have an underlying problem with overspending and overuse of credit. It dawns on them that, unless they do something about their spending habits, having more money won't really help them. They are now on their way to biblical wisdom.

They are on the way, but they will not have fully acquired wisdom until they apply what they know and understand. Such action is evidence of wisdom.

Applying What We Know and Understand

Most of us know what we ought to do most of the time. We understand what it takes to obey and please God. Becoming a perfect Christian means *doing* what we already know we should do. The couple in our illustration doesn't need more money. Instead they need to commit to handling wisely the money they already have.

I know a lot of Christians don't like to hear this, but let's talk straight. If you go to God without being willing to act on the knowledge and understanding He has already given you, why should He answer your prayer? Why should He give you more blessings to misuse?

Someone may say, "I need a new mate. My marriage is broken."

That may be a fact. Your marriage may be in shambles. But do you understand *why* your marriage is broken, and are you fulfilling your biblical responsibility to help fix what is broken?

Until that happens, don't expect much from God. As we saw at the beginning of the chapter, we are to demonstrate our good deeds "in the gentleness of wisdom."

Take any issue and ask these questions of yourself: What do I know?, What do I understand?, and What have I done about it? Until you get to the doing, you have not acquired wisdom. And until you get to wisdom, you have not experienced the power and deliverance of God.

I can't emphasize enough how crucial this doing, this applying, is to the biblical concept of wisdom. Paul warns, "Be careful how you walk, not as unwise men, but as wise, making the most of your time, because the days are evil" (Eph. 5:15–16).

You cannot make the most of your time without a plan. It's impossible. If you have no action plan attached to what you know and understand, nothing good is going to happen in your life. That is why Moses prayed, "Teach us to number our days, that we may present to Thee a heart of wisdom" (Ps. 90:12).

The Bible says that, on average, a person can expect to live seventy years or maybe eighty. With a limited number of years on this planet, we should indeed value our days so we can be wise before God. This biblical advice suggests an exercise I have done and intend to do regularly. I recommend it to you.

Multiply the number of days in a year by eighty. Then figure out your age in days and subtract it from the number of days in an eighty-year life span. Now you'll see how many days you may have left. Seeing that figure will help you realize that you have a finite number of days remaining in which to accomplish what God wants you to do.

An exercise like this is valuable because most of us don't really see the number of our days dwindling. We need to be reminded that we are on our way out of here and that each day counts.

How do we make each day count? Back to Paul: "So then do not be foolish, but understand what the will of the Lord is" (Eph. 5:17). We make the most of our time by planning to live as wisely as we know how under the direction and hand of God, based on our knowledge of His Word and His will.

Many of us ask to know God's will by praying, "Lord, lead me." But God will not lead you into His unrevealed will until He knows you're doing something with His revealed will—His Word. He will lead you in what is unclear once you are doing what is very clear.

The reason some of our prayers for God to reveal His specific will go unanswered is that God sees we are not doing anything with what we already know. We must make plans according to God's Word, but then we must hand our plan over to God for His adjustment and correction, for our sanctification and growth toward Christlikeness. God will make your plan into His plan as you build your life on His Word.

The Blessing of Wisdom

When we apply God's wisdom to our lives, when we live in accordance with what He has spelled out in Scripture, then we are in line for a blessing. Hear the promise: "'I know the plans that I have for you,' declares the LORD, 'plans for welfare and not for calamity to give you a future and a hope'" (Jer. 29:11).

Wisdom is the way to experience God's will, because wisdom is the application of God's Word to the practical issues of life.

Two Competing Kinds of Wisdom

Now that we have grasped something of the concept of wisdom, I want to contrast the two kinds of wisdom the Bible describes. It's important that we understand them, because they are diametrically opposed to each other.

God's Word teaches that there is a form of wisdom that is not "from above, but is earthly, natural, demonic" (James 3:15). In contrast, "the wisdom from above is first pure, then peaceable, gentle, reasonable, full of mercy and good fruits, unwavering, without hypocrisy" (v. 17).

Different Sources

For whatever reasons, people can be confused about what is and is not from God. But clearly, these two forms of wisdom come from different sources.

Look again at the wisdom that is not from God. First, it is "earthly," worldly, from below. Our society, and people in general, is trapped by this way of thinking, and that's not surprising.

What's unfortunate is the number of Christians who live by human wisdom rather than by divine wisdom. These believers are paying and will pay a high price for following the world's wisdom. The Bible says, "There is a way which seems right to a man, but its end is the way of death" (Prov. 14:12).

You and I need to determine from which source we are going to draw our wisdom. The Bible says, "How blessed [happy] is the man who does not walk in the counsel of the wicked, nor stand in the path of sinners, nor sit in the seat of scoffers! But his delight is in the law of the LORD" (Ps. 1:1–2).

You see, "the wisdom of this world is foolishness before God" (1 Cor. 3:19). On his best day, the unbeliever is still a fool before God if he is disagreeing with his Creator. Human wisdom is basically worthless when it comes to doing what God expects. And the Bible is clear that people apart from God don't know where to find wisdom since only God is all-wise.

As we saw above, earthly wisdom is fleshly, and we can find much evidence around us of people following fleshly wisdom. Consider the often-asked question, "If it feels so good, how can it be so wrong?" My question to someone who thinks that is, "If it's so right, how come your life is such a mess?"

A fleshly approach to wisdom puts feelings on a higher level than faith. It allows emotion to overrule God's revelation. What's important is how I feel, not what God says.

But godly wisdom says that our feelings must conform to God's revelation. We must adjust our feelings to our faith if we are going to be wise.

I once dealt with a woman who was getting ready to marry a non-Christian. Her argument was a familiar one: "If God didn't want me to marry this man, He wouldn't have brought him into my life."

That's worldly wisdom. The issue is "What does God's Word say?" It clearly says, "Do not be bound together with unbelievers" (2 Cor. 6:14). This unbelieving man may have captured this woman's thoughts and emotions, but what she needed to say was, "God, by the power of the Holy Spirit within me, I will adjust my feelings to Your Word."

When you can turn to the Holy Spirit like that in order to live according to God's revealed will, you are on the road to wisdom. You're also on the road to seeing God do some things in your life you wouldn't otherwise see.

Finally, the Bible also calls this earthly, fleshly wisdom "demonic," straight from hell itself. In other words, there is more behind the world's ideas and philosophies than just human thinking. Satan is the mastermind behind the world's false wisdom.

That's why it bothers me to realize that some Christians turn to the horoscope in the newspaper to see what they should do for the day. They know their Zodiac sign better than they know the Word. Others are getting someone to read their palms or calling the psychic network for advice and help.

Many people think this kind of stuff is harmless, but God's Word teaches otherwise. Consider King Solomon. We read that he had only one flaw. He did what was right before God *except* for the fact that he continued to burn incense and to worship at the high places, where idol worship was carried on.

I get the impression that Solomon just dropped by the high places every now and then. That's all. Just like the Christian who only reads the horoscope once a week or calls the psychic network a few times. That's all.

But Solomon's attachment to idolatry—as insignificant as it may have seemed—is what brought him down. He started marrying pagan women who brought all kinds of idolatry into Israel. The devil doesn't need much of an opening to drive home his hellish wisdom.

That's why God told the Israelites that anyone who practices any sort of divination or fortune-telling is "detestable" to Him (Deut. 18:10–12). That's also why God said He would drive the pagan nations out of Canaan: They were worshiping idols.

Appropriately, right on the heels of these words, Moses prophesied, "The LORD your God will raise up for you a prophet like me from among you, from your countrymen, you shall listen to him" (18:15).

This was a prophecy of Jesus' coming. And what did Jesus do when He came? He spoke God's Word, the wisdom from above. And how did God respond? He said, "This is My beloved Son, with whom I am well-pleased; listen to Him!" (Matt. 17:5).

The Word of God—with its account of the life of Jesus, God's Living Word—is the source of the wisdom from above. The Bible commands you to learn the truth, live according to its teachings, and to "set your mind on the things above, not on the things that are on earth" (Col. 3:2). Only those who are plugged into God's wisdom will know God's power.

But too many of us are like the man from the backwoods who bought a chain saw because the hardware store owner told him he could cut down a lot more trees each day with a lot less effort.

This guy had never seen a chain saw before, but he bought one. He came back a week later, saying, "Give me my money back. This is a piece of junk. I used this thing all day and I only cut down one tree. This thing doesn't work."

The clerk was amazed, so he took the saw from the man and pulled the cord. When the chain saw roared to life, the backwoods man jumped back and cried, "What's that noise?!"

Many Christians are like that backwoods man. They think they have tried God's wisdom, and they have concluded it doesn't work. They think they have been living God's way, but they're actually still stuck in the old way they have been used to for so long. How can that be?

Some believers come out of the world and into the church. But instead of discarding the earthly, natural, and demonic wisdom they learned from and preached in the world, they simply learn a few Bible verses and patch God's Word onto their old ways.

But the only way you can know God's power in your life is to use His wisdom His way. And that means totally disregarding worldly, human wisdom, not trying to mix some Christian ideas in with it.

Now did you realize that a very large percentage of rat bait is good food? It's not the food that kills the rats, but the very small percentage of poison that gets them.

In the same way, even a little bit of worldly wisdom mixed with God's wisdom spells spiritual death. That's why God wants our whole-hearted, unmixed devotion. He wants all of us. Godly and worldly wisdom originate from vastly different, mutually exclusive sources.

A man once said to another man, "You Christians are all brainwashed."

The Christian man replied, "Everybody's brainwashed. We've just chosen who we want to wash our brains."

It's as simple as that. Either you have been brainwashed by the world, the media, your friends, or whatever—or your mind has been cleansed by God. If I have to be brainwashed by someone, give me the Someone who can create and sustain the heavens and the earth!

Different Methods
Once you see the contrasting sources of earthly and godly wisdom, you won't have any trouble seeing the other points of contrast. Next,

these two contrasting kinds of wisdom operate in sharply contrasting methods.

The Bible says that earthly wisdom is characterized by "bitter jealousy" and "selfish ambition" (James 3:14). Jealousy says, "I am upset because you have what I want." Selfish ambition makes me upset because you hold a position I want to hold. That's how human wisdom thinks.

But divine wisdom is gentle, and gentleness has to do with an ability to submit to God. The world doesn't approve of submission to anyone, but the Bible shows us again and again the power that comes with serving and submitting to God.

Human wisdom says you have to get where you want to go your own way. Divine wisdom says, "If I submit to God, He will take me where He wants me to go. I don't have to worry about it, because God is in control. And I don't have to be jealous of you because God's plans for me are perfect."

Different Spirits

Now consider the sharp contrast between the spirit behind earthly wisdom and the Spirit who energizes divine wisdom.

We just saw that the spirit behind earthly wisdom stirs up jealousy and selfishness. That's because this wisdom is from the devil, who was jealous of God and let his ambition cause him to try to topple God from His throne.

But divine wisdom has behind it the gentle and peaceable Holy Spirit. No wonder His gift of wisdom is characterized by gentleness and peace.

Different Products

Finally, notice what these two kinds of wisdom produce.

The Bible says that human wisdom produces "every evil thing" (James 3:16). Divine wisdom, on the other hand, is the source of "mercy and good fruits" (v. 17). It produces positive things like peace and righteousness. It is pure, undiluted by evil.

Earthly wisdom leads us to "lie against the truth" (v. 14), to use and alter the truth to satisfy ourselves and promote our own agendas.

Human wisdom subordinates the truth to personal goals. But godly wisdom lifts up the truth. Clearly, these two kinds of wisdom could not be more different.

Cultivating Godly Wisdom

I hope you're saying by now, "Tell me how to get God's wisdom working in my life!" Let me suggest three ways to cultivate godly wisdom.

Fear God

The Proverbs say again and again that wisdom begins with the fear of God. Paul says the problem with mankind is that people have no fear of God (Rom. 3:18).

For us Christians, fearing God does not mean running away from Him in terror, but revering and honoring Him—in other words, taking Him seriously. We have to stop this "nod to God" way of life, the kind of Christianity that goes to church and gives God a nice spiritual compliment. Instead, let's start saying, "God, if this is what Your Word says, this is what I'm going to do. I am going to stop mixing Your way with my way."

You know what happens when you're driving down the highway and you see a police car parked by the side of the road. You slow down—and you may even start pulling your seat belt across your lap. (Tell the truth and shame the devil!)

Why do you do all that? The officer isn't even looking at you. That car is just sitting there. But on the side of that car is a symbol of authority that gets your attention whenever you see it. It arrests your focus and may cause you to alter your behavior—all because that car showed up.

That's the kind of fear we should show toward God. But some of us are speeding down the highway of life, and we don't even slow down when God shows up. There's no fear of God in our hearts. He doesn't even arrest our attention. If that's the case, we have to cultivate the fear of God by spending time getting to know Him. By reading His Word, we see more and more about our God, who is indeed worthy of all glory and honor, all fear and respect.

Abide in God

A second way to cultivate godly wisdom is to abide in God.

One way to do that, again, is to abide in God's Word. Listen to what God says so that you are able to judge things the way God judges them.

Also, abide in God's Son. The Bible says that in Christ "are hidden all the treasures of wisdom and knowledge" (Col. 2:3). The closer you draw to Christ, the more the hidden treasures of His wisdom will be accessible to you. Remember, now that you are a Christian, Jesus Christ lives in you and gives you access to everything that He has—including His wisdom.

Ask God

A third way to cultivate godly wisdom is to act on one of the greatest promises in the Bible. We dealt with it in an earlier chapter, but it bears repeating here. James says, "If any of you lacks wisdom, let him ask of God, who gives to all men generously and without reproach, and it will be given to him" (1:5).

With that kind of offer on the table, what's holding you back? What is keeping you from seeking God's wisdom for the trial, the test, or the everyday-life situation you're facing?

God is eager to grant you His wisdom. He will give it joyfully, gladly, without putting you down. He will give you more wisdom than you can even think to ask Him for.

Your prayer might be, "Lord, I need Your wisdom to know how to handle my finances. If You choose to give me more resources, that's great. But I want Your wisdom more than I want anything else."

If we would ask God for wisdom and apply the wisdom He has already given us in His Word, we wouldn't have to keep coming to Him with the same confession or the same requests for help year after year.

When you do ask for wisdom, you need to ask in faith without any wavering (James 1:6). That's when God will reveal Himself to you. Asking God in faith means that we treat Him like the supreme and sovereign God He is. He is not some human being who is simply going to give you His opinion or short-term assistance.

Asking in faith also means we believe that God is ready and willing to answer our prayer for wisdom. In fact, if you don't ask, God may intensify the trial until you do!

I've taken more than my share of airplane flights. I just buy a ticket and get on the plane. But for me to go from Point A to Point B, a lot of things have to happen. Hundreds of people have to build the airplane, and somebody has to be trained to fly it safely. Somebody else has to be in the control tower to guide the plane through a safe takeoff and a safe landing.

A lot of people have to apply a lot of knowledge to get me to my destination, but all I need to know is how to get in touch with a reputable airline. Then I find out where the plane is taking off from, and I get on board.

With that analogy in mind, you don't have to be a rocket scientist to be wise from God's perspective. All you have to do is be in touch with the God who possesses all wisdom and all knowledge. He has all the wisdom you will ever need, but if your life is going to take off, you have to go to Him. You have to know where God is taking off from and get on board.

Test Your Perfection I.Q.

- Wisdom is seeing life from God's perspective and then making decisions based on that understanding. Give yourself four points each for three times you relied on God's wisdom and note the results.

1.

2.

3.

- James outlines three ways we can cultivate wisdom.

—*Fear God.*

Proverbs 1:7 says, "The fear of the LORD is the beginning of knowledge." Are you fearing God, revering Him, honoring Him, taking Him seriously, and not trying to mix His way with your way? On this scale, "1" is "I give a nod to God, but I'll sing with Sinatra 'I did it my way'!" and "10" is "I do absolutely nothing without consulting God, and I cultivate my fear of God by spending time getting to know Him better."

1   2   3   4   5   6   7   8   9   10

—*Abide in God.*

Abide in God's Word: Listen to what He says and learn to apply His truth to everyday circumstances. Abide also in God's Son: Draw closer to Him through prayer, worship, meditation, and solitude. Are you abiding in God? On this scale, "1" means that you haven't taken root anywhere; as a result, the wisdom of the world is blowing you in ever-changing directions. "10" means that your roots go down deep in God's truth as you, a branch, abide in the vine of Christ.

1 2 3 4 5 6 7 8 9 10

—Ask God for wisdom.

Ask God for wisdom for trials, tests, and everyday situations—and ask in faith that doesn't waver, believing that God will answer. On this scale, "1" is "How can I ask? I don't know what door to knock on!" and "10" is "I'm a-knockin' all the time—and God is faithful to provide!"

1 2 3 4 5 6 7 8 9 10

Total Points _____

Chapter 9

How to Escape the Snare of Worldliness

Most people have long since stopped using the Susan B. Anthony dollar that was first issued a few decades ago. The primary problem was that the Anthony dollar looked and felt so much like a quarter that people kept getting the two confused.

A worldly Christian causes similar confusion. A worldly Christian is so immersed in this world and the world's way of thinking that people can't tell whether he's the real thing or not. A worldly Christian is worth a dollar, but looks like a quarter and spends like "chump change." A worldly Christian has great spiritual value because he has Christ within, but to others he looks like the fake stuff instead of the real thing.

A worldly Christian has one foot planted in the world and the other foot planted in Christ—and then tries to balance the two. That balancing act is impossible if you're truly on a journey toward becoming more like Jesus, if you want to be a perfect Christian.

Trying to be "a friend of the world" while claiming to follow Christ is a dangerous predicament for a believer to find himself in—or, more accurately, to get himself into. The term for this condition is *worldliness*, a word that has been batted around and misapplied until a lot of people don't know what it means anymore.

So let's begin with a definition and then we'll talk about how worldliness works against God's sanctification of us and what we can do to escape its snare.

A Definition of Worldliness

A lot of people would define *worldliness* with a list of do's and don'ts, things they believe a Christian should or should not do.

But making a list doesn't really capture the essence of worldliness, although God's rules and regulations are definitely involved. Consider some of the problems with using a list of no-nos to decide who is worldly and who isn't.

The Problems with Lists

One problem is that our lists of acceptable and unacceptable Christian behaviors are always too short. No matter what we put on our lists, we are going to leave something out.

For example, some people will leave off the no-no list things they enjoy doing or don't see as a problem, even though God may say these things are wrong. So their list will be too short.

Another problem with trying to define worldliness with a list is that our lists are also, in a sense, always too long. They will inevitably include things that don't belong there. Some Christians never get to enjoy many of the things that they could legitimately enjoy because someone once told them these things were sinful.

Now I'm not talking about questionable activities here. I'm thinking of such things as owning a television, listening to music, or even reading magazines. Of course we have to use discretion about what we put into our minds, but some people aren't given a chance by legalistic brothers and sisters even to make those decisions. No wonder the world thinks the Christian life is a boring affair that isn't worth the trouble.

Now don't get me wrong. It *does* matter what we believers do and don't do. And it's legitimate for institutions like Bible schools to set rules for their students' behavior. Our church in Dallas even has certain requirements for membership.

But here's the real problem with trying to define worldliness by lists of external behavior. The key word is *external*. Lists can only address externals. The problem? A person can keep all the rules of his particular group and still have a worldly, disobedient, rebellious heart toward God. Let me illustrate what I mean.

One day my granddaughter Kariss was eating potato chips in the den. I didn't want her eating in there, so I said, "Kariss, don't eat potato chips in the den." She went into the kitchen.

I came back a few hours later and Kariss was eating cookies in the den. I said, "I thought I told you not to eat in the den."

She said, "No, Poppy, that's not what you said. You said, 'Don't eat potato chips in the den.'" Then she held up the cookie. "This is not a potato chip." Cookies were not on the list of banned items!

My desire was that my granddaughter not eat food in the den. But her response was based on my earlier statement: As long as cookies weren't on the list of banned food, she was free to eat them in the den. The problem was that my unspoken list was too long, because I had in mind food of every sort. But Kariss's list was too short!

You can see why God did not simply hand us a list of rules and say, "Keep this list and I will be happy." He gave His people a list once—a perfect list called the Ten Commandments. Just ten rules, and nobody could keep them. That's another problem with external standards. Nobody measures up perfectly to the standard.

A Matter of the Heart

Being like Jesus—being a perfect Christian—is a matter of the heart, and God is indeed after the hearts of His people. That's why the Bible warns us not to become a friend of the world and not to adopt the spirit of this age—what Paul calls "the spirit that is now working in the sons of disobedience" (Eph. 2:2).

Worldliness is that attitude of a Christian's heart that reflects the spirit of this age, the attitudes and values of a system that is spearheaded by Satan. This system is characterized by thoughts and actions that exclude God.

Think about the unsaved world for a minute. Many lost people are fine, upstanding citizens and all of that—but they leave God out of their lives. They are worldly people. Their hearts are tied to this world.

We would expect that of the lost world. But when we as Christians begin to live as if God did not matter, we start looking just like the unsaved world. We become worldly Christians, and that's definitely a contradiction in terms.

Worse yet, the Bible says God sets Himself in opposition to those who become friends of the world—and you don't want God opposing you!

A worldly spirit makes us want to be independent of God's control. It makes us want to say, "I'm going to do it my way. God, when I have time for You and it's convenient for me, You are welcome to be part of my life. But don't call me. I'll call You."

Now that we have a picture of what worldliness involves, let's get to the bottom line. How do you and I know when we are worldly? The Bible gives us three signs or results of worldliness that we can use to determine the degree of our worldliness.

Worldliness and Conflict with Others

The first result of worldliness is conflict with others. A Christian who lives in perpetual conflict is revealing a worldly spirit. A husband and wife who fight all the time are revealing their worldliness, as are church members who constantly bicker with one another.

A Holdover from the Old Life

The Bible teaches that fussing and fighting are part of the old life that is supposed to be behind us (Titus 3:1–3). Now let me clarify that by "fussing and fighting" I don't mean legitimate disagreements or differences of opinion. Nor am I including the kinds of confrontations that need to take place, such as confronting a sinning brother or sister. I'm talking about conflicts that have their origin in self-centeredness, jealousy, pettiness, evil desires—in other words, a worldly attitude.

The Bible asks this question of Christians: "What is the source of quarrels and conflicts among you?" (James 4:1). Then the answer comes: The source of conflict is "pleasures that wage war" in the hearts of believers.

The New Testament contains plenty of examples of worldly-minded conflict in the church. Remember, for instance, the poor believers who were being discriminated against by the church in favor of the rich saints (James 2:1–13)? That's a perfect example of worldliness—allowing the world's spirit and values to set the church's agenda rather than the church influencing the world with God's values.

Sadly, Scripture includes other examples. The church at Corinth was the most carnal—or fleshly-minded—church in the first century. The believers there were taking their disputes with one another to secular court, dishonoring the name of Christ (1 Cor. 6:1–8). These people even turned the Lord's Supper into a source of conflict. And yet the Corinthians bragged about how spiritual they were!

Then at Philippi, Paul had to call on believers to reconcile two sisters who couldn't live in harmony with each other (Phil. 4:2–3). In his letter to the Galatians, Paul refers to Christians devouring one another like animals tearing each other apart (5:15). And, tragically, you may easily be able to point to evidence that worldly-minded conflict continues in the church today.

Unrighteous Anger

At the root of so much worldly-minded conflict is the anger that flares up when we don't get our way or someone messes with our little domain.

Now I'm not talking about righteous anger against sin, or taking a stand for God's truth, or confronting a legitimate problem, or seeking to settle a crucial doctrinal dispute. I'm talking about the "anger of man [that] does not achieve the righteousness of God" (James 1:20).

You see, some of us have been fussing and fighting for years about circumstances and people that bother us, and things still haven't changed. Do you know why? Because as long as we are determined to use human means to try to accomplish a righteous goal, God steps back, folds His arms as it were, and says, "You are on your own."

But the Bible is clear. You and I can't accomplish God's work when we're empowered by human anger. That's why we need to be "slow to anger" (v. 19)—slow to take matters into our own hands in an unbiblical way.

The Bible is also clear that there is to be no division in the body of Christ. The Corinthians I just mentioned were "walking like mere men," and the evidence was "jealousy and strife" among them (1 Cor. 3:1–3).

When a husband and wife who are both Christians turn their marriage into a battleground, the problem is not just personality differences. Those differences were there before they were married. The problem is also not just different likes and dislikes. The problem is that one or both parties is acting out of a worldly spirit.

Yet how many couples who are at each other's throats sit down and talk about their own worldly attitudes? What they usually talk about is what's wrong with the other person. But since human anger does not achieve God's purposes, a couple can argue for years and be no further down the road toward marital bliss.

Someone might say, "Well, I just have a bad temper." No, you don't have a bad temper. A bad temper has you. You're being controlled by a spirit of worldliness.

Let me say two things about worldliness and conflict. First, as long as we are quick to get angry rather than slow to get angry, we aren't going to fix many of our messes. Second, fleshly conflict among Christians would be eliminated if we would turn loose our worldly attitudes.

Worldliness and Conflict Within

Worldliness results in internal conflict, and that internal conflict is behind conflict with others. The Bible shows us that truth: "Is not the source [of conflict] your pleasures that wage war in your members? You lust and do not have; so you commit murder. And you are envious and cannot obtain; so you fight and quarrel" (James 4:1–2). The word *members* here is a reference to a believer's physical body, not to the members of the church. James is talking about the pleasures that battle internally for control over us.

The Problem Within

Scripture says it clearly. The source of our conflict with others is worldliness and therefore conflict within ourselves. So if you're looking at others as the cause of your attitude problems, you're looking in the wrong place. The problem is located in your own pleasures.

This word *pleasures* is the root of our English word *hedonism*. Hedonism, the pursuit of pleasure for its own sake, is the so-called Playboy philosophy. It is based totally on self-satisfaction and self-gratification.

When a man picks up a "skin" magazine and flips through the pictures, he is doing so to gratify a lust within himself. A woman who pursues her lust does so because it brings her some measure of self-gratification. X-rated movies are designed to stimulate and to feed such internal desires.

Besides being sinful in themselves, our attempts to feed our internal lusts also produce conflict with others. When someone interferes with the fulfillment of our pleasures, we lash out. But when we do that, we are actually revealing what is wrong within us.

Now we don't tend to think about conflict in these terms. We say, "He made me mad" or "She really has a problem." Such a statement may be true, but it may also be true that the other person merely hit your hot button because of a desire within that you are trying to satisfy.

Pinpointing the Problem

So illegitimate conflict can be traced to worldliness within. Until we identify and deal with the conflict within, we will never fix the crisis without.

The husband and wife who are in conflict with each other won't get very far toward making peace until one or both of them is willing to say, "Listen, maybe the problem is that we have been pursuing our own desires instead of seeking to please each other. We need to reassess how we're approaching our marriage."

Think back to the first marriage on record. Why did Eve commit the first sin in Eden? Scripture teaches that her decision was based on personal pleasure. Eve saw that the fruit was "good," "a delight," and "desirable" (Gen. 3:6). That tree was a "feel good" tree. Eve's pleasures waged war within her, and she lost.

Such internal warfare is aptly pictured in military terms of soldiers arrayed for battle (James 4:1). There is a war going on within us, even though we may take it out on others. When parents abuse their children or a man abuses his wife, those abusers are expressing what is messed up inside them. Similarly, the person who has no control over his tongue betrays with his words the sin within.

Internal problems will never be fixed as long as people play the blame game. We live in a culture where people refuse to take responsibility for their actions. The problem is always with somebody else.

Uncontrolled Desires

If we truly understood worldliness, we would see that it grows from desires, from our *uncontrolled* desires. These are things that characterize the unregenerate world and lead people to be "lovers of self, lovers of money, boastful, arrogant, revilers, disobedient to parents, ungrateful, unholy . . . without self-control . . . haters of good . . . lovers of pleasure rather than lovers of God" (2 Tim. 3:1–4). That's quite a list of the sins that pour out from within the human heart—and it's been edited!

The amazing thing is that the people who practice these things are then said to "[hold] to a form of godliness" (v. 5). That means it's possible to do all of the vile things mentioned in this passage and still go to church and look very religious.

How can this happen? The Bible says we "lust" after the things we want (James 4:2). This word effectively communicates the idea of trying to fulfill our pleasures at any cost. When you lust for something, you want it so badly that you will do almost anything to get it. James says the result of lust is murder.

Now I don't think this means the Christians of that day were bringing weapons to church in order to do one another in. After all, there is more than one way to destroy someone. When you use or abuse someone to satisfy your own desires, you can decimate that person spiritually, emotionally, or financially without ever using a gun.

God's Word goes on to say that when we envy what others have and can't get it for ourselves, we are ready to "fight and quarrel" to get it (v. 2). We are talking here about throwing spiritual temper tantrums.

Now most parents are not impressed when their children throw temper tantrums. In fact, that kind of behavior usually guarantees that the child will not get what he or she wants. The sad thing is that, in some cases, all the child has to do to receive the desired item is simply ask for it instead of pitching a fit.

Likewise, God is not moved by the spiritual tantrums we throw when we don't get what we want. The irony is that, as the Bible says, we don't have because we don't ask (James 4:2).

Asking God

Do you realize that God is saying we would have some of the legitimate things we desire if we would simply ask Him for them instead of trying to get them our own way? Now I'm not talking about God giving you a new BMW because you asked Him politely. We'll talk about that problem later. Let me give you an example of what I do mean.

Husband, do you want your wife to be more responsive to your leadership? You can go about achieving that desire several ways. You can try the worldly way of begging, bullying, or bribing your wife to be more responsive to you. Or you can ask God to make you the kind of husband she would be delighted to follow.

You see, the level of your prayer life will always determine the level of your spiritual health and growth. Worldly Christians will spend three hours fuming that things aren't going their way—and thirty seconds praying that God will do something.

This is backward. Instead, spend thirty seconds fuming and three hours praying, and you might find a solution to your problem. The worse the conflict, the more your desires battle within you, then the more these things should drive you to your knees before God.

But it is amazing the lengths to which people will go in order to satisfy their pleasures. David's son Absalom was willing to kill his father to satisfy his lust for the throne of Israel. Absalom tried to eliminate David, even though David loved Absalom more than anything and would have done anything for him.

Sometimes I counsel with couples whose pleasures aren't being satisfied in their marriage and who want to get a divorce. They give me the worst reason ever for divorce: irreconcilable differences. I've got news for these couples. Whenever you get two sinners living together in the same house, *something* is going to be irreconcilable!

A wife may say, "My husband didn't act like this when we were dating."

Of course he didn't. He was faking you out in order to win you. He was on his best behavior. Your slightest whispered wish was his command: "You want to go to the opera instead of the football game? Sure thing, baby."

You thought it was great that he liked exactly the same stuff you liked. But he was lying to you. And now you see the real him, and he sees the real you.

The key to making a marriage work is not to erase the differences between a husband and wife, but to transform those differences from a source of conflict into a source of complementary strengths.

But if a husband and wife are both operating out of selfishness, trying to get what they want their own way, they will never get around to asking God to work that transformation or to give them what they need as a couple.

And if you never get around to bringing God into the equation, let me tell you something: You will never get around to the bigger agenda, which is bringing Him glory. Let me explain why I say that.

The Wrong Prayer

Someone is going to say, "I've got you on this one, Tony. I'm in a conflict, a battle, and I've prayed about this thing. I don't mean just a thirty-second prayer either. I've prayed a lot about this thing, and it's as bad as ever. I'm asking. Why isn't God answering?"

Obviously, I can't answer that for every individual case. But consider this. There is a problem beyond the problem of failing to ask God. The Bible says, "You ask and do not receive, because you ask with wrong motives, so that you may spend it on your pleasures" (James 4:3).

Most worldly-minded Christians don't get around to praying.

But when worldly Christians do pray, they usually pray with the motive of satisfying their desires.

You see, there are only two ways to pray. It's either "Lord, Your will be done" or "Lord, my will be done." When we pray with selfish, worldly motives, we are asking God to endorse and accommodate our sin.

In other words, what motivates the selfish prayer is not the righteous glory of God. So if you get on your knees and say, "Lord, get me out of this marriage," that's the wrong prayer. The prayer that will bring God glory is, "Lord, change me so that I'm the right kind of mate in this marriage." Now He'll talk to you.

The wrong prayer brings no answer from God. So the obvious question is "How can we tell the right prayer from the wrong prayer?" It's very simple. Consider what glory God will get by answering it.

This question should occupy your mind every time you pray. What glory will God get out of answering my petition? When you pray with God's glory in mind, you'll see answers to prayer like you've never dreamed. After all, God has included you in His family for His own glory, and He responds to prayers that will mean glory for His name.

In sharp contrast is the worldly approach to prayer. Here the attitude is that God is in business to give me whatever I want and make me feel good. But such a "feel good" God is no God at all. We must accommodate ourselves to God, not expect Him to align Himself with our wishes and desires.

God knows us well. He knows that wrong motives often lie behind our requests. The Greek behind that phrase "wrong motives" (v. 3) means to be diseased or sick. A give-me-what-I-want-and-make-me-feel-good prayer is a sick prayer because it comes from a heart diseased by worldliness, a heart that is not in tune with eternal values but seeks only temporary gratification.

God also knows that we often ask for selfish reasons: We want to spend His blessing on our pleasures. The Greek word *spend* here means "to squander." It's the same word used of the prodigal son. He squandered his inheritance; he wasted his father's gift. The Bible says selfish prayers designed to acquire things so we can squander them on selfish goals will get no response from God. A prayer like that is not at all concerned with His glory.

Praying for God's Glory

What does a prayer that is concerned for God's glory look like? I think of the conversation that took place between God and Moses after the Israelites sinned by building the golden calf (Exod. 32:1–14). Let me give you an Evans paraphrase.

Because of the people's rebellion and disobedience, God said to Moses, "Step out of My way, Moses. I am going to wipe these people out and start over again with you."

But Moses interceded for Israel: "Lord, before You wipe Israel out, I just want to remind You that if You do this, Your name and Your glory are going to be tarnished. The Egyptians are going to say that You brought Israel out into the wilderness to kill them. You are going to look bad to the Egyptians, and I don't want that.

"Lord, I love my people and want to see them spared. But I also don't want Your glory to be tarnished. So, for the sake of Your own name and glory, I am asking You to turn away from Your anger and change Your mind about destroying Israel."

The Bible says that God heard Moses and "changed His mind about the harm which He said He would do to His people" (Exod. 32:14). God spared Israel. Why? Because God responds to requests to guard His glory.

When God hears our prayers, He wants to know how His glory is one of the concerns behind our requests. He wants to bless His people, but His first concern is bringing glory to His name. A worldly Christian does not pray or live with God's glory in view.

Worldliness and Conflict with God

When your life is characterized by worldliness, you not only have a problem with others and within yourself. You also have a much bigger problem than either of these. A Christian who is snuggling up to the world has God as an adversary. Worldliness always means conflict with God.

Spiritual Adultery

The Bible has a strong term for worldly Christians: "You adulteresses, do you not know that friendship with the world is hostility toward God? Therefore whoever wishes to be a friend of the world makes himself an enemy of God" (James 4:4). Worldliness is spiritual adultery against God. It is infidelity, the breaking of a covenant we have made with God to love Him with all our hearts, souls, and strength.

Worldliness is like a married person who has another love on the side. In this case, the other love is called the world. When we try to love God and love the world on the side, we can't expect to enjoy spiritual intimacy with God.

Such spiritual adulteresses are also called "friends of the world." The word for *friend* here has the idea of brotherly love, a relationship of genuine affection. God wants an intimate relationship with you, but He can't be intimate with you when you are being intimate with the world.

As we said earlier, the essence of worldliness is the desire to leave God out. So if you're hanging out with a lover who wants to push God out of your life, you are in bad shape.

Suppose a husband took his wife to dinner and said, "You sit here at this table and I'll sit over there at that table, because I don't want anybody to know we're together. I'll pay for your meal, but I don't want to be seen sitting with you."

Or, even worse, imagine a husband bringing another woman to dinner with him and his wife and announcing, "This woman is my other love. I want her to join us for dinner."

That would devastate a marriage relationship. So it is in our relationship with God. When we bring a rival into our relationship with Him, God becomes our enemy.

And when God is your enemy, nothing will work. Every time you try to take two steps forward, He will take you three steps back.

Everything you start on your own apart from Him, He will keep you from finishing. When Christians let themselves be compromised by the world, they put themselves in a position of hostility toward God.

Now God doesn't expect us to hide from the world. He knows we have to live in this age and place. What He wants is for us to move through this world the way fish move through salt water. Fish can swim in salt water their whole lives without tasting salty when we have them for dinner. In the same way, God expects us to swim in this world without becoming worldly.

A Jealous Lover

The reason God gets angry when you try to love Him and to love the world is that God is a jealous Lover. He gave His Son to save you from the deadly consequences of your sin, and He wants you all for Himself. So the Bible asks, "Do you think that the Scripture speaks to no purpose: 'He jealously desires the Spirit which He has made to dwell in us'?" (James 4:5).

There is no room for any rival in your relationship with God. That doesn't mean you can't do anything or enjoy anything in this world God created. But it does mean you can't do or enjoy anything and expect to leave God out.

That's why I don't allow rap music in my house. It is defiant music, and most of it is unrighteous. To have it playing means you have to exclude God. God created music, but the question with any music is whether He can listen to it with us. Is He snapping His fingers along with us?

God wants to be included in every area of our lives because He is jealous over us and doesn't want the world to stain us. Furthermore, we grieve the Holy Spirit who lives within us when we exclude God.

God's Greater Grace

We have been talking about worldliness and conflict, but I want to close this chapter with a powerful promise. The promise begins with, "But He gives a greater grace" (James 4:6). These words are so sweet. They say that if you will make Him your only love, God will open up the windows of heaven and pour out His grace—His favor—on you.

This is not a promise of grace for salvation, but a promise that God will give you more of Himself and His blessings than you could ever imagine if you will love Him only. But God is not going to give you more and more of Himself so you can squander your energy and affection on another love.

Two Kinds of Heads

That verse of promise ends with a closing statement on the issue of worldliness: "Therefore [Scripture] says, 'God is opposed to the proud, but gives grace to the humble'" (v. 6). Pride is at the heart of a selfish, worldly attitude that puts us in conflict with God.

God hates pride because pride prompts us to set ourselves up as our own god. God's opposition to such pride is expressed in a military term that means He arrays an army against proud people.

Pride is repulsive to God because it reminds Him of Satan, who rebelled against God and tried to dethrone Him. Every time we act independently of God, we remind Him of the devil. And God will not sit by passively; He will take action. He promises to put an end to "the arrogance of the proud" (Isa. 13:11).

Talk about conflict with God! You haven't known conflict until you've had God opposing you in your arrogant pride. How can you and I avoid this conflict? By humbling ourselves before God. Humility is the position we must assume in order to experience God's greater grace. Let me illustrate.

Once there were two brothers. One became a farmer, and the other became a brilliant, wealthy lawyer. The lawyer visited his farmer brother one day and said, "I can't believe you haven't made something out of your life. Look at me. I have investments on Wall Street. I have powerful clients who are millionaires. And you're stuck out here on a farm."

The farmer pointed out to his wheat field and replied, "Brother, there are two types of wheat heads out there. See the heads that are standing straight up? That's because there is nothing in them. They're empty. See the other heads that are bent over? That's because the heads are full of wheat."

Some Christians are standing straight up in pride, their posture saying, "Look at me. I'm somebody. I'm walking tall." That's because their heads and hearts have been emptied by worldliness.

Other Christians are bowed down low before God because their heads and hearts are full of love for Him and genuine humility before His grace and mercy.

Which position are you in today? The test is not what you have in your bank account or the awards you have hanging on your wall. It's what you have in your heart that counts. Until God gets your heart, you won't get more of Him. Humble yourself before Him, cry out to Him, and let go of your worldliness. Then you'll be on the path toward Christlikeness and becoming that perfect Christian.

Test Your Perfection I.Q.

- Give three reasons why worldliness can't be defined by a list of do's and don'ts—and give yourself four points for each reason.

    1.

    2.

    3.

- Worldliness results in conflict on at least three levels—conflict with others, conflict within yourself, and conflict with God.

—Conflict with others.
A Christian who lives in perpetual conflict reveals a worldly spirit rooted in self-centeredness, jealousy, pettiness, and evil desires. Consider how well you're getting along with folks. On this scale, "1" is "Worldly Christian's my name; fussin' and fightin's my game!" and "10" is "Dying to self and seeking to please the Lord in all things."

    1 2 3 4 5 6 7 8 9 10

—Conflict within.
When worldly pleasures battle for internal control over us, we know conflict within. That conflict comes when we want to pursue our own (often uncontrolled) desires, making personal pleasure of paramount importance, and, more subtly, acting with wrong motives. On this scale, "1" is "I want what I want—and I'll fight for it!" and "10" is "I'm asking God to give me what He wants me to have, concerned about His glory as well as my growth and determined to be a good witness in the world."

    1 2 3 4 5 6 7 8 9 10

—*Conflict with God.*

Friendship with the world means hostility towards God. We commit spiritual adultery when we try to love God and love the world on the side. How faithful are you being? On this scale, "1" is "I'm standing straight, just like that wheat that is hollow. My head and heart have been emptied by worldliness" and "10" is "I'm bowed down low before God, my head and heart full of love for Him and genuine humility before His grace and mercy."

1 2 3 4 5 6 7 8 9 10

Total Points _____

Chapter 10

How to Pursue
Intimacy with God

One thing I love about the Word of God is its wonderful balance. The Bible never tells us to give up or avoid something wrong without replacing it with something positive that honors God.

The balance and the wisdom of Scripture really shine through as we move on from God's call to avoid worldliness and its devastating effect on our Christian lives. If our goal is to be like Jesus, to be perfect Christians, we definitely need to flee from a worldly, selfish spirit that causes us to look, act, and think like the world—and worse, like the devil.

But God doesn't just want us to run *from* something wrong. He wants us to run *toward* something right—intimacy with Himself. The Christian who is focused on drawing closer to God won't have to worry too much about leaving worldliness behind. You can't go in both directions at once!

Now some people think the best way to avoid worldliness is literally to flee from the world by taking refuge in a monastery or convent. Sincere Christians have been doing that for centuries.

But God does not intend for us to lock ourselves in the church and hide from the world. In fact, the night before His death, Jesus prayed for us specifically, "I do not ask Thee to take them out of the world, but to keep them from the evil one" (John 17:15). God wants us to go into the world to serve Him and live for Him without becoming worldly, without letting the world's value system capture us.

The challenge of the Christian life, then, is to pursue a deeper, more intimate relationship with God right where He has put you. Let's talk about three ways the Bible says you can do this.

Submit to God

The first step you need to take in your pursuit of God is to submit to His authority in your life.

The command is stated very plainly in Scripture: "Submit therefore to God" (James 4:7). That's about as clear as it gets.

But what does the "therefore" point back to? The value God places on humility before Him. An attitude of humility is the key to submitting ourselves to God. A person with an arrogant spirit isn't about to submit to anyone—not even the Lord God Almighty.

Submission has never been a popular concept, even in Christian circles. But you can't skip it if you want to walk the road of sanctification and become more like Jesus. A mature and, yes, perfect Christian is a submissive Christian. Besides, we are going to see that God has a load of benefits and blessings in store for the believer who is fully submitted to Him.

This principle of submission appears throughout the Bible. We are commanded to submit to duly constituted government (Rom. 13:1). A wife is to submit herself to the authority of her husband (Eph. 5:22), and children are instructed to obey their parents (Eph. 6:1).

Now it's true that there are exceptions, as when an authority may tell us to do something directly contrary to God's Word. But submission to authority is the rule.

Submission is a military term meaning "placing yourself in your proper rank." It means to place yourself under the authorities God has placed over you—and, ultimately, to place yourself under His authority.

Get an Alignment

We could say, then, that submission to God requires a new alignment of our lives.

When your tires are out of alignment, you may feel your car pull to one side or the other. At other times, you can't detect the problem. But one way you can know your car needs an alignment is when the front tires begin to wear unevenly.

Some Christians look at their lives and see the uneven wear. They may even feel themselves being pulled to one side or the other by the world, the flesh, and the devil. They may be experiencing more defeats than victories. They find themselves unable to cope with the constant battle with sin that Christians must fight every day. They know there's a problem, so they keep changing "tires," hoping to solve it. Let me explain.

Christians who don't feel fully aligned with the Lord may keep changing churches, hoping to find something that can pull them back in proper alignment with God. Or they may go after a certain spiritual experience that promises something new, running from this conference to that seminar in search of help.

But if the front end of your car is out of alignment, changing tires won't fix it because the new tires will simply begin to wear out like the old ones.

The same is true spiritually. You can change your spiritual tires every week, but that won't help unless you submit your life to God on a daily basis. Until you bring your heart into its proper alignment under God's authority, you are still going to be a worn-out believer.

Many of our marriages and personal lives are being worn down by the world, and we think the answer is to change our spiritual tires. We want to change churches, change environments, or even change mates.

If this is your situation, check your alignment. More specifically, if you want to prevent the kinds of problems that come when our lives are not in proper relationship to God, check to see if you are in alignment with the Lord and submitted to His authority.

Submission to God means saying to Him on a day-by-day basis, "Not my will, but Your will be done. I subject my desires to Your desires, my dreams to Your dreams, my purposes and plans to Your purposes and plans." What I am talking about is utterly abandoning yourself to God's control.

Now if you've been lined up with the world, taking your orders from the culture and from your old sinful nature, you'll find it tough to get yourself back in rank under your Commander, Jesus Christ. But this is a necessary first step in experiencing the kind of relationship with God that grows you into maturity and Christlikeness.

Leave the Warm Spot

Here's another way to look at this issue of submission. You know what it's like to be in bed on a dark, cold winter morning, comfortable in that spot you have warmed up, and hear the alarm go off.

You know what that means. It's time to get up. But that spot in your bed is so warm and comfortable. You're all covered up, and you don't want to be interrupted. You don't want to leave your bed and put your feet on a cold floor.

But you get up anyway. You choose to get out of bed and go to work. Why? Because you know that the rewards of going to work, of earning a living so you can provide the house that holds your warm bed, are greater than the temporary pleasure of a few extra minutes in a warm bed.

Now you may not feel like getting up on that particular morning. But the price tag for turning over and staying in that warm spot is too high to pay.

Can you see where I'm going? Submitting to God requires the choice (an act of the will) to leave that little warm spot we have developed in the world. I don't know what your "warm spot" is, but most Christians have one.

God is calling us to leave that temporary comfort for the greater reward of getting ourselves in proper rank under Him. God can empower you to make that decision, but He will not make it for you. Submission to God involves a conscious decision to throw back the covers of a lesser, temporary comfort in order to seek the greater blessing of intimacy with God.

Resist the Devil

Like a magnet with positive and negative poles, submission to God also has a negative pole: "Resist the devil and he will flee from you"

(James 4:7). Drawing closer to God will help you resist Satan's attempt to influence you.

Remember that Satan has no power over you that you don't allow him to have. The devil is not invincible. He has been "render[ed] powerless" by the death of Jesus Christ (Heb. 2:14).

Since the devil cannot overcome us by power, he has to attack us with deception and temptation. Satan can make you *want* to sin, but if you are a believer, Satan can no longer *make* you sin. He simply makes sin look attractive and easy for you to commit.

The devil is smart. As I said before, he doesn't waste his time tempting you and me in areas where we are not vulnerable. He is a student of our lives. He has a game film on us, and he studies it like a football coach who watches hours of film on his next opponent so he knows his opponent's habits, tendencies, and preferences.

Satan's film on your life goes all the way back to your unsaved days. He and his demons have studied that tape so long that they know what you like to do, what you like to think about, the places you like to go, and the people you like to hang out with.

Knowing all of this, the devil's strategy is to put before you circumstances and people that will bring out the sinful tendencies you have. So when you see how the devil has lined up against you, what you need to do is draw on the power of Jesus Christ and call a new counter play at the line of scrimmage—what is termed in football an audible. You change the play so that the devil's knowledge of your tendencies and weak spots does not give him the power to control your thoughts and actions.

The greatest example of resisting the devil is Jesus Christ. In Satan's temptation of Jesus we find the keys to resisting Satan in our lives.

We first read, "Jesus was led up by the Spirit into the wilderness to be tempted by the devil" (Matt. 4:1). Notice that this temptation was on God's terms, not the devil's. God opened the door to this opportunity, and Jesus Christ confronted the devil head-on.

Now we aren't to go looking for the devil, but we need to remember that Satan can only attack us on God's terms. The devil can't go any further than God allows him to go.

Next we see that although Jesus was God in the flesh, He did not take the devil's temptation lightly. Jesus "fasted forty days and forty nights" in spiritual preparation (v. 2). Even Jesus did not meet the devil without being prepared. Beforehand, He spent a lot of time in His Father's presence, an example of perfect submission to God.

This point is critical. You can't resist the devil if your spiritual immune system is weak. When your body's immune system is weak, you become vulnerable to illness. Your resistance—spiritual as well as physical—gets low when there are not enough disease fighters in your system.

What does it take to keep your spiritual resistance high? Jesus fasted and prayed. He sacrificed bodily comfort for spiritual strength.

If you have little desire for spiritual things, if you are making few or no sacrifices of creature comforts in the pursuit of God, your spiritual resistance will be low.

And Satan knows when you are weak. So even though you may tell him to leave, he won't budge because he knows you don't have enough strength and energy to resist him.

The devil cannot hurt or defeat the Christian whose immune system is strong because that person is living in submission to God. But if you are living in perpetual spiritual defeat, your resistance is down. Your spiritual immune system is deficient in the basics that keep a believer strong against Satan. When you submit to God, you find the strength you need to resist the devil.

Jesus may have been physically weak, but He was spiritually strong after forty days of preparation. You can read the account of the temptation in Matthew 4:3–11. I want to make several observations about this temptation.

First, the devil acted in character. He tempted Jesus to act independently of God and create food, put on a show, and take the kingdom apart from God's will.

But Jesus defeated the devil at each turn by quoting the Word: "It is written" (vv. 4, 7, 10). Jesus used the Word of God, the one thing that gets past the devil's immune system.

You see, the devil has an immune system, too. He can handle all of our promises and resolutions to do better, and our attempts to resist him in our own strength. But the Word of God always takes the devil down.

Obviously, then, to resist the devil, you need to know your Bible. I don't mean merely owning a Bible, I mean being so thoroughly immersed in the truth of Scripture that you can quote it on the spot to ward off the devil's attack.

After Jesus had hit the devil three times with the Word, the devil's resistance was so low he had nothing left to fight with, and he left. He couldn't hang out there anymore.

So instead of the devil weakening your immune system and making you sick, you should be making him sick by being submitted to God and skilled in the Word. We Christians should be learning and memorizing the Word, not so we can impress others and win Bible-quoting contests, but so we can win at life.

I recently ministered at a treatment center in New Jersey that has the most phenomenal program I've ever seen. When men with drug and other addictions go there for two weeks, they have to sign an agreement to abide by the rules of the program, which are very strict.

This program saturates people with the Word of God. The men who enter the program have to read the Word, quote it, memorize it, and study it. The idea is to help them increase their resistance and build up their spiritual immune systems before they start dealing with the specific problems that have led to their addictions.

I was told that 80 percent of the men who go through the program leave in victory and that only 5 percent have to come back. When I commented on these great statistics, the director told me the key is strengthening the spiritual immune system before trying to deal with the addiction.

Otherwise, he said, if they try to fix an addiction problem without strengthening the addict's spiritual weaknesses, the help is only temporary. But if they can show a man how to build up his spiritual strength, then the effects of the other counseling are lasting.

Submitting to God will help you resist the devil. Resist him with prayer, spiritual discipline, and the Word, just as Jesus did, and the devil will have to leave. He cannot function in that environment.

Draw Near to God

The story is told of a little boy who was being beaten up by a bully every day on his way to school. The boy's friends told him to go to school a different way. But the bully found out about that route, met the boy on his way to school, and beat him up.

Another friend advised the boy to carry a stick to school. He carried a stick one day, but the bully took the stick away from him and beat him with it. Nothing this boy tried worked to get rid of the bully.

One day as the boy was walking to school, the bully jumped out and clenched his fist. But instead of being afraid, the boy said, "Come on, I'm ready. I'll take you right now."

The bully couldn't believe this little kid had become so brave. But as the bully got ready to pounce on him, the boy's father stepped out from behind a bush; he was about 6'10", 275 pounds. The bully said, "Uh-oh."

The moral of the story is, stay close to your Father. The closer you are to God, the more that bully the devil will leave you alone. That's why the Word of God tells us, "Draw near to God and He will draw near to you" (James 4:8). This is the second part of the Bible's formula for realizing greater intimacy with God.

And that intimacy is key to growing into the believer God wants you to be. After all, you cannot avoid worldliness and beat the devil at his game if you're maintaining a long-distance relationship with God. You cannot be a part-time Christian, an "S.M.O." (Sunday Morning Only) saint, and be the maturing Christian God wants you to be.

The closer you draw to God, the more like Him you are going to become. You can't help but be affected, the way you can't help but sweat if you're out in the hot sun. Greater closeness to God produces in you a greater likeness to Him.

Plan for Closeness

But you don't draw close to someone by chance or by accident. You have to plan for closeness. Intentionality is necessary to achieve intimacy. It doesn't just happen.

If you are married, chances are good that you and your mate did not simply drift to the altar. You drew near to one another as you got acquainted and began to spend time together. You talked on the phone. You went out on dates.

And when you weren't on the phone and weren't together, you wished you were. You began thinking about each other all the time. Your investment in nearness produced an intensity of relationship, which led to the marriage altar.

Most marriages start off with a passionate intimacy, but what often happens as the years go by? It's easy for a couple to drift apart emotionally because now they find themselves dealing with other agendas and looking after their children.

If a married couple have no ongoing plan to continue drawing near to one another, they can drift dangerously apart. Then one day they look up and the marriage is weak and in trouble.

Your relationship with God is a lot like a marriage relationship. Intimacy with Him won't happen by chance. You need to make an intentional commitment to pursue God and seek greater intimacy with Him so that He can grow you into a greater likeness to Jesus Christ.

When we make that commitment, we have the tremendous promise that He will draw near to us. Just as in a good marriage, the commitment is not one-sided. God is eager to bring us near.

Now someone might ask, "If God wants me closer, why doesn't He draw near to me, and then I'll draw near to Him? Why do I have to initiate the process?" The answer is simple. He's not the one who pulled back. He's not the one who left. That brings us to the issue of sin.

Deal Seriously with Sin

Suppose a man walks out on his family, gets his own apartment, establishes a separate life, and then says, "If my family will draw near to me, I'll draw near to them."

That's not right. He has it backwards. He's the one who left home; it's his job to repent, return, and draw near to his family. It's the same in our relationship with God. Our sin breaks our fellowship with Him and puts distance between us. When we return to God in repentance, willing to change our ways, we'll find that He never left.

So what exactly does it take to draw near to God? The Bible answers in no uncertain terms: "Cleanse your hands, you sinners; and purify your hearts, you double-minded" (James 4:8).

Clearly, James is talking to Christians here because non-Christians can't cleanse their hands and be clean. They first need a "whole-body" cleansing by the blood of Christ. These words are addressed to Christians who are living like sinners.

Why does James tell us to wash our hands? Handwashing was part of the cleansing ceremony that Old Testament priests performed before they could offer sacrifices to God. The act symbolized the getting rid of the defilement of sin.

Hands represent our external actions, just as the heart represents our internal attitudes. Cleansing our hands means that we say to God, "I know this is sin. I know it is defiling me, and I'm going to stop it." God wants us to make that kind of decision to change any of our actions that are sinful.

But one reason we don't get nearer to God is that we are reluctant to call sin what it is. We call it everything but sin: a weakness, a problem, a mistake, a bad choice, an issue. God will only deal with you if you are ready to deal openly and directly with your sin.

Dealing with sin means being cleansed and purified. It also means being focused on the Lord and His ways. The opposite of that is being double-minded, being unable to make up your mind whether you want to line up with God or line up with the world. It means wanting to be a saint and a sinner at the same time. God wants you to know that this kind of spiritual indecision is deadly, because He pulls back when He sees a believer who flops back and forth between commitment and compromise.

Some of us are being double-minded when we hang around the edges of sin just to keep in touch. We don't really want to plunge into the dirtiness of sin. We just want to collect some of sin's souvenirs so we can put them in the attic and get them out every once in a while.

But God calls us to clean out the attic, too. He wants us to get rid of the reminders of the world. He says, "Don't let your heart be divided." And He invites us to go to Him as David did. David knew, "Against Thee, Thee only, I have sinned" (Ps. 51:4). When you and I remove the sin, then God will be free to draw near.

We hear that promise throughout Scripture: "The LORD is near to all who call upon Him" (Ps. 145:18); "You will seek Me and find Me, when you search for Me with all your heart" (Jer. 29:13); "Draw near with confidence" (Heb. 4:16); and "Draw near with a sincere heart" (Heb. 10:22).

In case we somehow miss the intensity of God's desire that we deal with sin, James adds, "Be miserable and mourn and weep; let your laughter be turned into mourning, and your joy to gloom" (4:9).

Now doesn't it bother you when something serious is going on, and somebody who should be taking it seriously is laughing it off as if it were no big deal? God says, "Don't brush off sin as if it were nothing serious. It's serious." If you want to draw near to God, you have to adopt His attitude toward sin. You have to weep bitterly over your sin as Peter did when he denied Jesus three times. You need to grieve and agonize over your sin as King David did (Ps. 51). And he didn't blame his sinful deeds on childhood abuse or other extenuating circumstances.

You need to "be miserable and mourn and weep" over your sin. That's evidence of sincere repentance. If you don't think your sin is bad enough to cry over, if you're comparing your "little" sin to some of the really bad sins being committed out there, you don't understand how God views sin. All sin is a deep affront to His holiness. We cannot enjoy nearness to God, real intimacy with Him, when sin is present. Sin never fails to choke off our fellowship with our Lord.

Humble Yourself Before God

The third step in this biblical formula for seeking God is found in this command: "Humble yourselves in the presence of the Lord, and He will exalt you" (James 4:10). Here is yet another great promise from the Word.

If we are busy lifting ourselves up, why should God do any lifting? Humility means you go low so God can lift you high.

Remove All Pride

We know true humility when God has removed all fragments of pride from us. As we see in the Bible, the people whom God lifted up were always taken down first.

Joseph was taken down to Egypt to become a slave and do time in prison before he became prime minister of the land. Moses was sent out into the desert for forty years before he was ready to lead Israel. David had to hang out with the sheep and spend years running for his life before he could be king. These men—and many others—had to learn humility before God trusted them with great positions and responsibilities.

If you want God to raise you up in usefulness, in power, in victory, and in strength, you have to go low. Why? Because there is no room for two Gods in this universe. You see, if you are able to raise yourself up, to be God over your life, the true God will have no room to work.

But if you can't raise yourself up and you realize you are in desperate need of God, you can go low before Him in humility. When you need mercy, you say please. When you need grace, you ask humbly.

Then you will know a sweet intimacy with your Lord. Arrogant people don't know such intimacy or nearness to God. He does not invite the proud to draw close. So you must let go of all pride if you are to reach God's heart. His elevator to the top always starts by going down.

Lift Others Up

God's Word not only tells us to humble ourselves, but it gives a great illustration of what humility looks like in real life. Not surprisingly, one example has to do with the way we use our tongues. That passage reads:

> Do not speak against one another, brethren. He who speaks against
> a brother, or judges his brother, speaks against the law, and judges
> the law; but if you judge the law, you are not a doer of the law, but
> a judge of it. (James 4:11)

Humbling yourself before God means, in part, realizing that you shouldn't use your tongue to hurt other people and drag them down. That realization comes more easily when you are able to acknowledge your own sin and shortcomings. Pride causes us to exalt ourselves and treat other people with contempt. Humility causes us to see that we are all on level ground before God. Since that's the case, attacks on a fellow believer have no place in the life of a Christian who is pursuing intimacy with God.

"Who are you who judge your neighbor?" the Bible asks (James 4:12). Put differently, how dare you and I tear down a brother or sister when we ourselves cannot stand before God because of our sin? If God started keeping accounts, none of us would be around long. Humility demands that we deal with our own shortcomings rather than look at other people's sin. Looking at other people's failings tends to lead us to "speak against" them. To "speak against" a fellow Christian here means to slander the person, to speak viciously with the evil intent of destroying another person's reputation. The opposite of such slander is speech that is "good for edification according to the need of the moment, that it may give grace to those who hear" (Eph. 4:29).

Do you use your words to tear people down or to build them up? Your speech matters a great deal to God. Notice that slandering a fellow Christian is a violation of God's royal law, which says, "You shall love your neighbor as yourself" (James 2:8). Slander is not treating your neighbor the way you want to be treated. No one wants to have his or her reputation destroyed! In fact, when we fail to exercise humility as we talk about others, we actually set ourselves above God's law and treat it with contempt. That is a very dangerous thing to do.

Jesus summarized all of God's law by saying we should love God with our whole being and our neighbor as ourselves (Matt. 22:37–40). The Ten Commandments (Exod. 20:3–17) are really commandments that have to do with love. Let me show you.

The first commandment forbids another God: Our love can't be fickle; it must be single-minded. The second commandment forbids idols: Love must be loyal. The third commandment forbids taking

God's name in vain: Love must be respectful. The fourth commandment says remember the Sabbath and keep it holy: Love must be focused in its affections.

The next six commandments address our relationships with others. The fifth commandment commands us to honor our father and mother: Love must be submissive to legitimate authority. The sixth commandment forbids murder: Love values other people. The seventh commandment rules out adultery: Marital love is to be pure, undefiled, and loyal.

The eighth commandment says do not steal: Love is not to be selfish and take from others what belongs to them. The ninth commandment tells us not to bear false witness: Love must be truthful. And the tenth commandment forbids coveting: Love must be content and thankful.

Clearly, love is built into the Ten Commandments. Therefore, love must govern the way we talk about others. The person who speaks against a brother or sister breaks God's law.

Now don't misunderstand. The Bible does not say we can never judge other people. At times, judgment is appropriate, and even necessary for that person's spiritual well-being. The key is the attitude with which we make our judgments. Again, the Bible is balanced in this regard.

Jesus Himself teaches that the issue is not *whether* you judge, but *how* you judge. He also warns that the standard you use for judgment is the standard by which you yourself will be judged.

So if you are judging others with evil intent, God is going to bring that back upon your own head. (I'm convinced that some of the things I see believers going through are the result of this principle being carried out in their lives.)

God is very protective of His children. Even though He has kids who need to be corrected for the wrong they have done, the correction is always to be done with the goal of restoring them to fellowship and building them up. The only time any of us can do this effectively is when we have removed the log from our own eye, and that important surgery requires humility before God.

Again, the problem with slander and wrong judgment is that you set yourself up as judge, jury, and executioner. You are playing God.

But there is only one God, the Bible says. "There is only one Law-giver and Judge, the One who is able to save and to destroy; but who are you who judge your neighbor?" (James 4:12).

God is the only One able to render righteous judgment perfectly. If you try to judge others, you are setting yourself up for a big fall. That's why the Bible warns us, "Let him who thinks he stands take heed lest he fall" (1 Cor. 10:12). This is clearly a call to humility. When we see someone caught up in sin, pride causes us to look down on that person and say, "That could never happen to me." But the humble person knows better: "But for the grace of God, that could be me." When you understand this, you are indeed humbling yourself before God.

I think of the story Jesus told about two men who went to temple to pray. The Pharisee stood up proudly and said, "God, I thank Thee that I am not like other people" (Luke 18:11). As he went on to list various sinners, he noticed a tax collector standing next to him—a perfect example of the kind of sinner he was talking about. So the Pharisee thanked God that he was not like that low-life tax collector.

But the tax collector had a different attitude as he prayed. He would not even approach the altar, but stood back, beat his chest in agony over his sins, and cried out, "God, be merciful to me, the sinner" (v. 13).

Jesus said the tax collector went away justified, while the Pharisee went away condemned. Why? Because the person who thinks he is high will be brought low, but the one who goes low will be lifted high.

That tax collector knew what it meant to pursue God. Despite his sins, despite his evil deeds, he wanted to draw close to God more than he wanted anything else. He also knew what God required in order to draw near to Him: a humble awareness of his sin and need for God.

What about you? Do you have a desire for God that will not be satisfied with anything less than deep, satisfying, personal intimacy with Him? Wherever you are right now in your spiritual life, you can still decide to pursue God with greater intimacy.

One thing I love about the game of football is halftime. At half-time, the teams stop playing and regroup. No matter what happened in the first half, they still have time to do something. The game isn't over yet.

Right now, it's only halftime in your spiritual life. You still have another half to get back out on the field and play to win. Don't listen to the crowd or to anyone else except Jesus Christ. He is calling you to intimate fellowship with Himself. Go for it!

Test Your Perfection I.Q.

- Let's begin with a quick review! What three instructions does James offer for pursing intimacy with God (4:7–10)? Give yourself four points for each answer.

1.

2.

3.

- Now let's see how you're doing on each count.

—*Submit to God's authority.*
Have you placed yourself in proper rank under your Commander, Jesus Christ? Do you daily pray, "Not my desires, dreams, purposes, and plans—but Yours"? On this scale, "1" is "That submission stuff is from the Dark Ages!" and "10" is "Not my will, but Yours be done."

    1 2 3 4 5 6 7 8 9 10

—*Draw near to God.*
Are you intentional in your pursuit of intimacy with your heavenly Father? Are you working to get rid of the sin in your life? On this scale, "1" is "Intimacy will just happen, won't it? I don't buy this business of sin choking off fellowship!" and "10" is "My bitter tears and genuine grief over my sin enable me to be close to my holy Father, and He's honoring my intentional efforts to draw near to Him."

    1 2 3 4 5 6 7 8 9 10

—*Humble yourself before God.*

Removing all pride is key to knowing intimacy with God, and using your tongue to build people up rather than tear them down is evidence of a humble opinion of yourself. On this scale, "1" is "At least I'm not like that sinful person!" and "10" is "There but for the grace of God go I."

1   2   3   4   5   6   7   8   9   10

Total Points _____

Chapter 11

How to Include God in Your Plans

I wasn't allowed to attend many movies when I was a kid, but I do remember the old 3-D movies. We were given a pair of glasses that made the images on the screen really come alive.

Now to be cool, you had to wear those glasses. If you didn't, something like a haze seemed to hang over the screen, and you could hardly tell what was happening. But when you put on the 3-D glasses, not only could you see clearly, but the action seemed to leave the screen and jump right into your lap.

I would like to suggest that growing in Christlikeness and becoming a perfect Christian calls you to put on a pair of 3-D glasses and see life in an entirely new dimension. More specifically, when you put on your "Holy Spirit glasses" and look at life from God's perspective, things start falling into place and making sense.

Looking at life as God does is an exciting way to live, just like watching a 3-D movie was an exciting way to spend a Saturday afternoon. As we continue on our journey of sanctification in pursuit of God's perfect standard, we want to put on our Holy Spirit glasses and apply the reality we then see clearly to what I call the planning of life.

Let me give you the principle right up front. To be like Jesus, we must plan our lives in complete dependence upon God. Our plans need to reflect God's character and His will for us.

Unless we plan with our Holy Spirit glasses on, life is going to be hazy and unclear. So let's find how life is supposed to look when we view it from God's perspective.

Submit to God's Sovereignty As You Plan

Recognition of God's sovereignty needs to be the starting point for all our planning. With that acknowledgment we are saying that God is in control, and we aren't. Making plans without submitting them for His review, correction, and approval is an act of arrogance on our part that God will not let go unchallenged.

This is why the apostle James wrote, "Come now, you who say, 'Today or tomorrow, we shall go to such and such a city, and spend a year there and engage in business and make a profit'" (4:13). Hold on a minute. Did you ask God? Did He get to vote?

The Worldliness of Arrogant Planning

Remember our definition of *worldliness*? It's a worldview that excludes God from every area of life.

It's no surprise, then, that lost people act worldly, because they don't know life with God. But "worldly Christian" is an oxymoron, a contradiction. Yet it is also a reality. The Bible helps us believers see our own worldliness by inviting us to consider how we approach the everyday details of life.

In today's language, God is saying, "Get real! Don't give Me that stuff about you not being worldly when you exclude Me from your plans."

With the word *shall*, James's hypothetical speaker is saying, "This is what I am going to do. This is my plan, and I'm going to make sure it happens. I've already figured out the time frame (today or tomorrow), the location (such and such a city), the activity (engage in business), and the result (make a profit)."

Do you see the arrogance in this statement? Do you see any room for God to lead or even to offer an opinion? This finite human is making fixed, airtight plans as if he or she has total control over every detail of life, but the truth is that we can't control anything.

The reason you and I can't make fixed plans is that, unlike God, we are dependent by nature. God, on the other hand, is totally independent by nature.

The independence of God simply means that He does not need other things to happen in order for Him to do what He wants to do. God's plans are not contingent upon the weather or human actions or anything else.

You and I might make plans to fly to a certain city on a certain day and take care of some business. But those plans depend on the airlines, the weather, the business climate, and a lot of other things we can't control.

Whenever we make plans, we are assuming that we will wake up tomorrow with our bodies in working order. We assume the transportation we need is going to be available.

Now I know life calls for us to make plans. You may even be able to take out your planning calendar today and show me where you plan to be and what you plan to be doing a year from now.

I often have to plan my schedule a year or more in advance. But there are too many uncertainties and unknowns between now and next year for me to say confidently, "This is what I am going to do—period." I am not independent, and neither are you.

Again, don't misunderstand. God does not condemn human planning. The Bible urges us to plan (Prov. 6:6). But God is the Author of the eternal timetable. According to God's plan, Jesus was crucified and the plan of salvation was set before the earth was ever created.

The Danger of Excluding God

It's not sinful to plan. In fact, it's sinful *not* to plan. We need to be good stewards of the life God has given us. What God condemns, though, is independent planning that leaves Him out, schedule-making that does not allow for His review. These plans will never succeed.

Making plans without God is like hacking through a jungle without a map or being at sea without a compass. You'll wind up lost. It's like sewing with a needle but no thread or using a pen without ink.

Without God, your plans will fall apart; you'll have nothing to show for your efforts.

My older daughter Crystal loves puzzles. When she was a child, she always wanted a puzzle for Christmas. As Crystal grew older, I would buy her more complex puzzles.

One year, I bought her a one-thousand-piece puzzle for Christmas. She took the puzzle back to her bedroom, joyfully anticipating the challenge ahead of her. But after spending the better part of the day in her room, Crystal came out and was ticked off at me. She wanted to know why I had bought her this puzzle.

I asked her, "What's the problem?"

She came back with a classic answer: "Dad, this puzzle has too many pieces."

That's true of life, too. It has too many pieces. No matter how smart you are, you can't put this puzzle together without help. That's why the puzzle-maker puts a picture on the box. As long as you get help from the puzzle-maker, you can put the pieces together. But you can't force a piece to fit where the puzzle-maker didn't design it to fit.

The Bible is saying that to plan your business, your travel, or your day-to-day life without including God is a sign of worldliness—and it is sinful. It's not enough to acknowledge God on Sunday morning. He must be part of the warp and woof of existence.

If you exclude the sovereign God from your plans, you are in trouble. When something happens that you didn't anticipate—and it will—chances are that you won't know how to handle it because you haven't allowed a place in your plans for God's activity.

Too many Christians have handed God their Declaration of Independence. Like the devil, they are telling God, "I will, I will, I will. These are my plans, God, and I'm going to make them happen." That's planning for disaster. We need to do our planning in dependence upon God's sovereign direction.

Rely on God's Infinite Knowledge As You Plan

Another important aspect of planning that pleases God is planning in dependence on His infinite knowledge. After all, He knows the end from the beginning. The Bible reminds us that we human beings "do not know what your life will be like tomorrow. You are just a vapor that appears for a little while and then vanishes away" (James 4:14). We really don't know what we think we know because our knowledge—like our life—is limited.

Our Knowledge Is Too Limited

You and I don't even know what tomorrow holds, the Bible says, so why are we talking so confidently about what we will and will not do? Words like that betray our worldliness and lack of humility.

It's easy to demonstrate just how limited our knowledge is. Don't all of us make plans only to be disappointed when something unforeseen happens?

Remember when you thought you were going to get that raise or promotion? Confident that it was coming, you went out and bought stuff before the raise actually came through—then for some reason it didn't.

Or you thought everything was moving along well and the new house was going to be yours. Or you thought you would be able to afford the new car payment, but then something in the house broke and now you're strapped. How did you get into that mess? Because you're not God, and you can't see what's coming next.

In Psalm 73, the psalmist got shook up when he looked around and noticed that evil people seemed to have everything going their way. They grew rich and fat and never had trouble, while the righteous went from problem to problem. So the psalmist pointed this apparent injustice out to the Lord. When he did, God showed him the real deal, which is that the wicked have one foot on a banana peel and the other foot in hell.

When the psalmist saw things as they really are, when he put his "Holy Ghost glasses" on, he said he felt "senseless and ignorant . . . like a beast before [God]" (v. 22). We would say today that he slapped his forehead and said, "Duh! Of course! Why didn't I see that?"

We are indeed like senseless animals when it comes to advising God on how to run His universe. You don't go to your pet for advice on how you should conduct your life. In God's sight, our knowledge is like that of a dog or cat.

Again, the best proof of our limited knowledge is that we don't even know what's going to happen tomorrow. That's why the Bible says, "Do not boast about tomorrow, for you do not know what a day may bring forth" (Prov. 27:1).

In fact, we can't even be sure we are going to make it through today. The emergency room is full of people who had plans for tomorrow. So is the cemetery.

Our Lives Are Too Short

We need to lean on God's infinite knowledge, first, because our knowledge is limited. Second, we need His knowledge because our days are limited.

"Life is short." How many times have you heard that? You hear it a lot because it's true. Life truly is short, and the older you get, the faster time moves.

When you're a child, time creeps along. Why is it taking so long to become a teenager? Then when you finally become a teenager, time starts to walk a little bit. You can see the day ahead when you will leave the house and go to college or work.

When you become an adult, time starts to run. Life is going by faster. Then when you are older, time just flies. You wonder where it went. And you can see the day when your time on this planet will run out.

Oh, we use terms such as *young* and *old* to describe people's ages, but these terms are relative because we don't know how long our lives will be. But one thing is sure. Our lives are just a vapor, a puff of smoke, because God measures our days against eternity.

So you and I don't know much about much of anything when it comes to the issues of life. The reason you need to include God in your planning is that He knows what you don't know. He sees every factor, takes into consideration all possibilities, and gives you the best option. Let me compare this to an everyday situation.

If you live in a city that has regular traffic reports on the radio, you know what it's like to want to go somewhere and wonder if there's a traffic tie-up on the freeway you want to take. When I need to get across Dallas, I tune in to a local station that has a helicopter in the air checking on traffic.

I want to take the most direct route to my destination, but my knowledge of the current traffic situation is extremely limited. I don't know if traffic is backed up just around the corner. I don't know if there has been an accident on my route, because I can't see any farther than a few feet in front of my car.

But the radio station can help me, because it has an "eye in the sky" that can take in the traffic scene all at once. I'm down low on the ground, but the person in the helicopter is up high. So I rely on the helicopter for information in planning my route across Dallas that day. The pilot can suggest an alternate route if my original route is stacked up.

As you navigate your way through life, you are so low, but God is so high. He can see all the possible routes, and He can show you the one that can save you from winding up in a mess. But God will only share His infinite knowledge with you if you include Him in your planning. Because life is so short—and we are so finite in our knowledge—we can't afford to exclude Him.

The writers of Scripture also knew that life is short, and they were faithful to remind us: "Our days on the earth are like a shadow" (1 Chron. 29:15); "My days are swifter than a weaver's shuttle" (Job 7:6); and "Teach us to number our days" (Ps. 90:12).

All of us have made decisions without God's direction. If given the opportunity to turn back the clock, we would undoubtedly do things differently. Hindsight is always better than foresight.

Well, the bad news is we can't go back. Time is like a coin. You can spend it any way you want, but you can only spend it once.

But the good news is you're still alive, and that means you still have the opportunity to make better and wiser decisions today. You can't change yesterday, but you don't have to make today look like yesterday if you will plan in dependence on God's perfect knowledge.

Defer to God's Will As You Plan

Earlier saints used to finish their sentences by saying, "The Lord willing." They also used to come to church and sing praises that God had brought them safely through another week.

Those folks understood something we have forgotten today. Maybe because life was more harsh and uncertain in the old days, God's people in earlier generations learned to say, "If the Lord wills, we shall live and also do this or that" (James 4:15). But this is what all of us ought to say.

God Has a Will for Us

With our limited knowledge and limited life span, we are wise to defer to God's will when we are making plans. We do well to punctuate our pronouncements about the future with a spiritual proviso. But saying "If the Lord wills" should be far more than just a phrase to make you sound spiritual. These words need to reflect an attitude that says, "Lord, these are my plans, but I subject them to Your will because You are infinitely greater than I am." That attitude includes God in your planning.

Since God's will for you is the expression of His infinitely perfect plan, you won't go wrong submitting your plans to Him. But if you leave God out, you may miss out on some blessings He wanted to send your way. You may also miss out on His protection from some danger if you are fixated on what you want to do.

Have you ever met people who are rigid and inflexible? They're tough to deal with because their plans leave no room for anyone else's will—even God's.

Jesus said, "My food is to do the will of Him who sent Me" (John 4:34). Doing God's will was as satisfying to Jesus as a good meal is to most of us. When you include God's will in your planning, you know God's satisfaction. And His will is so satisfying because it is "good and acceptable and perfect" (Rom. 12:2).

God Wants Us to Know His Will

The fact that God's will satisfies is good news for those of us who desire to obey God. And there is more good news. God wants us to know and understand His will. He wants us to test and prove His will, and He wants us to obey His will.

The Bible says that, because of the intimate relationship God had with Moses, God "made known His ways to Moses" (Ps. 103:7). If you have a growing, intimate relationship with God, He is going to let you in on what He's doing with your life.

But if your relationship with God is shaky because you're an "S.M.O." (Sunday Morning Only) Christian or because you won't let God into your business or your family life, then He will say, "Fine. Do it on your own."

Many of us want a "911 God." We want to say to God, "This is my plan, and I don't want You messing with it. But stay close in case of emergency."

When I first met my wife, Lois, I liked her right away, but the feeling was not mutual. So I decided I would try to win her heart. I began to intrude into her life and her plans. I reached back for my best Baltimore rap.

I remember one day when we walked out on the seawall and I was talking about naming the stars and all that stuff. I didn't know what in the world I was talking about, but I was pulling out my best rap.

And it worked. Lois started out saying, "I don't like him." Then it progressed to "Well, he's all right." Then it was "He's kind of nice." And from there, it was the marriage altar! Lois didn't necessarily plan for things to happen that way, but that's what happened.

God wants the opportunity to "rap" about His will with you and to intrude in your affairs. He may bring along things you didn't plan on, but when you give Him the right to work out His will in your life, He will be God for you. Otherwise, you'll get stuck being God in your life, and we'll see what kind of universe you come up with.

Finally, Jesus prayed that He would not have to go to the cross. But He ended His prayer with "Yet not what I will, but what Thou wilt" (Mark 14:36). This is the prayer of a person whose plans are made in dependence upon God's will.

Honor God's Holiness As You Plan

This final point takes us right to the heart of the planning issue. The way we plan our lives is a matter not just of intelligence or convenience, but a matter of holiness. To plan apart from God is sin.

The Sinfulness of Godless Planning

The Bible says, "But as it is, you boast in your arrogance; all such boasting is evil. Therefore, to one who knows the right thing to do, and does not do it, to him it is sin" (James 4:16–17). As always, God is clear. Godless planning is not just bad planning. It's sinful, unholy planning. We insult the character of God when we deliberately exclude Him from our lives.

One of the fundamental truths of Scripture is that God is distinct from His creation. He is with us, He is close to us, but there is a dividing line between Him and us much like the line between parents and children.

Parents don't always tell their children everything. They reserve the right to keep some of their plans and intentions private. In those cases, when the child asks why, the parent doesn't say much. At other times, parents explain things more fully to their children.

Likewise, God reserves His right as Creator to step into our lives and ask us to obey even when we don't understand exactly what is going on. But because He is perfect and holy and loving, we can trust Him.

But the people to whom this passage was addressed were not just being worldly in their planning, they were bragging about their independence from God. The word *boast* here suggests a peddler trying to sell something.

The Foolishness of Bragging

You may remember the peddlers in the old Westerns who pulled into town in their wagons, opened the side of the wagon, and started selling an elixir that they claimed could cure any illness. It was pure chicanery. The peddler was giving people the impression that this potion could do things it wasn't really capable of doing.

Well, that's what is happening when people brag about how they don't need God. They give you the impression they can do stuff that they really can't do.

And that's evil. God says, "Let not a wise man boast of his wisdom, and let not the mighty man boast of his might, let not a rich man boast of his riches; but let him who boasts boast of this, that he understands and knows Me" (Jer. 9:23–24).

In other words, don't brag that you have a lot of money; God can take it away from you in a heartbeat. Don't brag about your degrees; they may only be good as wall decorations. Don't brag because you work out at the gym; you can get hit with a cold that will put you in bed for a week.

If you want to brag, tell people that you know God. Brag about Him, not about the great plans you have made. The Bible calls that arrogance.

Furthermore, this kind of boasting leads to spiritual rebellion, and that leads to sin. Sin is more than just doing something wrong. You and I sin when we know what is right and yet fail to do it.

The tragic story of the ocean liner *Titanic* is a classic example of the boastful arrogance that leads to disaster. The people who put that ship in the water were convinced it was unsinkable. The company that owned the *Titanic* was so confident about its seaworthiness that they made more passenger rooms in the space that should have been used for lifeboats. Advertisements for the *Titanic* boasted of its safety. One passenger, however, told her husband she didn't want to sail on the *Titanic* because she believed the owners were tempting God by bragging that their ship could never sink.

A Biblical Example of Foolish Planning

Jesus told a story that offers an even better example of arrogant planning. It's the story of the foolish farmer:

> The land of a certain rich man was very productive. And he began reasoning to himself, saying, "What shall I do, since I have no place to store my crops?" And he said, "This is what I will do: I will tear down my barns and build larger ones, and there I will store all my grain and my goods. And I will say to my soul, 'Soul, you have many goods laid up for many years to come; take your ease, eat, drink, and be merry.'" (Luke 12:16–19)

This guy sounds like a lot of people on those television "infomercials." They have their investments all made and secured, and they are looking forward to retirement. They already know where they are going to retire to, and how they are going to play golf, travel, and do all the things they've always wanted to do.

Now we have already said that God is not against our planning for the future. He is not offended when we dream. But—as we have been saying all along—just don't leave God out of your plans. Or, worse, don't wave your plans around as if to say to God, "Here's what I plan to do, and You can't stop me."

The farmer Jesus talked about was a fool because God was nowhere in his thoughts or plans. And God said to him, "You fool! This very night your soul is required of you" (v. 20). The party was over before it started for him.

This farmer must have been in pretty good health, because he clearly figured he had a lot of years left. He also thought he had the money to enjoy his health because his barns couldn't contain his wealth. But he died utterly broke spiritually and financially. I say that because everyone dies broke. No matter how much money you have when you die, you leave it all behind and it belongs to somebody else. So you are penniless when you leave this life.

Now if the foolish farmer in Jesus' parable had put his faith in God, he could have left this world as a fabulously rich person with all the wealth of heaven at his disposal.

And that was Jesus' point: "So is the man who lays up treasure for himself, and is not rich toward God" (v. 21).

This man told himself, "I'm going to live a long time." God said, "You fool, today is your last day on planet earth." Now wouldn't a person be a fool to be planning for the next thirty years when he is not going to make it through the night?

The farmer had success, satisfaction, and security. But Jesus saw him as a man facing death. What this man did was to decide how well off he was spiritually by looking at what he had accumulated materially. The farmer looked at his barns, but started talking to his soul.

Now you may look at your bank account and start talking to your body. You may say, "Body, today you are going to wear designer clothes and diamond jewelry. You are going to drive the finest car available and live in a palatial home." You can look at your bank account and talk to your body.

But what you can't do is look at your bank account and tell your soul that it is well off. The foolish farmer spent his life on himself, but he never made any investments for his soul.

Spending or Investing Your Life?

I want to ask you a question as we close this chapter: Are you spending your life or investing it?

If you spend all your time and plans on yourself and the things of this life, you may not have anything left when life takes a turn and you are face-to-face with the reality of God's evaluation of your life.

Ever since I started giving my younger son Jonathan an allowance, it has been a battle teaching him to save. When he got a one-dollar allowance, we made him take out ten cents for his giving and ten cents for saving. We taught him to give, save, and spend in that order.

Like a lot of kids, Jonathan didn't like having to save. But one day the investments he had been making in his savings account came in handy because he wanted some special tennis shoes like the ones worn by a basketball star.

I told Jonathan I didn't have the money for those expensive shoes. But then he looked me square in the eye and said, "Dad, don't worry about it. I have the money in my bank account." Because I had made Jonathan save for the future, he didn't have to depend on me to buy the shoes. The investment had already been made.

Now there are things you are going to want in the future that no one else can buy for you. You're going to need something in your spiritual account to afford the peace, blessing, and other spiritual riches God has available.

The question on that day will be "Did you make plans for your life that enabled you to make the spiritual investments you are going to need?" Jesus says we must invest in that which is eternal. Not to do so is to be a perfect fool.

I don't believe you want to make foolish plans for your life. I believe you want to be a perfect Christian, not a perfect fool. Do your plans—made in submission to God's sovereignty, relying on

His infinite knowledge, deferring to His will, and honoring His holiness—reflect that desire?

Test Your Perfection I.Q.

- What are the four guidelines for including God in your life plans? Give yourself three points for each answer.

  1.

  2.

  3.

  4.

- In general, how much are you including God in your short-term and long-term plans for your life?

—*Submitting to God's sovereignty and deferring to His will.*
Do your prayers, attitudes of the heart, and decision-making process reflect this position? On this scale, "1" is "Never! I have my life wired!" and "10" is "Always! If Jesus Himself submitted to God's will, I should, too!"
1 2 3 4 5 6 7 8 9 10

—*Relying on God's knowledge and honoring His holiness.*
How regularly do you rely on God to guide you and seek His will and His fine-tuning of your plans? On this scale, "1" is "Planning with God? Waddya mean?" and "10" is "Planning without God? Never! That's absolutely inconceivable."
1 2 3 4 5 6 7 8 9 10

—The question one day will be "Did you make plans for your life that enabled you to make the spiritual investments you are going to need?" Are you spending ("1") or investing ("10") your life right now?

1 2 3 4 5 6 7 8 9 10

Total Points _____

Chapter 12

How to Avoid the Corrupting Power of Wealth

What would cause those of us who claim to know Christ to plan our lives as if He did not exist? What would make us say with an arrogant attitude, "I'm going to go here or there for this amount of time and cut this business deal and make this much profit"—without consulting God or His will?

I want to suggest that at the core of this arrogant mentality is a spirit of materialism—which, as the name suggests, is the worship of material things. One powerful motivation for a person to plan life independently of God is a passion for wealth.

At some time or other you have probably watched one of those television programs that takes you inside the mansions and the playgrounds of wealthy people. Maybe as you watched the program you thought, *I could get used to living like that.*

Now if you had a thought or two like that, you would not be all that unusual. The pull of materialism is so strong that we all feel it at times. Wealth has the power to help and bless, but built into it is also the power to corrupt the human heart.

Simply hiding from the problem won't solve it. The Christian growing into the image of Christ is the brother or sister who learns how to defeat the problem of materialism and handle possessions in a way that honors God. Let's find out how we can conquer the corrupting power of wealth.

God's Word has a lot to teach us about this subject. God does not shy away from the issue. Jesus told thirty-eight parables in the New Testament, sixteen of which deal with the subject of money. One of every ten verses in the New Testament mentions possessions. The Bible contains five hundred or so verses on prayer, and about another five hundred verses on faith. But there are more than two thousand verses in the Bible on money.

Why is this? Because God knows materialism is a barometer of our spiritual temperature and can stifle our spiritual development. If our focus is on wealth, its brilliance can blind us spiritually. We cannot grow in our Christian lives if we have the wrong view of possessions.

That's why the Bible tells rich believers not to let their wealth go to their heads. After all, their possessions will all fade away someday like dead grass or flowers (see James 1:10–11). Furthermore, money can tempt us to treat other believers according to their wealth or lack of it (see James 2:1–3). That's not just bad taste, it's sinful.

Since I'm convinced it's impossible to live in this culture and not be tempted by the sin of materialism, let's learn how to handle it.

The Concept of Materialism

First, what is materialism, anyway? It isn't just having material things, because we all have them to a greater or lesser degree. There's more to materialism than that. Materialism is a sinful attitude toward the things you have.

A Sinful Attitude Toward Wealth

Lest there be any misunderstanding, let me say right off that when the Bible speaks against the sin of materialism, the issue is not how much a person has. God's primary concern is not how much money you have in the bank, how many cars you have in your garage, or how much tax you have to pay at the end of the year. God's concern is your attitude toward what you have.

Some of God's choicest servants were in fact very wealthy people. Abraham and Job come to mind. Satan himself knew that God was the One who enriched Job (Job 1:10). It was true, and God gave Job even more at the end of his life than he had at the beginning (see Job 42:10–17).

God did not apologize for enriching Job. The Bible says, "It is the blessing of the LORD that makes rich" (Prov. 10:22). Moses told the Israelites, "It is [God] who is giving you power to make wealth" (Deut. 8:18). So materialism is not a matter of how much you have, but instead how you treat what you have and how you respond to the God who gave it to you.

You see, if you have the wrong attitude toward what you have, you can be poor and still be a materialist. And most certainly, you can be rich and be a materialist. A materialist is someone who has taken gold and turned it into God.

We are heading toward the sin of materialism when we start looking at God's blessings as an end in themselves instead of as a God-given opportunity to serve His eternal purposes. The materialist expects gold to do what only God can do.

When you look at what God has given you and somehow decide that this has all come about by your own ability—when you see no relationship between God's goodness and the resources you have— you are on dangerous ground.

The sin of materialism (what the Bible calls being covetous) is listed in the Bible alongside some other sins we wouldn't be caught dead committing: drunkenness, murder, swindling, and homosexuality (1 Cor. 5:11; 6:9–10).

Not a very nice list, is it? The Bible puts materialism in the same neighborhood as these others because all sin is disobedience and rebellion against God. While many believers would decry these other sins, they have a sin that God says they better come to grips with, and that's the sin of materialism.

You may be wondering, "How can I tell if I'm a materialist?" Ultimately, the answer to this question is between you and God. But here are a few tests you can take to help determine your attitude toward money and possessions.

First of all, are you content with what you have, or will you be discontent until you get more? If the latter, how much more do you need to be content?

For example, you may be in an apartment hoping and saving for your own house. Or you may be in a two-bedroom house wishing you had a three-bedroom house. There's nothing wrong with wanting to take that step.

But until that day arrives, are you at peace where you are? Could you be satisfied with God's blessings if the move up never comes? If not, you have no guarantee that a bigger house or a better job will bring you contentment.

The reason is that peace, joy, and tranquillity can only come from God. If you haven't learned to find these blessings in your relationship with Him, no amount of material possessions can give you those things.

Too many of us are using credit cards to acquire what only God can give us. In fact, some of us can't move from a two-bedroom to a three-bedroom house because we have been trying to buy peace and joy on credit. Remember, a materialist is someone who expects gold to do what only God can do.

Here's a second test, and it's critical. When God and gold come into conflict in your life, who wins?

Think back. When you had fewer possessions, did you have more time for God—and, conversely, now that you have more stuff, do you have less time for God? Have God's blessings pushed Him to the fringes of your life? I know men who never missed church when their businesses weren't doing too well. But now that they are successful, they "worship God on the golf course."

If God is losing in your choices between Him and money, you are being choked by the sin of materialism that will stifle your spiritual growth and keep you from growing in Christlikeness.

A Loss of Perspective

Proverbs 11:28 says, "He who trusts in his riches will fall." And Jesus said it is almost impossible for rich people to get to heaven (Mark 10:25). That's not simply because they're rich, but because they have been seduced by the corrupting power of wealth. We need to keep this heavenly perspective before us here on earth.

I recently came across a good story that illustrates what can happen when we lose God's perspective on material things and let possessions possess us.

A man was driving his new BMW down the highway when he came to a sharp turn and lost control of the car. As it careened toward a steep embankment, the man realized he was going to go over the cliff so he unhooked his seat belt and threw himself out of the car. But as he did, he got his arm caught and the force of his fall and the moving car tore his arm off.

The man lay dazed on the side of the road, blood pouring from his shoulder. A truck driver who stopped to help ran up to the injured man and heard him sobbing, "Oh no, my BMW! My BMW!"

The trucker said, "Mister, you'll bleed to death if I don't get you to a hospital. You've lost your arm!"

The man looked down, saw that he had no arm, and began crying, "Oh no, my Rolex! My Rolex!"

A materialist loses perspective and majors on the insignificant, not on that which has ultimate value.

Yet finances can seem anything but insignificant. Some couples fight day and night over money. The subject can't even be brought up in the house without a battle erupting. That's because somebody in that marriage—maybe both parties—is a materialist. I even know couples whose disputes about money issues were so severe they opted for divorce instead of dealing with their finances.

"But," you say, "how can I be a materialist? I don't have any money. I'm as broke as a skunk."

It's easy to be as broke as a skunk and still be a materialist, because materialism is an attitude. You can be poor and still have mixed-up priorities if the love of money consumes your heart and life. Again, materialism is not measured by your wealth or lack thereof, but by your attitude toward wealth.

Anyone who has money and is miserable has a spiritual problem. And anyone who doesn't have money and is miserable has a spiritual problem, too. The reason is that Christian joy and godly contentment have nothing to do with economic well-being.

I can introduce you to some poor folks in old neighborhoods who are a lot happier than some people who have moved up and out of those neighborhoods.

Why does that happen? Why are so many people who have so

much so unhappy? Because money is like an atomic bomb. It can produce a lot of energy, and that energy can be very destructive.

The Cost of Materialism

Businesspeople often talk about "the cost of doing business" when they discuss expenses. There is a cost attached to all of our decisions about money.

The sin of materialism comes with a price tag, too, and the Bible spells it out: "Come now, you rich, weep and howl for your miseries which are coming upon you" (James 5:1).

Misery Is Coming

People caught up in the sin of materialism can anticipate misery because they are flying in the face of God's plan. That becomes more apparent as James continues: "Your riches have rotted and your garments have become moth-eaten. Your gold and your silver have rusted" (vv. 2–3). First the Bible says misery is coming for the materialist, and then the text says the misery is already here.

This misery is something like cancer. Cancer is invisible initially, and you don't know it's there. But by the time its presence becomes obvious, a lot of damage may already be done.

James mentions garments because, in biblical days, clothes were one measure of a person's wealth. Many poor people would only be able to afford four or five garments in their lifetime. Only the rich could afford a closet full of clothes.

But for the person whose accumulation of wealth is an act of sinful materialism—for those who, to borrow a phrase, are sinfully rich—God has a way of making sure the bank account runs dry and the moths throw a party on the expensive clothes. When that happens, those who are rich in the wrong way will howl in their misery.

Resources Diminish

When you substitute gold for God, you will never get much benefit out of the gold you have put in His place. Sometimes God will make sure your water heater breaks down or your new car quits running so you will learn to trust in Him, not in your possessions. Or maybe

He'll let you enjoy all those new things you're spending your money on for a while so that you will discover that those material things don't provide the self-fulfillment you were really seeking.

Sooner or later you will discover that your possessions can never give you the satisfaction you desire. You will never be content until God becomes more important than anything you own.

We need to remember what money can—and cannot—do.

Consider the fact that some people are in more debt today than they were when they made a lot less money. How did that happen? Did they just lose track of their finances, or is something else going on? Maybe that water heater broke down because God told it to break down. Maybe that car won't keep running because God said, "I don't want it to run."

You see, when materialism is your sin, God has many ways of bringing His judgment against it. He can have a lot of moths and rust-producers eat up your wealth when you put other things ahead of Him. And your life won't smooth out until God becomes more important than anything you own.

We need to remember what money can—and cannot—do. Money can buy you a bed, but it can't buy you sleep. It can buy you books, but it can't buy you brains. Money can buy you food, but it can't buy you an appetite. It can buy you finery, but it can't buy you beauty. Money can buy you a house, but, as too many of us know, it can't buy you a home.

The list goes on. Money can buy you medicine, but not health; amusements, but not happiness; companions, but not friends; flattery, but not respect. So if you are trying to use money to acquire all these things in the second category, you will find yourself paying a high price for your materialism.

The Ultimate Cost of Materialism

In fact, do you realize that materialism has cost some people their eternal destiny? The rich young ruler's love of his wealth cost him heaven when he refused Jesus (see Luke 18:18–27).

The parable of Lazarus and the rich man also illustrates this tragedy (Luke 16:19–31). Lazarus the beggar went to heaven, while the rich man went to hell. In hell the rich man asked Abraham to send Lazarus with a drop of water to cool his tongue in the flames.

But Abraham said to the rich man, "During your life you received your good things" (v. 25). The rich man had been so busy "living in splendor every day" (v. 19) that he never got around to taking care of his soul. And his negligence cost him eternity. The cost of materialism is indeed high.

Now there are three classes of people when it comes to material things: the "haves," the "have-nots," and the "have-not-yet-paid-for-what-they-haves." I suspect many of us are in this latter category, so let me make this statement.

Excessive, long-term debt is primary evidence of materialism. When your liabilities outweigh your assets, when you owe so much for the stuff you have that all you can do is tip God a few bucks each Sunday, you are a materialist, not a growing Christian. I'll leave that one right there.

God says there is a price to be paid for the sin of materialism. When gold replaces Him, it's time to weep and howl because these riches are a "witness against [us]" (James 5:3) that we have let possessions displace God.

Clues of Materialism

What does materialism look like in practice? The Bible gives us several clues to look for in ourselves as evidence of materialism. One bit of evidence is the excessive debt we mentioned above. Let me give you three other clues that warn of the sin of materialism.

The Sin of Hoarding

First, consider this exclamation: "You have stored up your treasure!" (James 5:3). The people whom James was addressing were hoarding their riches.

Now hoarding is very different from legitimate saving. God does not mind you saving. In fact, Paul says it is the parents' job to save up for their children and have something to pass on as an inheritance (2 Cor. 12:14).

And, in His parable of the talents, Jesus said the lazy servant should at least have put his master's money in the bank to draw interest (Matt. 25:27). Saving is not a sin, but hoarding is. Solomon said, "I have seen . . . riches being hoarded by their owner to his hurt" (Eccl. 5:13).

How can you tell whether you are saving or hoarding? The difference is whether your accumulation is tied to a legitimate biblical purpose. The Bible gives several reasons for saving: to invest in God's work, to provide for our needs, to provide for our family's future, to have something on hand in times of emergency, and to help meet the needs of others.

But a hoarder collects and stores out of greed, simply to accumulate more for himself without regard for others.

So when someone says, "I want to become a millionaire," the question to ask is "Why?" The answer to that question will tell you whether that person is a hoarder or has legitimate economic goals. A hoarder can't give you any reasons for wanting wealth beyond his own self-aggrandizement.

Again, there's nothing wrong with saving for retirement or in case you can't work or so you have something for a rainy day. But to accumulate wealth just so you can talk about what you have, or put it on display to impress your friends, is to commit the sin of hoarding.

You may say, "Keep talkin', Tony. I pass this test. I've never wished to be a millionaire just for the sake of having money."

That's fine. That's wonderful. But money is not the only thing you can hoard. What about that closet stuffed with clothes you never wear? Many of us have closets so full of clothes, shoes, and other accessories we can't even get into the closet. Our motto seems to be, "I shop, therefore I am."

Rather than being a clothes hoarder, you would do well to give some of those clothes away and meet someone else's needs with your abundance.

Moving on, how many people do you know who have a living room that is nothing but a showcase for their finest furniture? No one is allowed to sit on that furniture. The kids don't dare go into that room. It's for display only, a museum piece to materialism.

Now I understand that we don't want the kids taking food and drinks into the living room. And some of us may have special family heirlooms that mean a lot to us and can't take a lot of handling. The problem doesn't lie in either of these situations. I'm talking about the mentality that says, "Let me show off how wealthy I am and all that I have by displaying it in my living room." That's the attitude of a hoarder, a materialist: The accumulation is not tied to any legitimate purpose. "I want to be rich" is an illegitimate statement. The question to be answered is "Why do you want wealth?"

We all know godly people upon whom God has poured abundant material blessings. The key is that they are godly people who know how to handle wealth to God's glory.

Now someone may say, "Oh, I get it. I'll be godly so God will heap the gold on me." No, you just missed the whole point. Only a materialist would think like that.

The Sin of Using Others

As bad as it is to hoard material things, it's even worse to use people to get what we want. The Bible warns: "Behold, the pay of the laborers who mowed your fields, and which has been withheld by you, cries out against you; and the outcry of those who did the harvesting has reached the ears of the Lord of Sabaoth" (James 5:4).

This is a disturbing verse because of the dishonesty involved. First, the landowner was cheating the laborers out of what they had earned. Second, in biblical times, it was important that a laborer be paid each day so he could buy food for his family. Withholding the wage a laborer had earned, even for a few days, was to condemn that person and his family to hunger.

People who use others like this come under the gaze of the "Lord of Sabaoth," which means the "Lord of hosts" or "Lord of armies." In other words, the materialist who robs people will be dealt with by a God who is big enough to do something about it.

Now I hope that cheating and dishonesty are not major problems for most people reading this book. You and I are more likely to yield to the temptation of looking down on others and using them in more subtle ways to help us advance.

The world helps us in such pride. You know how it goes. You get a regular credit card. You pay a few bills on time, and then it's the gold card. Then you qualify for platinum, and now you're really somebody. Look out, world!

Then it becomes easier to start using people at work to make yourself look good or to begin cultivating friendships solely for what the other person can do for you. But it's evil to look down on other people and use them like that. If God has blessed you, two things ought to happen.

First, you ought be thankful. Your blessing ought to make you more generous and more sensitive to others in need because you know that, except for the grace of God, that person with less could be you.

Second, God's blessing ought to make you more helpful, more willing to reach back and help someone else the way God helped you.

In sharp contrast to these attitudes is the attitude that views others as put on this earth for your benefit. The people James was warning had gotten rich by fraud, by not paying their workers. A laborer would harvest their crops, and they would tell him "Your check is in the mail"—except that it wasn't in the mail. In fact, they had no intention of paying this worker.

God takes dishonest business dealings very seriously. The law He gave Moses was very clear that a worker was to be paid for his work the same day so he could feed his family (see Lev. 19:13; Deut. 24:14–15). Otherwise, that person could cry out to God and get a quick hearing, and the one withholding the pay would be judged.

The Sin of Perverting Justice

Closely related to the sin of using others is the sinful perversion of justice.

The Bible says to these sinfully rich people, "You have condemned and put to death the righteous man; he does not resist you" (James 5:6). The righteous person couldn't resist the rich people, because he didn't have the legal or financial clout to do so. The rich people had bought the courts and the judges.

I get tired of seeing all the injustice in this world, and I'm sure you do, too. The world's "Golden Rule" is that he who has the gold gets to rule. But remember that the righteous person's cry for justice does not fall on deaf ears.

Many materialists will resort to injustice to keep what they have and to get more. On the individual level, you may even be the victim of injustice and unfairness at work. If so, talk to God about it. Such prayer isn't a cop-out. It's acting on a promise that the Lord who commands heaven's armies will take the situation in His own hands.

The Sin of Indulgence

Let me mention one more clear mark of a materialist: "You have lived luxuriously on the earth and led a life of wanton pleasure" (James 5:5). Materialists live for luxury, and they are always ready for the party.

Now there's nothing wrong with having a party. But for a true materialist, the good times are the main attraction of life and God is an afterthought—if He's there at all.

So the Bible says of these people, "You have fattened your hearts in a day of slaughter" (v. 5), a reference to the calf that people in biblical times used to fatten up for a big party. God is saying to the materialist, "You don't know it, but you are the calf I am fattening up for My judgment party. I am going to give you more riches and more luxury until your heart is fat, so that when I judge you the reason for your eternal destiny will be clear."

You cannot afford to love money instead of God because when God takes you down, He takes you down hard.

The Cure for Materialism

Here's the good part—what we can do to make sure we are not being drawn into a life of materialism. Jesus Himself offered the cure for this sin. In the Sermon on the Mount, He said:

> Do not lay up for yourselves treasures upon earth, where moth and rust destroy, and where thieves break in and steal. But lay up for yourselves treasures in heaven, where neither moth nor rust

destroys, and where thieves do not break in or steal; for where your treasure is, there will your heart be also. (Matt. 6:19–21)

Now let's unpack this teaching.

Don't Be Self-Centered

One of the key ideas is the issue of where you are laying up your treasure. Jesus tells us not to lay up treasures on earth, which is what we have been talking about. Jesus is certainly speaking against the self-centered accumulation of material possessions.

But there's more here. Jesus is telling us not to get too focused on earthly wealth, because it will all eventually pass away. None of it will transfer to heaven. So when we think about our money and possessions, we need to think in terms of using what God has given us to advance His work and to help bring more people into His kingdom. That's being others-centered instead of self-centered.

But if the things you have are only for your use on this earth and are not connected to any eternal purposes, then your eternal, spiritual bank account in heaven will be awfully low when you arrive. The stuff of this earth stays here. Only what we do for eternity will survive into eternity.

Acknowledge God As Owner

The only way you can keep this eternal perspective on your possessions is to acknowledge God freely as the Owner of all you have. And that biblical perspective is definitely the wise way to go.

Why? Because if God is the Owner of your stuff, then what happens to it is His responsibility—and providing you with what you need is His responsibility, too. I don't know about you, but that sounds like a much better deal than trying to do it all myself.

Besides, even though you may think you own and control your stuff, you don't. You can't control what happens to it. You can't keep the rust and moths from taking their toll. Thieves may come in and steal all you have. The stock market may take a plunge and take your fortune to the bottom.

If your stuff is all invested in this life rather than in any eternal purposes and you're trying to hang on to it as the owner, then when earthly things go down, you'll go down with them.

But if you are using your earthly wealth to lay up heavenly treasures, then the glory of God is involved, and He will take care of you. God doesn't allow moths or thieves to mess with His stuff. He doesn't let inflation or recession upset His plan. Stock markets don't determine what happens to His possessions.

This is why I encourage believers to dedicate not only their children, but their homes and cars and everything else to God and His kingdom. I invite them (and you) to say, "Everything I have, including my family and my very self, is Yours. And since everything I have is Yours, Lord, I'm not going to worry about it because I know You can take care of Your things better than I can. In other words, I am giving back to You what You gave me. Use it for Your glory."

This cure for materialism is crucial because, as Jesus said, "Where your treasure is, there will your heart be also" (Matt. 6:21).

Now don't misread what Scripture teaches. It would seem logical to say that our treasure will follow our hearts, that we will spend our money on the things we love. But Jesus said just the opposite. He said that you will come to love what you spend your money on—so be careful where you put your money! Let me give you an example of this.

Suppose you were sitting in church listening to your pastor's sermon when someone came to you and whispered that your house was on fire. Chances are your heart would race, and you'd get up and leave immediately. Why? Because your most valuable possessions were being threatened.

Of course there's nothing wrong with rushing to your home if it's on fire. My point is simply that your heart is tied to your home because so much of your time, talents, and treasures are tied up there, too. Your heart follows your treasure, so make sure you are investing in things of eternal value.

Now let me drive this point home. How many times have you told yourself that, since things are tight this week, you really don't have any money to spare for your giving? Why is it that, when things are tight, it's always the Lord's money that gets left out?

Are you like the farmer who had two prize-winning calves? He decided to give one to the Lord and keep one for himself. One day one of the calves died, and the farmer told his wife, "Honey, something awful happened. The Lord's calf just died."

In Psalm 62:10 we find a wise word to those of us who want to be perfect Christians: "If riches increase, do not set your heart upon them." It's OK to prosper; just don't let your heart be captured by the material things God allows you to have.

One day an old man asked a young man, "What are your plans for life?"

The young man replied, "Well, I'm going to go to college and get a good education so I can get a good job and make a lot of money."

"What then?" the old man asked.

"I'm going to get married and raise my children and then send them to the best possible college so they can get a good education and get good jobs."

"And what then?"

"Well, after the kids are gone, my wife and I will travel around the world. Then we'll retire and live off the investments we have made."

"That's fine," the old man continued. "But what then?"

"Well, when it's all over, I guess I'll die."

The old man looked at him and said, "And what then?"

That's the question a lot of people can't answer. But we need to answer it because one day we will stand before Jesus Christ. On that day the issue will not be how much we left behind, but how much we sent on ahead. What is God gaining in heaven from the stuff He has given you here on earth?

Test Your Perfection I.Q.

• Materialism is a sinful attitude toward the things you have—substituting gold for God. What evidence of materialism can you find in your life? Give yourself four points for each.

1.

2.

3.

• How can you tell if you're a materialist? Ultimately the answer to this question is between you and God. But these two tests may help you learn something about yourself.

—Test #1. Are you content with what you have? If not, how much more do you need to be content? On this scale, "1" is "Maybe I'll finally be happy if I have X or Y or Z" and "10" is "'All I have needed Thy hand hath provided'—and peace, joy, and contentment besides!"

1 2 3 4 5 6 7 8 9 10

—Test #2. When God and gold come into conflict in your life, who wins? When you had fewer possessions, for instance, did you have more time for God? On this scale, "1" is "Interesting! More stuff does seem to leave less time for God!" and "10" is "God's the Giver of all good things! He's my priority!"

1 2 3 4 5 6 7 8 9 10

—If God has blessed you materially, two things ought to happen. First, you ought to be thankful as well as more generous and sensitive to others in need. Second, God's blessing ought to make you more willing to help someone else the way God helped you. Are these traits evident in your life? On this scale, "1" is "Grab those bootstraps, big guy! God helps those who help themselves!" and "10 " is "There but for the grace of God go I—and it's my joy and privilege to help!"

1 2 3 4 5 6 7 8 9 10

Total Points _____

Chapter 13

How to Cultivate Patience

Do you know any impatient people? You can probably give me several names without trying too hard. All of us know at least one person who is low on patience. We often call it "having a short fuse."

Well, a perfect Christian is at the opposite end of the spectrum. A Christian who is growing to be more like Jesus is patient. The fascinating New Testament term literally means to be "long-fused" or "long-tempered."

In the Bible, God calls us again and again to be patient in the face of whatever trial or circumstance He may send our way.

One day a doctor called a patient to tell him, "I have some bad news, and some *really* bad news, for you."

The man gulped and said, "What's the bad news?"

"You only have twenty-four hours to live," the doctor replied.

"That's awful!" the man cried. "What could be worse than that?"

"I should have called you yesterday."

Sometimes life is like that. One day is bad, but the next day is worse. We need patience to hang in there when things are going downhill and God's timing is not the timing we want.

Sometimes it seems that God is taking an awfully long time to get us where He wants us to go. But if we lose patience, if our fuses are too short and we burn out too quickly, we may miss what God wants us to learn from the situation or the benefit He has for us in it. Either way, we may have to stay in the trial longer to learn the lesson.

Now some people don't like to read about the believer's need to be patient because they feel guilty before they ever start. If that's the case for you, stay with me because I want to help you understand what biblical patience is and how to put it into practice in your life on a consistent, daily basis.

How to Practice Patience

Let's begin with a fundamental statement on patience. The Bible says, "Be patient, therefore, brethren, until the coming of the Lord. Behold, the farmer waits for the precious produce of the soil, being patient about it, until it gets the early and late rains" (James 5:7).

Be Productive

Patience means to be long-tempered, to hang in there and not let your fuse burn down too quickly. But what exactly does this quality look like in everyday life? How can we practice patience?

The Bible gives us both a great illustration that helps us understand patience and some precepts that will help us put it into practice.

The first thing we are told is to be patient until the Lord's coming. But that does not mean sitting with our hands in our laps until Jesus comes.

Instead, our patience is to be like that of a farmer. You can't be a farmer if you're impatient. My son once had the school assignment to plant a seed and watch it grow. He planted the seed on Monday, and Tuesday morning he was nearly in tears because nothing had happened yet. He definitely did not have a farmer's patience!

A farmer can wait patiently for "the precious produce of the soil" because he has done something important. He has sown the seeds of the crop he hopes to produce.

This illustration helps us understand what the Bible means by being patient until the Lord's coming. Patient waiting does not mean sitting and doing nothing, seeing nothing, thinking nothing, and saying nothing. Patience is not meant to result in a passive Christianity.

Any farmer who tried to produce a crop by passively waiting would starve to death, as would everyone else who was depending on him for food. The farmer's patience comes not from doing nothing, but from understanding his limitations.

A farmer needs to be faithful to till the ground and plant the seed, but he has no control over "the early and late rains." He is totally dependent upon God to supply the rain—and if God doesn't supply the rain, the farmer's work is largely a waste of time.

On the other hand, even if God supplies rain, the result will still be a waste if the farmer hasn't prepared the ground and planted his crop. So, like the farmer, you need to do all that God expects you to do before patience becomes an issue. Once you've sown the seed, then you can trust Him to do what is impossible for you to do.

Again, being patient doesn't mean being passive. So if you are undergoing a trial and need patience, you must ask yourself, "Have I done what God has commanded and expected me to do?"

If not, then maybe the reason your trial is still going on is not because God has withheld His rain. Maybe the problem is that you haven't given Him anything to water.

Some of us are going through trials that could have been over a long time ago except that, since we haven't been faithful to plant the seed, there has been no growth even though there has been rain.

Remember, God's goal is to perfect us, not just to make us comfortable or keep us free of hard times. Therefore, we need patience along the path to spiritual perfection.

Now how does the illustration of a farmer relate to the Lord's coming? I would like to submit that the Bible is not talking about Christ's Second Coming in this passage, although His coming is mentioned three times (vv. 7–9).

Instead, I believe the focus here is the Lord's coming to us here on earth to deliver us through (not necessarily *from*) life's trials. This is not Christ's *ultimate* coming, in other words, but an *intermediate* coming—His invasion of your circumstances to deliver you through whatever you are facing because it's time for the spiritual crop in your life to grow.

That's why the farmer illustration is so appropriate here. A farmer plants in order to produce growth, not just to fill up time. God sends trials and other challenges your way in order that you may grow in grace. But you need to be patient as He works to produce maximum spiritual growth in you.

Then, when the rain comes from heaven, when the Lord comes to invade earth, He will bring forth the crop in you that He wants to produce. When that part of the process is complete, you will be ready to move on to the next growth experience.

You say, "Excuse me. Did you say more trials and challenges are coming?"

Of course. A farmer doesn't plant just one crop and then expect to have food for the rest of his life. He has to continue being productive year in and year out. So it is in the Christian life. Do you see why we need patience?

Strengthen Your Heart

In order to have patience, you must strengthen your heart. Why? Because a weak heart won't hold out in times of trial. God's Word tells us, "You too be patient; strengthen your hearts, for the coming of the Lord is at hand" (James 5:8).

Strengthening your heart means strengthening yourself spiritually so you can handle the external pressure of the trials that will attack you—and this effort is crucial to your journey of faith. Many believers fall apart in trials because they have not been building themselves up. When a trial hits, it destroys them.

These believers who have weak hearts know they're not ready for trials. Their prayer is "Lord, please don't try me because I'm not ready yet."

Now God cannot let a situation like that continue. It would be like a child saying to his mother at the end of the summer, "Mama, please don't send me back to school. I'm not ready yet." That child needs to get ready because school is coming.

How do you strengthen your heart? Mary of Bethany is a good

model. When Jesus came to visit, Mary sat at His feet listening to His words while Martha was busy in the kitchen (Luke 10:38–42). Jesus told Mary she had made the better decision.

We need to take time to sit at Jesus' feet as Mary did if we're to be strong spiritually. But the local church itself has a crucial ministry to carry out in strengthening believers. Paul knew that, so he wanted to go to Rome to impart spiritual gifts to the believers there so they would be established (see Rom. 1:11). He also sent Timothy to the church at Thessalonica to "strengthen and encourage" the believers (1 Thess. 3:1–3). Paul also prayed that these believers' hearts might be established (vv. 10–13).

Strength also comes to the body of Christ as we minister to one another using the gifts God has given us. The pastoral leaders of the church also have an essential role to play in strengthening and equipping the saints for the trials they will inevitably face.

Don't Complain

The Bible identifies something else we can do—or, rather, not do—to increase our patience: "Do not complain, brethren, against one another, that you yourselves may not be judged; behold the Judge is standing right at the door" (James 5:9).

This command makes good common sense as well as good biblical sense. In those situations where things are tense and everyone is a little edgy, nothing makes things worse than for someone to start complaining about everything in sight.

Such complaining is serious stuff because, James says, the Judge—that is, God Himself—is at the door. He's listening to what you say, so be careful what comes out of your mouth when you're going through a trial. Instead of complaining about the people and circumstances God has placed around you, ask Him to give you patience.

The Judge is also at the door in the sense that He's ready to come and invade your circumstances, as we said earlier. But if He hears you complaining against other believers because of the trial He is putting you through, you have just become a candidate for judgment. God may come through the door not to aid you or deliver you, but to judge you. (It's hard enough to endure a trial successfully. You don't need a spanking in the midst of the trial!)

The reason we need to be warned against complaining is because, when we get upset, our tendency is to take out our frustration on anyone who is near us. Parents do that when they snap at a child for no other reason than that the child happened to walk into the living room at the wrong time.

Now you may be saying, "Come on, Tony. Let's be practical. How can I go through a hard trial and not complain?"

You can do it when you realize that God is up to something good in your life—even in the bad times. He is undoubtedly using a hard trial to help you grow. God is at work in your circumstances to bring about something so good you can't even imagine it.

That's why the Bible says so much about giving thanks. No matter what you are going through right now, you can find something to give thanks for if you look for it.

Now sometimes our children will get very focused on what they don't have. Then we hear questions like "When are you going to get me this?" or "Why can't I have that?"

Never mind that they have eaten three times that day, that they don't sleep outdoors, or that it's always warm when they come home in the winter and cool when they come home in the summer. Never mind saying thanks for all of that. They want to discuss the latest computer game they don't have.

That's exactly what you and I do to God sometimes. But if we spent more time praising Him rather than complaining, we would get through our trials a lot faster.

So the essence of patience is doing what I'm supposed to do—sowing the seed and strengthening my spiritual life—while I wait without complaining for God to send the rain that will produce the growth I want in my life.

Some Examples of Patience

A farmer serves as a good example of biblical patience, but the Bible is also filled with real-life models of patience: "As an example, brethren, of suffering and patience, take the prophets who spoke in the name of the Lord. Behold, we count those blessed who endured" (James 5:10–11).

James does here what you and I are supposed to do with the Old Testament. He points us back to the Scripture and says, "Remember the prophets of God and how they exercised patience!" After all, the history and teachings found in the Old Testament were written for "our instruction" (Rom. 15:4). We need to learn from what we read there.

The Example of the Prophets

The Old Testament prophets not only waited patiently, but they witnessed to or proclaimed God's truth in the meantime. Put differently, they "spoke in the name of the Lord." Elijah did so—and Queen Jezebel and King Ahab came after him to take his life. But again and again God supernaturally intervened and saved Elijah.

First, God sent ravens with food for Elijah then the widow of Zarephath fed him. God also encouraged Elijah with the news that He had seven thousand men who had not bowed their knees to Baal.

Later, the prophet Daniel was being tested at the hands of an ungodly king named Darius. God didn't keep Daniel from the lions' den. Instead, He just joined the prophet there! Daniel not only patiently endured and remained faithful to God, but he was counted as blessed even by the evil king.

Jeremiah the "weeping prophet" was lowered into a muddy pit for speaking in the Lord's name. But God sent people to Jeremiah to encourage and strengthen him even in the midst of his tears.

Many other prophets and believers had to endure hard times patiently. God asked Noah to preach righteousness for 120 years without a convert, and Noah patiently obeyed. We definitely count him as blessed because he and his family survived the Flood when no one else on earth did. Habakkuk was another prophet who waited for God to bring the justice he was praying for.

Now, did you notice that James mentions suffering along with patience? No one said it would be easy to live out the kind of patience God wants us to have. Certainly the prophets never found it easy! But those who endure trials patiently are "blessed," or happy.

And that patience marks the difference between a miserable Christian and a joyful Christian in trials. The key factor is not the severity of the situation, but the response of the Christian to the trial. Has the Christian strengthened his or her heart—or is the believer complaining all the way through? If you need encouragement and strength in your trial, look to the prophets' example.

Also, don't forget that the prophets were God's witnesses even in their hard circumstances. So if you are going through a hard time, talk about the Lord more, not less. Praise Him more, not less. Share Jesus Christ with others more, not less. Being a witness makes the waiting a lot better.

The Example of Job

The prophets offer us a great example of patience, but the quintessential illustration of patience is the patriarch Job: "You have heard of the endurance of Job and have seen the outcome of the Lord's dealings, that the Lord is full of compassion and is merciful" (James 5:11).

We've considered Job's example on a number of occasions in this book, so I won't recap his circumstances. You are probably already familiar with Job's calamities.

Earlier we noted that most of the book of Job is comprised of the accusations of Job's friends and Job's defense of his uprightness. Understandably, Job was distressed and depressed by what God had allowed to happen to him.

Now it's certainly OK to be discouraged when things aren't going well. There's nothing wrong with feeling bad if there is something to feel bad about.

It's even OK to question God when you don't understand what He is doing. There's no use pretending you never do. Besides, we all do this. And God knows when you're questioning Him in your heart, stumbling around looking for answers to your trial. Your questions are no secret to Him.

That's why the Word invites you to ask God for the wisdom you need to persevere and be victorious in times of trial (James 1:5). God knows when you're confused, and He wants you to ask Him for wisdom.

Well, Job's friends thought they had God's perspective on Job's calamities, and they let him know it. This ordeal alone—having to listen to his friends go on and on—is evidence of Job's patience, but that's just the beginning.

Consider the statement Job made rather early in the onslaught of his friends' many words: "Though He slay me, I will hope in Him" (13:15). Here was Job, who had experienced every calamity possible—except death itself. He had been stripped of everything else that made life worth living.

By the way, before we examine Job's bold declaration, do you know why Job did not die? Because God had His hand on the thermostat of Job's "fiery furnace," and God wouldn't let Satan turn the fire up any hotter than it already was. In the same way, our sovereign God has His hand on the thermostat of your trial, too, and things will only get as hot as He allows them to get.

But Job looked at his circumstances and said, "Even if God does the only thing left to me that can be done to me, which is take my life, even then I will go to my grave believing that God is faithful."

My friend, that is enduring patience! No complaining from Job, only praise and trust.

But the real significance of Job's story lies not in his calamities or his defense before his friends, but in his deliverance and restoration. His story culminated in a great chapter that reveals the real spiritual payoff for patience.

At this point, notice that Job freely confesses that God and His ways are far too big for him to figure out. If you want to become exasperated and lose your patience (as well as your mind), just try to figure out everything God is doing and why He is doing it. You'll flip out because God is beyond figuring out. His ways aren't our ways. He is the inscrutable God. But Job is gaining some new insight: "I have heard of Thee by the hearing of the ear; but now my eye sees Thee" (42:5).

This statement is so powerful that you need to take a few minutes and let it sink in. Job was saying that everything he thought he knew about God was just hearsay compared to seeing God for himself through the lens of his trial. (Read that sentence again!)

Do you understand what Job is saying? His statement means that you can go to church all year and hear other people talk long and passionately and truthfully about God. You can listen to the pastor's sermons each week, listen to Christian radio every day, and watch each religious program that's on television. You can hear all about God—and yet never really experience Him for yourself.

Now don't misunderstand. I'm not saying a person who does all this hearing is not a Christian. Job was a longtime believer—and a strong believer—when his problems hit. But I am saying that it's possible to know God and yet not really see Him for yourself, not really see how He is working in your life.

That's why God sends you trials—so that you can see with your own eyes what you hear about God doing in other people's lives. God wants you to see Him for yourself. He doesn't just want you to know about what happened to Job or Noah or Daniel or Habakkuk. God wants you to be able to get up and give your own testimony: "I thought I had seen God, but now I have really seen Him for myself. Let me tell you what He did for me."

But you can't really see God in this sense until He puts you in a place that demands enduring patience. Job got a new view of God, but only in the midst of a great trial.

And notice Job's response when he saw God: "Therefore I retract, and I repent in dust and ashes" (42:6). As he saw God more fully, Job also got a new view of himself.

Now Job was the most spiritual man living at that time. If anyone was all right with God, it was Job. Even Job thought he was OK before God.

The prophet Isaiah thought he was fine, too—until he saw God in the temple. And Peter was fine as long as he was fishing. But when he saw Jesus, no longer was he OK. Likewise, when Job had an awesome revelation of God, he could only fall on his face and repent.

Until you read Job 42, you don't see the full reward of Job's patience. The fact that Job was patient during a painful trial is only the first part of the story. The rest of the story is that his patience paid off in a new view of God and a new view of himself.

Job learned that he needed God desperately and that God needed to increase in his life while Job decreased. That is the heart of Job's lesson.

Now the Bible says we can learn of God's compassion and mercy through Job, and we do see that in the way God restored Job's fortunes. And most people want to camp there, because they read that Job had more at the end of his life than he had at the start—and Job was a very wealthy man when this trial began.

But let me tell you something about all of Job's stuff. The reason he had more possessions and a bigger bank account is that, after Job got a new view of God and a new view of himself, God knew He could trust Job with more possessions.

Job's stuff came because of his spiritual life, not because he named it and claimed it. God is not in the "stuff" business. Someone who wants the kind of wealth Job had needs to be ready to endure as Job endured.

But most of us don't want that deal, do we? Comfort is more important to us than character, convenience more important than commitment, and cash more important than Christ. But God wants to switch that order around, and He will try us until we get things in proper perspective.

The Evidence of Patience

Now that we know something of the essence of patience, and have seen some great examples of patience, let's talk about the evidence of patience—how we can tell when it is operating in our lives.

The Bible gives us this important word about patience: "Above all, my brethren, do not swear, either by heaven or by earth or with any other oath; but let your yes be yes, and your no, no; so that you may not fall under judgment" (James 5:12).

This statement comes on the heels of a discussion about the trials God sends our way to teach us patience and help us grow into mature Christians He can use in mighty ways. But what do trials and patience have to do with making vows and swearing? The connection is more obvious than you might think.

Have you ever noticed that, when you're in the midst of a painful trial, you are tempted to make all kinds of promises you don't mean? Do you find yourself praying, "Lord, if You'll get me out of this mess, I'll serve You the rest of my life" or "Lord, if You'll raise me up from this sickbed, I'll go anywhere You say."

Now there is nothing wrong with making commitments to God. But "foxhole" promises usually don't stick. Almost every soldier getting shot at has made God a rash promise. If God held you and me to all the promises we have made, I wouldn't be here to write this book and you probably wouldn't be here to read it.

James says that if you are exercising godly patience in your trial, you won't be making all kinds of rash vows because you won't be so impatient to get this thing over with.

Jesus also said special vows aren't necessary for those whose word is trustworthy. He wasn't referring to oaths like those you make in a courtroom before testifying (although some people apply it that way), and neither was James. Jesus' focus, and that of James, is on our everyday conversation.

One problem with making oaths, especially when you invoke God's name or swear by heaven, His throne, is that you are trying to obligate God to do things He may feel no obligation to perform. When you swear by heaven, you are out of bounds because you have no authority there.

So you say, "Well, I'll swear by the earth." But the earth was created by God, it's His footstool, and you can't make things happen down here either.

Jesus told the leaders of His day not even to swear by themselves, because human beings don't have control over their own bodies, much less anything else. The point? Don't say anything that God can't or won't back up.

Peter got in trouble making a rash vow: "Even though all may fall away because of You, I will never fall away" (Matt. 26:33). Peter was serious. He was sincere. But he made a vow he was not qualified to make. Not only did Peter break his oath and deny Jesus, but he used another form of oath-taking when he cursed and swore and said he never knew Jesus.

Do you know why Peter cursed? To add emphasis to his lie.

That's why people who regularly use profanity to punctuate their speech can't be trusted. The same warning applies to the person who is telling you something and has to add, "I swear to God" or "I swear it's the truth." If a person is speaking the truth, why does he have to add profanity to his words?

If you are a person of integrity, you don't need to add anything to give your words more weight. That's what Jesus meant when He said, "Let your statement be, 'Yes, yes' or 'No, no'" (Matt. 5:37). James picked up on Jesus' teaching.

When you are experiencing a trial, that is not the time to start making worthless, impatient promises to God. And it's definitely not the time to curse your circumstances, the people around you, or your bad luck. God does want you to use words (as we'll see in the next chapter). He does want you to pray.

When you squeeze a lemon or any piece of fruit, what do you get? You get whatever is inside. And when you squeeze a Christian by putting him or her in a trying situation, guess what you get? Whatever is inside.

When God squeezes a Christian, He wants to see what comes out. Does worship come out? What about prayer or praise? This is why the Bible tells you to strengthen your heart, so that when you are in the squeeze of a trial, what comes out is the righteousness you have built up inside.

The Rewards of Patience

I want to close with what I hope is a very encouraging word for you: Godly patience brings great reward.

The Reward of a Full Harvest

Jesus wasn't in Bethany when He got word that His friend Lazarus was sick, and He waited two days before going to the village. He arrived after Lazarus had died and been buried. Understandably, Mary and Martha wondered why in the world He had not come earlier and saved their brother, sparing the family a painful trial of heartache and loss. But Jesus had delayed His coming on purpose.

Do you ever feel as if you are about to die in a trial—and yet God has delayed His coming to you? You need to know that His occasional delays are always for a greater purpose. He wants us to develop patience, and when He doesn't come right away, we (like Mary and Martha) have no choice but to wait.

God may delay His arrival—He may leave us in our trial longer than we think is necessary—to help us develop patience. But here's the payoff, the reward for patience. The longer God leaves you in a trial when you are doing the best you can to be faithful, the greater the reward will be at the end.

In other words, borrowing from our earlier farming analogy, the longer the spiritual "growing season," the greater the harvest at the end.

You see, if God bails you out of your trial too soon, the spiritual fruit He is growing in you will be underdeveloped. He knows just the right amount of time required to produce the greatest harvest. You don't want God to come too soon because the fruit won't be ripe.

A popular bumper sticker reads, "When the going gets tough, the tough go shopping." That's what a lot of Christians do. When the going gets tough, they say, "Let me out of here. Take me to the mall. Let me get this trial off my mind."

What we need to do when the going gets tough is go to our knees and say, "Lord, I'm waiting on You because I want the harvest of patience You are producing in my soul. I'm not going to make rash promises and swear and curse. I'm going to strengthen my heart so that what comes out of my mouth and heart honors You."

You may say, "But, Tony, I don't know what to do. I'm trying to hang in there, trying to wait for the Lord. But I'm running out of strength." God has something good for you.

The Reward of New Strength

Isaiah 40 is a prophecy about the Israelites returning from exile. The Jews were on their way back home, but they didn't know how they were going to make the long trip. So they were saying, "My way is hidden from the LORD, and the justice due me escapes the notice of my God" (v. 27).

But the prophet answers, "Do you not know? Have you not heard? The Everlasting God, the LORD, the Creator of the ends of the earth does not become weary or tired. His understanding is inscrutable" (v. 28).

Here's what this great, powerful, limitless, beyond-our-understanding God does for those who wait patiently for Him:

> He gives strength to the weary,
> And to him who lacks might He increases power.
> Though youths grow weary and tired,
> And vigorous young men stumble badly,
> Yet those who wait for the LORD will gain new strength;
> They will mount up with wings like eagles,
> They will run and not get tired,
> They will walk and not become weary. (vv. 29–31)

These words are sweet! God offers three levels of help for those who look to Him and wait for Him. I call them His intervention, His interaction, and His inner action.

Eagles' wings represent God's intervention, those times when He swoops down to supernaturally intervene in your circumstances and bear you up, the way a mother eagle bears her babies on her wings. Eagles' wings may bring you the job you need, the mate you've been praying for, or the deliverance you seek.

When God runs with you so that you don't get tired, that's His interaction. You're running along, wondering where this strength is coming from. Maybe you're running the race of the Christian life as a single person, and you're doing fine. God is running with you, talking with you along the way, saying, "Keep going. You're going to make it."

But there are other times when you're tired. You can't run anymore. Well, God has something for you, too. He will walk with you so that you do not become weary.

This is God's inner action, in which He comes to your spirit, puts His arm around you and says, "I know you're tired. Let's just walk. You've been running for Jesus a long time. Let's just walk for a while."

He builds up your inner strength even when you are weak on the outside. God becomes your spiritual pacemaker, sustaining your strength even though your heart is weak.

Whatever your need may be, in each case God brings new strength. So if you are in a trial right now, be patient. Wait for the Lord, and He will renew your strength. And when the trial is over, you'll see how far He's brought you along the path toward being a perfect Christian.

Test Your Perfection I.Q.

- The essence of patience is doing what you're supposed to do—
sowing the seed and strengthening your spiritual life—while you
wait without complaint for God to send the rain that will produce
the growth. How well do you tend to do on each count? Which
statement best reflects the kind of patience you have in the midst
of trial, or where do you fall in between?

—*Be productive.*
Do what God commands and expects. Sow seed so that when the
rains of trial come, spiritual growth will result. On this scale, "1"
is "I can't find the seed, and I'm not even gonna look," and "10"
is "I've been plowing, sowing, weeding, tending, and it's a full-
time job!"

1 2 3 4 5 6 7 8 9 10

—*Strengthen your heart.*
You need to strengthen yourself spiritually to handle the pressure
of trials. On this scale, "1" is "Strengthen my heart? I can hardly
get out of bed in the morning!" and "10" is "Sitting at Jesus'
feet—there's no better place to be as the fires rage around me."

1 2 3 4 5 6 7 8 9 10

—*Don't complain.*
Instead of complaining about the people and circumstances God
has placed around you, ask Him to give you patience. No matter
what you're going through right now, you can find something to
give thanks for if you look for it. On this scale, "1" is "Why me,
Lord? What did I do to deserve this mess?" and "10" is "I know
God is up to something good in my life—and I'm very grateful!"

1 2 3 4 5 6 7 8 9 10

- Consider the experiences of Job; Mary and Martha when Lazarus died; and the people of Israel returning from exile. What are three rewards of patience? Give yourself three points for each answer.

    1.

    2.

    3.

May these truths keep you cultivating patience in your life!

Total Points _____

Chapter 14

How to Know the Power of Prayer

So how are you doing in your journey toward the perfect Christian life? We've covered a lot of ground, but we're almost finished. Hang in there because—as you'll see here—if you can begin to master the discipline of prayer, your spiritual life will soar.

Now we Christians love to talk about prayer. We love to hear people tell about answered prayer. We thrill to the stories of great Christians from the past who had unbelievable prayer lives and saw God do unbelievable things. We love everything about prayer—except the actual discipline of praying.

Why do I say that? Because it is estimated that most Christians pray three to five minutes a day. Take out the mealtime prayers, and that amount probably goes down to even less time.

If you want to know how far you need to go in your prayer life, let me suggest this test. Compare the time you spend complaining to the time you spend praying. Or compare the time you spend talking to people about other people to the time you spend talking to God about other people. Do you now have a pretty good idea where you are in your prayer life?

We all need to get better, a lot better, in prayer. One reason is that God has so ordered His world that there are many things He will not do in the life of the Christian apart from prayer. Let's see what a powerful and much-debated passage of Scripture has to say about prayer.

The Priority of Prayer

First, we need to acknowledge the priority of prayer in the life of a believer. James asks, "Is anyone among you suffering? Let him pray" (5:13). Prayer is to be the first course of action.

The word *suffering* here is key to understanding this verse as well as what will follow. The Greek word can refer to any kind of affliction: physical, emotional, circumstantial, financial, familial, or any other category you can name. But the specific context here is the kind of suffering that comes with the trials God takes us through to mature our faith.

Notice the straightforward simplicity of the command. If you are hurting in any way, you ought to pray. Prayer ought to be the priority, the action you take first instead of last.

Prayer Accesses Grace

Prayer is the priority because of its power. And prayer is powerful because it is intimate communication with the Almighty God. When you pray, you enter into God's presence, and when you do that, you gain access to His grace.

If you are suffering under a trial, you need grace. Why? Because the problem will not necessarily go away just because you pray. In fact, if the situation is a trial sent from God, it will not end until God is finished teaching you the lesson He wants you to learn.

Prayer is not a magic wand to wave over your problems to make them magically disappear. No, prayer is your link to God's immeasurable store of grace that will enable you to deal with any problem, and that connection with your heavenly Father is much better than a mere change of circumstances.

The Bible reports that God's throne is characterized by grace, and He invites us to come for grace "to help in time of need" (Heb. 4:16). When Paul was wrestling with his "thorn in the flesh" (2 Cor. 12:7), he asked God to remove it because it was so painful. But God said no. The Lord wanted Paul to have a lesson in humility and dependence on Him because of the great spiritual privileges Paul had been given. God refused Paul's request, but gave him something better: the all-sufficient grace of providing His strength in Paul's weakness. Paul's response was, "Keep the thorn!"

Unlike Paul, some of us are mad at God because He hasn't taken away our affliction. But the question is "Have we tapped into the grace God makes available to us?"

I don't know what trial you're facing right now, but I can tell you that sufficient, even abundant grace is available to you. You'll find it at God's throne, and you gain access to the throne through prayer. That's a promise from Scripture: God gives "greater grace" to those who humble themselves and pray (James 4:6).

Prayer Leads to Praise

Right on the heels of this call to pray comes the question: "Is anyone cheerful? Let him sing praises" (James 5:13). What better reason for cheerfulness than answered prayer. So when God answers prayer and the good times come, then praise Him for delivering you!

Notice that the command to sing praises is linked to the command to pray because praise (like prayer) brings us into God's presence and puts us in intimate communication with Him.

You see, whether we're experiencing suffering or good times, both come from God. And since that's true, we ought to be praying or praising and therefore in touch with God all the time.

If you want to see this dynamic in action, read the Psalms. David is constantly moving back and forth between making petitions for help and offering soaring praise for help given. Why? Because that's the way life flows. Reasons for prayer and reasons for praise compel us to maintain the constant communication with God that we need.

When you seek God in days of darkness, He gives you songs for the long night. The story of Paul and Silas in jail at Philippi shows us this link between prayer and praise in a dramatic way.

These guys had been beaten. They were in the middle of a terrible trial. But they prayed and sang praises through the night (see Acts 16:25), and God delivered them.

Why is it, then, that you and I don't pray more if prayer is supposed to be our priority? Is it because we don't care enough about being in communion with our Lord? Is the problem that we haven't heard enough sermons on prayer?

No, I believe most of us already know we ought to pray more—and most of us really want to pray. But we don't pray because we don't plan to pray.

Plan to Pray

Let me make a blanket statement: If you don't plan to pray, chances are you won't pray. It's as simple as that.

One reason you won't pray without an intentional plan is that Satan will make sure you stay too busy to pray. Now he doesn't mind if you shoot up a little "quickie" over dinner, or say, "Now I lay me down to sleep" at bedtime. What the devil does not want is for you to cultivate a life of prayer that puts you in intimate communication with God.

I hope you don't think prayer is a spur-of-the-moment, whenever-the-Spirit-moves-you conversation with God. Now of course you can pray spontaneously. But approaching prayer as something you just sort of drift into is like getting up one morning and suddenly deciding you want to take two weeks off and leave on vacation that afternoon.

Do that, and you will be in for a forgettable vacation. Why? Because you were not in contact with your boss to request the time off. You were not in contact with anyone for your transportation or reservations. You were not in contact with family members to let them know you're coming.

A trip to Disneyland to visit Mickey Mouse takes planning. How much more should we plan to visit with the God of heaven? So let me ask you, Do you have a prayer plan? If not, make one!

As I write this, my son Anthony is away at college in another state. We have a toll-free 800 telephone number that allows him to call anytime.

Like a lot of college students, Anthony often calls either when he needs money or when he knows his grades are coming home in the mail and he hasn't done too much studying that semester. But he also calls when something good or exciting happens.

But wouldn't it be foolish for Anthony to be in a crisis and not pick up the phone to make a call he doesn't have to pay for to somebody who loves him and has only his best interests at heart?

God has given you your own toll-free number called prayer, and it's never busy. The problem with too many of us is that we hardly ever pick up the phone and call. We must plan to pray. So don't throw in the towel before you have thrown up the prayer.

The People of Prayer

A second issue in prayer is what we might call the people of prayer. God's Word tells us, "Is anyone among you sick? Let him call for the elders of the church, and let them pray over him, anointing him with oil in the name of the Lord" (James 5:14). This verse refers to two people or groups of people.

The Sufferer

The first person is the one who needs prayer. James describes this person as "sick."

Again, we need to understand what the original language of Scripture is saying here. The word *sick* means "weak." It can refer to all kinds of weakness, and the Bible uses the word in various ways.

The most obvious form of sickness or weakness is physical illness or pain. But there are other kinds of sickness. For example, we say things like, "I'm sick of being broke," or "I'm sick to death of this job." You're referring to a situation that is beating you down and making you feel weak. Perhaps that situation is the trial you're currently facing and the suffering it's causing you.

But the Bible is not talking about minor inconveniences. It's talking about those things that weigh you down and beat you down until, in your weakness, your knees are buckling. If you are in that situation, you need help to stand. You need prayer, and it's time to call on the church for help.

The Leaders of the Church

Now comes the controversial portion of this passage. But I propose that if we unpack what the Word is saying, a lot of the controversial questions will take care of themselves.

The Bible clearly teaches that a hurting believer who needs the ministry of prayer is to call for the elders of the church, the spiritual leaders of his or her congregation. Not all churches call their leaders "elders," of course. But the idea is to call on those who give the church spiritual guidance.

When you're feeling weak and beaten down, you may not feel you are getting through to God. You may even feel too weak to pray effectively. Or you may just need the ministry of the body to help you deal with your need. So you ask the elders to pray for you.

Now let me say something at this point that I believe needs to be said. In our age of "media religion," a lot of people are offering to pray for Christians who need the ministry of collective prayer.

I'm thinking of the so-called faith healer who wants to send you a blessed handkerchief for your donation. Or the guy who will send you water from the Jordan River for a contribution.

But Scripture says that when we are in need, we are to go to the spiritual leaders of the local church. God has ordained the local church to minister to the needs of His body. So the spiritual leaders, representing the church's authority and ministry, are the ones who are to go to you when you need support and help you pray about your weakness.

This passage also says that the elders are to anoint the person with oil. Many people think that the ceremony somehow gives the elders special power to heal the person of a physical illness. Let me make several observations about this.

First, God can heal anytime, anywhere, and by any means He chooses. He may sovereignly decide to heal a person who is obeying this instruction. But James is not talking about some magical healing service that is supposed to work every time. Furthermore, he was referring to the common, everyday oil used in that day.

This oil was used for refreshment and for grooming, as when Jesus told the Pharisees to anoint themselves so they would not appear to be fasting. It also had a medicinal use: The Good Samaritan poured oil on the beaten man's wounds.

Since there were no hospitals in those days, people had to use what was available, so they used oil much like our grandmothers used castor oil. If you remember that stuff, you know that Grandma used it for whatever ailed you: headache, backache, cough, cold, sniffles. Whatever the symptom, get the castor oil! The oil of Jesus' day was the same kind of all-purpose product.

Now here's the real issue. Does James mean that the elders need to go to the homes of believers with a jar of oil for anointing? I don't think that's the real meaning behind this phrase. Let me explain.

To anoint a person with oil was to provide refreshment and restoration. Oil was a tangible means of bringing soothing relief to a sore muscle or a wound. So I believe that, along with their prayers, the elders are to minister tangible encouragement, assistance, and refreshment to the person who is weak.

And here's how I believe this works. A believer who is struggling with a weakness of some kind calls on the church's spiritual leaders. They come and pray, but in the process of ministering they also learn what the church can do tangibly to alleviate the struggling person's suffering.

In other words, I believe that the anointing oil is a symbol of the body of Christ in action, ministering to the needs of a member who is suffering.

Now if someone in my church asks me to anoint him or her with real oil, I will do that. In Scripture, oil was a symbol of God's choice and His blessing, as when the Israelites anointed priests when they were ordained and kings when they were crowned.

But the anointing in James 5:14 is a symbol of the church coming alongside to bear up a member who is weak, providing whatever practical assistance is needed.

Psalm 23 offers an example of this symbolic reference to anointing oil. David said of God, "Thou hast anointed my head with oil" (v. 5). David has in mind a shepherd pouring oil on a wounded sheep.

Now God didn't literally anoint David's head with oil. What God did was come down to encourage and refresh David in the midst of his suffering. God anointed David with the oil of encouragement He brought to the king.

Likewise, the elders of the church are to go and pray for a weak member, providing along with prayers any practical encouragement and tangible help the hurting person needs. This assistance is the refreshment and comfort God calls the church to provide.

And this encouragement is to be offered "in the name of the Lord" (James 5:14). This instruction does not mean repeating the name of Jesus as if it were a magical incantation. When the Bible talks about a name, it is pointing to the person behind the name. After all, the person behind a name gives significance to that name.

So to anoint someone in the name of the Lord Jesus is to identify with Him and stand in His authority with full access to the throne of heaven. In fact, it is because of Jesus that we are able to approach the throne of God and receive the grace we need—in this case, the answer to our prayer.

Clearly it's foolish for you and me *not* to pray, and *not* to call on the church to help when we are struggling. It's like trying to push a bus out of a ditch all by yourself when Clark Kent is sitting on the bus. You're not using the real power available in the situation. Anointings in the name of Jesus mean that you have access to a power infinitely bigger than your own.

The Promise of Prayer

When you give prayer its proper priority in your life and have the people God has designated praying for your need, the Bible makes this great promise: "And the prayer offered in faith will restore the one who is sick [weak]" (James 5:15).

The Promise of Restoration

As I said above, some people want to apply and even limit this promise to physical healing. I see several problems with this.

First, if this passage were referring only to physical healing, every time a believer got sick, all we would have to do is have the elders go over with a vial of oil and the person would be healed. But life doesn't work that way, partly because of what I'll say next in my second objection to this limited interpretation.

This objection has to do with a reality we see throughout Scripture, which is that God—in His sovereignty—sometimes allows sickness in the lives of His people. Our old friend Job is a prime illustration of that fact. Physical healing is not always the will of God. So when you see Christians suffering physically, you may not be seeing a spiritual problem at all, but the outworking of God's sovereign and loving plan.

The promise is that the prayer of faith (which we will discuss next) will restore the one who is weak or weary. This restoration comes with the divine refreshment and encouragement provided by the elders ministering in the Lord's name.

Many of us can endure a lot if we can just have some encouragement along the way. And that's exactly what the church is designed to provide—a ministry of encouragement to the members of Christ's body.

Now the church can't solve all your problems, but it can help you by praying for you and bringing you godly encouragement. The Lord will use this refreshment in the weak person's life to "raise him up" (v. 15) from whatever it is that has beaten him down and caused his weakness.

The Prayer of Faith

But what exactly is "the prayer offered in faith"? John says it is prayer offered "according to [God's] will" (1 John 5:14).

In other words, the prayer of faith is prayer that is confident of God's will. In the case before us, it is not God's will for you or any other believer to be miserable and mystified in the midst of your trials.

How do I know this is not God's will? Because the Bible tells us what God's will is in this situation. We are commanded to "consider it all joy . . . when you encounter various trials" (James 1:2). How can we be joyful? Because we know that God is using our trials to perfect our faith (see 1:3).

Even if you're in a serious trial, God's will for you is to be joyful and informed instead of miserable and mystified. When you and the spiritual leaders of your church pray for you to know joy and encouragement, you are offering prayer in faith.

Mark 2:1–12 is a wonderful example of this ministry in action. Remember the sick man in Capernaum who was lowered through a roof by four of his friends so they could get him to Jesus?

This man was too weak to get to Jesus by himself, so the other men went to him, lifted his pallet, and carried him to the house where Jesus was teaching. Then they tore a hole in the roof, put ropes under his pallet, and lowered him down right in front of the Lord.

Notice what the Bible says next: "And Jesus seeing *their* faith said to the paralytic, 'My son, your sins are forgiven'" (Mark 2:5, emphasis added).

Did you get that? Jesus wasn't only looking at the weak man's faith, but at the faith of his friends. Responding to the collective faith of these men, He forgave the sick man and also healed him. What a picture of the church in action!

Now you may be reading all of this and saying, "Tony, this is fine, but I'm not really all that weak right now. In fact, I'm feeling strong in the Lord."

Great! Then go and put a rope under the pallet of a brother or sister who is weak and suffering right now and help that person get to Jesus. And remember that one day you will be the one on the pallet who is too weary and weak to get to God by yourself. Hard times come to all of us, and we need each other.

So this prayer of faith is prayer that is confident of God's will. Such prayers can bring healing as well as forgiveness for any sins the hurting believer may have committed: "If he has committed sins, they will be forgiven him" (James 5:15). "If" tells us that not all sicknesses or other problems are the result of sin. And the Greek verb translated "committed sins" is in the perfect tense, which signifies a past action with lasting results.

In other words, one reason a believer may be weak or sick or weary is because of that person's sinful lifestyle. In such a case, the prayer of faith only comes into effect if the sinning Christian is willing to confess and deal with the sin involved.

If sin is at the root of the problem and the believer comes clean about it before the elders who are present, the promise is that God will forgive the sin and remove the weariness resulting from the sin.

But if a Christian is not willing to confront the sin in his or her life, that person doesn't need to call for the elders because they can't do anything in a case like that. Sin always blocks our access to Jesus Christ and the grace He offers.

Paul said some believers in Corinth were suffering physical sickness because of their gross sin in abusing the Lord's Supper. Some had even died prematurely for their repeated sin. If you harbor sin, expect to be weak. But know, too, that once you deal with it, the weariness will be lifted.

All we have said about prayer so far means that God will meet you in your struggle. While He may or may not bring that struggle to an end, depending upon His purposes for you, He will strengthen you by His grace and give you His peace in the midst of the hardship.

I'm reminded of the two artists who were asked to paint portraits of peace. The winner would get a large sum of money.

The first artist brought in his portrait to be judged, and it was magnificent. It was a picture of serenity, with the ocean kissing the horizon, the sun beginning to set, no movement on the water, and all the trees calm. The crowd applauded.

Then the second artist unveiled his portrait—and instantly, he was declared the winner. His portrait depicted not a picture of serenity and calm, but a thunderstorm, with lightning splitting the dark sky, the waves crashing, and the sun hidden behind fierce clouds. A picture of chaos covered the canvas.

But tucked in the corner of the scene was a rock with a cleft in the middle of it. And huddled in the cleft of the rock was a little bird, singing serenely.

Peace isn't always calmness and serenity. Sometimes peace is having God hold you in the cleft of His hand while the lightning of trial strikes and the days are dark. Peace is when God meets you at night and gives you a daytime experience.

Remember the man who was born blind and healed by Jesus? Jesus' disciples thought the man or his parents must have sinned, or else he wouldn't be blind. But Jesus said that nobody sinned. The man's blindness was so that "the works of God might be displayed in him" (John 9:3). The man was blind because God wanted to reveal His power.

Sometimes God allows negative things to happen so He can show you His power in a way you've never seen before. So go to God in your trial and pray, "God, show me what You want to show me. And accept my prayers and the prayers of the elders for Your peace and victory in these circumstances."

The Productivity of Prayer

This call to pray, praise, and be prayed for ends with a word about prayer: "Therefore, confess your sins to one another, and pray for one another, so that you may be healed. The effective prayer of a righteous man can accomplish much" (James 5:16).

Praying for Results

Now we have moved beyond the ministry of the elders to the wider fellowship of the saints in the church. We are to pray for one another, but we need to use common sense and discretion here.

Confessing your sins to one another does not mean you share your problem with everybody. Nor does it mean airing dirty laundry in front of the entire congregation. The idea is to search out spiritual people who, like the elders, have the ability to pray with faith in accordance with God's will. Don't go to carnal believers for prayer. They themselves need somebody to confess to! Instead, seek out people who know how to pray.

And why should we pray for one another? Because prayer works. It's productive. The word *effectual* is the root of the word *energy*. This is energized, focused, passionate praying, not the kind of quick, "lay me down to sleep" praying we mentioned earlier.

When children really want something, they don't just ask politely one time and then let it alone. They ask with energy—so much energy, in fact, that they wear us out. That's like energized praying. It accomplishes things.

What enables us to pray with energy? A right relationship with God, when our sin account is cleared. That's why we need to confess our sins. It's the prayer of the "righteous" man or woman that moves heaven.

I call this "gut praying." It's when you roll up your sleeves, latch onto God, and say like Jacob, "I will not let you go until you bless me" (Gen. 32:26).

I well remember the time that my associate pastor, Martin Hawkins, and I went to the hospital to visit a child who was hovering between life and death. Brother Hawkins and I removed our suit jackets, took off our ties, and got down on our knees. It was time for some gut praying.

King Hezekiah knew about gut praying that brings results. When he was told his illness was terminal, Hezekiah turned his face to the wall, wept, and cried out to God for mercy. He called on heaven, and God granted him fifteen more years (see 2 Kings 20:1–6).

A Biblical Example of Productive Prayer

Having declared that prayers by the righteous get results, the Bible does what it does so often, which is put flesh on its principles. Our example this time is the prophet Elijah:

> Elijah was a man with a nature like ours, and he prayed earnestly that it might not rain; and it did not rain on the earth for three years and six months. And he prayed again, and the sky poured rain, and the earth produced its fruit. (James 5:17–18)

I love this illustration, because it tells us we can pray with energy and power. We can pray as the prophets of old did.

You see, Elijah was not from Krypton. He was an ordinary man. We know Elijah was ordinary because Queen Jezebel ran him out of town after he had defeated the prophets of Baal in what is perhaps the greatest example of energized praying in the Bible. When a woman can run you out of town like that, you're an ordinary man!

So if you are simply a Christian in love with Jesus Christ, Elijah had nothing on you. He was ordinary, but he became super-ordinary in prayer. The phrase "prayed earnestly" (v. 17) literally means Elijah "prayed in praying." He didn't just pray, in other words. He got serious with this thing, and God answered by shutting off the rain for three-and-a-half years.

You say, "Tony, I want to pray with that kind of power!" So do I, and we can learn much from Elijah's prayer. But first, I need to set up the context of his prayer.

Israel was deep in sin. King Ahab and Queen Jezebel had turned the place into a nation of idol worshipers. God was ready to judge Israel, so Elijah got down on his knees and said, "Lord, Your people are not obeying You. So let Your people see Your power. Act upon Your word and shut up the heavens."

Do you know where Elijah got the idea to pray that God would shut off the rain? He got it from Deuteronomy 11:16–17. Moses had warned Israel that if they turned away from God and began worshiping idols, "He will shut up the heavens so that there will be no rain and the ground will not yield its fruit."

I want you to see that Elijah prayed *biblically*. He knew the Word. The reason you and I don't get more answers to our prayers is that we don't know God's Word well enough to know how to pray.

Let me give you an example. People will often quote Philippians 4:19 when they have a financial need: "My God shall supply all [my] needs according to His riches in glory in Christ Jesus."

That's a great verse, a wonderful promise. So how come more believers aren't seeing their needs met? Because they haven't read this verse in its context. The promise of verse 19 comes on the heels of verses 14–18, which tell us that the Philippians could expect God to meet their needs because they had been investing in the work of Christ even though they were poor.

If you just pray for God's financial blessing while ignoring the prerequisite for blessing, you're using God like a jack-in-the-box toy in which the little man has no choice but to pop out when you play his tune. God doesn't come because we play a tune. He comes because we know Him and know how to pray. Elijah prayed biblically, and he also prayed *specifically*. None of these vague "Lord, bless me today" prayers for Elijah. If you want God to answer prayer, give Him something to answer. Pray specifically.

A sister in the Lord once told me that she needed a car and was asking God to provide a blue and green car, since those were her favorite colors.

When she went car shopping, she found a green car that was just right for her. But it had no blue on it. She said, "Lord, I don't know if this is the car You have for me, but this is the car I want." As the salesman was showing the car to her, he opened the hood to show her the motor, and she shouted, "Glory!" The motor had been painted blue!

Some of us will never know whether we've heard from God because we pray so vaguely. Elijah did not just say, "Lord, show Ahab something powerful." He prayed for a specific demonstration of God's power.

Besides praying biblically and specifically, Elijah also prayed *humbly*. When it was time to pray for God to send rain again and end the drought, Elijah went up to Mount Carmel, crouched down low on the ground, and put his face between his knees to pray. Elijah humbled himself before God.

Now some of us can't physically do what Elijah did. He must have been a skinny guy with a high metabolism rate. But all of us can humble our hearts before God.

Next, Elijah prayed *persistently*. According to 1 Kings 18:43, Elijah prayed for rain seven times as he kept sending his servant to look for the rain clouds. Elijah did not pray once and then quit when God didn't answer immediately.

Finally, this ordinary man prayed *expectantly*. In fact, before Elijah ever prayed, when God told him it was time to end the drought, he told King Ahab to get out his umbrella and listen for "the sound of the roar of a heavy shower" (v. 41). And Ahab did what Elijah said because he knew this prophet was in contact with God.

Elijah's confident expectation that God would answer is also apparent in the routine he went through with his servant. Elijah prayed for rain and then sent the man to look for rain. The servant came back and reported, "No rain yet."

So Elijah prayed again, sent his servant out to look again, and got the same report. This happened six times, but the seventh time the servant came back and said, "A cloud as small as a man's hand is coming up from the sea" (v. 44).

Elijah said, "That's it. A storm is coming. Ahab, get out of here before your chariot gets bogged down in the mud!" It hadn't rained yet, but Elijah was so expectant that he got everybody ready for a cloudburst.

Praying with Power

It's wonderful to read the promises of God concerning prayer. And it's exciting to read about people like Elijah who knew how to move heaven with their prayers. But how can we learn to pray like that?

We can start by getting rid of our double-minded praying. We can stop trying to believe God and listen to the world at the same time. And we can start praying and not let go until God answers.

One night when the disciples were in a storm on the Sea of Galilee, Jesus came walking to them on the water. Peter said, "If it's You, Jesus, let me walk to You on the water" (see Matt. 14:28).

You know the story. Peter started out and did fine as long as he looked at Jesus. But when he began to look at the dark, stormy waves surrounding him, he began to sink.

If your prayer life is sinking beneath the waves of a stormy trial, if you feel like you're about to be engulfed by the waves, you're looking in the wrong direction.

Stop looking at your circumstances, stop complaining against other people, and look instead to Jesus. Peter cried out, "Lord, save me!" (v. 30). That was a great prayer: biblical, specific, humble, expectant. Jesus answered Peter's prayer—and He's waiting to hear from you.

If you want to read the temperature of your spiritual life, take a look at the thermostat setting on your prayer life.

Test Your Perfection I.Q.

- List three characteristics of Elijah's effectual prayers. Give yourself four points for each characteristic.

  1.

  2.

  3.

- Reasons for prayer and reasons for praise compel us to maintain the constant communication with God that we need.

—Where are you in your prayer life? On this scale, "1" is "Three to five minutes is a generous estimate of my prayer time! Sigh . . ." and "10" is "I'm praying at all times, praying without ceasing, and praying just as Elijah did!"
1 2 3 4 5 6 7 8 9 10

—Most of us don't pray because we don't plan to pray. On this scale, "1" is "Oh, I pray when the Spirit leads—and He seems to be pretty quiet!" and "10" is "I've made a commitment to pray, and I keep my daily appointments with God as conscientiously as I do my other appointments."
1 2 3 4 5 6 7 8 9 10

—Effective prayer is biblical, specific, humble, persistent, and expectant, offered by one whose sins have been forgiven. How do your prayers measure up when the storms of trial and the challenges of life come? On this scale, "1" is "Look how big those waves are, and I've never seen lightning fill the sky like that!" and

"10" is "Like Peter when he first stepped out of the boat, I'm keeping my eyes on Jesus and walking through the storm!"

1 2 3 4 5 6 7 8 9 10

Total Points _____

Chapter 15

How to Restore the Straying Believer

There is probably not a mother alive who has not warned her child about the danger of running into the street to chase a ball. And few are the parents who have not warned their teenagers about the danger of hanging out with the wrong crowd and going down the wrong road in the name of friendship and fun.

We parents do all of this warning and pleading and praying because we want our children to make good choices. We want our younger children to stop and think before they run into the street. We want our teenagers to make right choices so they won't defect from the faith and turn away from the Lord's "narrow road."

Likewise, God is a good Father who is vitally concerned about the road His children take. He knows that, in the midst of suffering and trials, we are sometimes tempted to stray from the path, to decide the Christian life isn't worth the pain. Or we allow serious, untreated sin to develop in our lives and throw us off.

Either way, the result is falling away, a defection from the faith. It even happens to people who were raised in the church. Their faith somehow fades away as they reach adulthood. Or they move away from home and go to college, which gives them opportunity to veer off the path they were raised to walk.

God knows that such defection is a possibility for believers, because we are still sinful, imperfect Christians. He loves us with the perfect love only the perfect Father can give—but because He is also a good Father, He will not simply sit by and watch His children ship-wreck their lives.

Therefore, the Bible contains several very serious warnings to those who stray from God's truth and His ways. But the Word also urges faithful brothers and sisters to draw the erring believer back to the Lord and to restore him or her to fellowship and usefulness. This effort is an obligation of every believer who is following Jesus and pursuing spiritual perfection. Furthermore, you'll find that there are some tremendous promises to go around when a wanderer is brought back to the Lord.

With these truths to share, I can conclude this book with words of encouragement. First, I want to exhort you yourself to remain faithful. But you may discover at some point—if not right now—that you are one of those who need to turn back. If something in this chapter can help lead you back, that's great.

If you are currently walking faithfully with the Lord, my hope is that the message of this chapter will encourage you to reach out to a brother or sister around you who is going astray.

So even though we are going to discuss the problem of spiritual defection, what the saints before us called "backsliding," we will end on an upbeat note of restoration and renewal.

The Reality of Defection

The starting point is the acknowledgment that defection from the faith is always possible as long as we are in these sinful bodies and in this fallen world.

The Bible doesn't try to hide, much less deny the problem. Paul openly stated that people will defect from the faith during the last days. Without doubt, it's possible for a saint to stray. The word picture being drawn here in the Greek is that of a planet or other celestial body going off course, straying from its orbit.

Identifying the Defector

Now let's be clear right up front that if the defector is a true believer, the issue is not losing one's salvation.

It's true that defection may lead to physical death if not corrected. (John speaks of a "sin leading to death" [1 John 5:16].) But a straying believer is still saved. The Bible is addressing messed-up saints, people who have named Jesus as their Savior and Lord but, for whatever reasons, are not living as He commands.

Now some people may look like backsliders because they were once active in the church and no longer are. But if they were never "frontsliders"—that is, if they were never saved in the first place—when they act up, they're just acting like the lost sinners they are. Reaching them is an evangelism issue, not a restoration issue. The appearance of their faith was just that—an appearance rather than a commitment of the heart.

The biblical term for a backslider is a carnal or "fleshly" Christian (1 Cor. 3:3). In this spiritual state, a Christian knowingly and persistently lives to please and serve self rather than Christ. Such a person is regressing, not progressing, in the faith.

And these are the only two options: regression or progression. There is no such thing as static Christianity. A Christian cannot shift life into neutral or idle for a while. You can move forward, or you can slide backward. If you're not moving forward, you are automatically drifting back.

The Bible offers a number of examples of backsliding saints—some who were restored and others who were not. Peter comes to mind. His defection at Jesus' crucifixion was serious because Peter had made a vow never to forsake the Lord.

But we also have the record of Peter's restoration. Even before the denials actually happened, Jesus told Peter, "I have prayed for you, that your faith may not fail; and you, when once you have turned again, strengthen your brothers" (Luke 22:32). Peter was restored to fellowship with Jesus, and his Lord's prophecy was fulfilled as Peter played a key role in the early church.

Mapping the Road to Defection

One ministry of the local church is to identify the straying believer. We can better do that once we understand the process and more clearly see the definite downward road that the defector takes.

The first step on the downward road to spiritual defection is *spiritual neglect.* The writer of Hebrews said, "If the word spoken through angels proved unalterable, and every transgression and disobedience received a just recompense, how shall we escape if we neglect so great a salvation?" (Heb. 2:2–3).

You don't have to commit any horrible sins to be neglecting your faith. Neglect is characterized by a nonchalant attitude that just doesn't do much of anything good rather than bold, outright sin. Neglect is like the neighbor who lets his house and yard get rundown. He may be a fine person and a friendly neighbor, but he's neglectful.

A believer in this condition has started taking his or her salvation for granted—and that's not good, because our salvation is too great to be ignored.

Any neglected wife or husband can tell you what neglect feels like. A husband who is guilty of neglect may argue, "Hey, I work hard every day, I bring my money home, I'm not mistreating her." That's fine, but that's not all there is to a marriage.

The next step on the road to defection from the faith is *spiritual insensitivity.* In other words, sin doesn't seem as sinful as it used to be. This is a more serious stage.

In Hebrews we read this warning:

> Take care, brethren, lest there should be in any one of you an evil, unbelieving heart, in falling away from the living God. But encourage one another day after day, as long as it is still called "Today," lest any one of you be hardened by the deceitfulness of sin. (3:12–13)

When a brand-new Christian sins, he feels very, very bad. But sometimes—not always, thank the Lord—after a few more sins he only feels sort of bad. A few more sins, and he feels funny. Then, if the process isn't reversed, you start hearing things like, "No big deal. Everybody's doing it."

This kind of thing happens as calluses form on a believer's heart, and it becomes hardened by sin. Then sin can work its deceit because it doesn't look so sinful anymore.

The third step on the road to defection is *spiritual dullness.* The author of Hebrews said he had a lot more spiritual truth to explain to them, but they had a problem: "You have become dull of hearing" (Heb. 5:11).

The word *dull* here means mule-headed, stubborn. Now the believer is not just merely insensitive to sin. Instead, when someone tries to point it out or help, the defector stubbornly resists.

The writer goes on to tell the Hebrews that, although they should have been teaching spiritual truth to others by this time, they were still in kindergarten learning their ABCs. They had made no progress. Why? Because they stubbornly refused to grow.

This continued stubbornness leads to *spiritual drift.* At this point, the straying saint pulls away from the fellowship of believers. To counter that tendency, the Bible cautions: "Let us hold fast the confession of our hope without wavering . . . not forsaking our own assembling together, as is the habit of some" (Heb. 10:23, 25).

A person this far along the road to defection doesn't want to go to church. He or she doesn't want to be in an environment of accountability anymore. Drifters gradually disappear from the assembly of believers. They simply don't care to make the effort anymore.

The final step downward is *flagrant rebellion.* Hebrews 10 gives this stern warning:

> For if we go on sinning willfully after receiving the knowledge of the truth, there no longer remains a sacrifice for sins, but a certain terrifying expectation of judgment, and the fury of a fire which will consume the adversaries. (vv. 26–27)

In other words, when you get to this point, the blood of Christ will no longer protect you against God's temporal judgment. The same anger that God shows toward unbelievers will be unleashed on those who bring the blood of Christ into ridicule and shame—a very serious condition indeed. Although this believer is not at risk of losing his salvation, he is saying, "I know I'm sinning, and I know I'm trampling the blood of Christ that saved me—and I don't care. I'm going to live like this anyway."

That person is in danger of being taken out of here by the Lord if he persists in that attitude.

Our Responsibility to Defectors

Since spiritual defection is so serious, the natural tendency is for other Christians to pull back from the defector perhaps for fear of getting tainted.

But that's not what the Bible calls us to do: "My brethren, if any among you strays from the truth, and one turns him back, let him know that he who turns a sinner from the error of his way will save his soul from death, and will cover a multitude of sins" (James 5:19–20). Our responsibility to defectors is to try to turn them back to the Lord.

A Misunderstood Principle

Many believers don't like to hear about this responsibility. But to sit by and do nothing while a brother or sister strays from the truth and the Lord is like standing on the corner watching a child about to run out in front of a car and saying, "That's none of my business."

You wouldn't stand by and let a child run in front of a car if you had the power to stop the child. Why? Because the results of doing nothing are too terrible even to consider.

No father in his right mind would say of his teenager, "Well, if he wants to hang out with drug dealers, it's no business of mine." A father knows the high cost of hanging with the wrong crowd. He would do everything possible to turn his child around.

The prophet Elijah intervened on behalf of an entire nation of backsliders. Because the prophet was a faithful man of effectual prayer, God responded, and Elijah saw God bless Israel, a land that had been under the curse of idol worship and God's judgment in the form of severe drought.

To put this command another way, the church is supposed to be a spiritual hospital where the spiritually ill can be healed. But this healing work requires believers to care enough to become involved in one another's lives, to nurse one another back to spiritual health, and to get one another back on the road to spiritual perfection.

We've heard God's call to "confess your sins to one another, and pray for one another, so that you may be healed" (v. 16). This kind of ministry requires that we become others-centered rather than self-centered. One way you know your faith is others-centered and therefore Christlike and genuine is when you see a fellow believer straying from the truth and care enough to help turn that person back.

But what happens too often when we see someone in sin? We pick up the telephone: "Girrrrl, let me tell you what I just found out! Turn off that soap opera. I've got something better than that. Now, I'm only telling you this so you can pray about it, but . . ." Not only is that not helpful, that's sin.

The Risk of Involvement

So let's admit it. It's not easy to reach out to a straying brother or sister. There is a risk involved in such caring. The sinning believer may not let you or even want you to care. You may get your concern thrown back in your face with a curt, "Stay out of my life! Who asked you to get involved?"

Yes, there is a risk. But anytime you love someone, you take risks. And taking a risk is better than doing nothing.

The Reward of Involvement

We need to get involved because God commands us to. Consider, too, what a privilege it is to offer another the help you may someday need and see that brother or sister return to the flock. Furthermore, as you'll see, the rewards for both helper and the one helped are so rich when a straying believer responds.

A believer who is turned back from defection enjoys a restored relationship with God, and the rest of the body enjoys a restored relationship with that member.

But you cannot be a passive Christian and enjoy the rewards of seeing an erring brother or sister restored. You need to seek out the one who is going astray and bring him back before God has to discipline him—or, in the most severe cases, take that person home to heaven so he won't shame God's name any further.

The Restoration of the Defector

James 5:20 says the restoration of a spiritual defector saves him from death and covers a multitude of sins. First, what does the term *death* mean here?

Normally the term *spiritual death* is used of a lost person, an unbeliever who is experiencing the death that separates him from God forever.

But the Scripture also uses the term in another way, to describe the loss of fellowship that occurs between God and a straying believer. You may not think such a loss is all that serious, but let me show you otherwise.

The moment Adam and Eve sinned, they died spiritually. Their perfect, unbroken fellowship with God was shattered, and they had to leave the Garden of Eden.

When Adam and Eve lost that intimate fellowship, their whole world deteriorated and their lives fell apart. Adam had to fight thorns and thistles to make a living. Strife, self-centeredness, jealousy, and competition were all introduced into the marriage relationship. Their son Cain rose up in anger and killed his brother, Abel.

All this happened because Adam and Eve had entered the realm of spiritual death. They were no longer in fellowship with God. But God did make provision for their sin, and—to use the New Testament term—they died as saved people.

But whenever we experience a loss of fellowship with God (as Adam and Eve did), we also experience a deterioration in our life. God removes His divine protection.

It's true that, in His grace, God may not give you everything you deserve for your sin, but life still hits the skids when you stray from Him. Again and again I see people try everything to fix a serious problem when they haven't fixed it spiritually first—and that's always a tragedy.

If the root of your problem is a loss of fellowship with God due to a backslidden life, then only by reestablishing fellowship with God will your problem be fixed. Otherwise, He will see that the core spiritual problem breaks everything else you try to fix, too.

Saved from Physical Death

But death in James 5:20 and elsewhere has another meaning, and that is physical death. Some Christians die before their time because they have strayed so far from God and become so rebellious that God refuses to let them trample His Son's blood any longer.

The story of Ananias and Sapphira is a powerful illustration (Acts 5:1–11). This husband-and-wife team crossed God's line by lying to the Holy Spirit.

Theirs wasn't just a slip of the tongue. Ananias and Sapphira conspired ahead of time about their story, and God took them home. They had withheld funds needed by their destitute brothers and sisters. Their greed caused these folks further suffering, even as it dishonored the name of God and His fellowship.

The Blessing of Intervention

Now God says that you and I have the power to step between Him and a sinning believer who may be about to take an untimely trip to heaven.

One of the great illustrations of this ministry of intervention is Moses' prayer for Israel in Exodus 32. The people had crossed God's line by building the golden calf, and God was ready to destroy them. But Moses placed himself between God and the people, and in a prayer that reminded God of His promises and argued in defense of His reputation, pleaded for God to change His plan. As a result, God backed off from His wrath.

Likewise, when you and I stand between God and a Christian who is defecting, we can help prevent the full wrath of God from falling on that person and maybe even preserve his life. Clearly, this is not some casual situation. It can be life-or-death, like a mother who runs into the street to pull her child out of the path of an oncoming car.

A generation ago, many of us were raised in communities that operated with this kind of connection and accountability. An adult could correct a neighbor's child who was doing something wrong without worrying about being sued or attacked by the child's parents—or being blown away by the child.

The child's parent was glad for the help, because then the attitude was "Let's look out for each other because we live in the same neighborhood."

But that sense of community is long gone. God forbid that we lose it in the church! Let's obey what the Bible says and, if you see someone in your community straying from the truth, go after him.

Now we are to do so "in a spirit of gentleness" (Gal. 6:1). When a bone is broken, it needs to be set and mended, not damaged further.

Another reason to turn the defector back gently is that we may be there someday, and we'll want a gentle hand. Or perhaps we've already been there and know all too well that anyone can fall away. Besides, when we intervene with a gentle spirit, the blessing can be tremendous.

The Seriousness of Straying

One of the problems in the church today is that we often fail to take this matter of spiritual defection seriously enough. But given the broken families and scarred lives we see all around us, we really don't have any reason to treat lightly those who are falling away from the faith. But maybe part of the problem is we just don't draw close enough to other believers to see when somebody is going in the wrong direction.

I had dinner with an actor in California who had gone through a highly publicized divorce from his actress wife. They were both Christians, but in Hollywood they strayed, and that meant the death of their relationship and a lot of other things as well. His former wife was now remarried.

This man looked at me and said, "If I knew then what I know now, we would be happily married today. But nobody told me." What a shame.

It's a shame, too, that a young man is in prison because no godly man ever taught him what a man was supposed to be like. It's a tragedy when a young girl works the streets because nobody stopped her and said, "You don't have to lower yourself to this level. You are more valuable to God than you could ever imagine." This stuff of turning back a defector is serious business and part of the requirements you and I must meet in our pursuit of spiritual perfection.

Now you'd be petrified if your doctor came in with a diagnosis of cancer and then told you, "Take two aspirin and get plenty of rest." You'd be horrified if your house was on fire and the firefighters told you, "Don't worry. It will burn itself out after a while." You'd be shocked if a police officer watched a gang beating up an old man and said, "Well, boys will be boys."

Doctors, firefighters, and police officers who respond this way clearly don't know their jobs. And a Christian who sees a brother or sister straying and says, "That's not my concern" doesn't understand the job God has assigned us. You and I are to save endangered souls from death.

The Renewal of the Defector

Now for the best part. Along with saving a soul from death, our God-blessed and successful efforts to turn a straying Christian back to the truth "cover[s] a multitude of sins" (James 5:20).

The book of Proverbs says, "Hatred stirs up strife, but love covers all transgressions" (10:12). A lot of people quote the well-known phrase, "Love covers a multitude of sins," but it's another thing to put that truth into practice.

The Sacrifice of Love

The essence of Christianity is *agape* love, and the essence of *agape* love is giving oneself for the person who is loved. Biblical love simply does not exist without sacrifice.

Love in the Bible is not a giddy feeling or butterflies in the stomach. A husband who says he doesn't love his wife anymore is usually saying he doesn't feel about her the way he felt about her when they got married.

But love cannot be defined by how we feel. Biblical love is not discussing whether you feel what you felt on your honeymoon. Biblical love is measured by the sacrifice you are willing to make for the benefit of another. That's the model God Himself gives us: "God demonstrates His own love toward us, in that while we were yet sinners, Christ died for us" (Rom. 5:8). Love is measured by sacrifice.

I just wanted to set the record straight on the meaning of love before we apply it to the case of a straying saint.

The Covering of Sin

When a caring believer makes a sacrifice of love on behalf of a straying saint, something wonderful happens. A multitude of sins are covered.

Now don't misunderstand. Covering sin has absolutely nothing to do with condoning sin, ignoring it, or sweeping it under the rug. I'll explain what the Bible is talking about.

Let's say your Christian brother John has strayed. He has been deceived by sin and has wandered far away from God. He is out in the world, living like an unbeliever.

You see what is happening to John, and you realize you have several options when it comes to exercising your responsibility to help turn John back. First, you can simply look the other way. But we have learned that, if the spiritual defector goes far enough away from God and no one tries to stop him, his straying could cost him his life. So doing nothing about John's sin is a poor choice.

A second option is to spread the word about John, giving everyone who knows John the full lowdown on his sin. Instead of covering his sin, you could expose it to people who have no reason whatsoever to be part of the story.

The awfulness of gossip is that each of the twenty people you told will tell twenty more people, and soon you need a calculator to figure out how many people know that John is living in sin. No progress has been made toward solving the problem, but a lot of damage has been done.

Now let's talk about the third option, the option of biblical love that covers sin. Love provides a covering for sin so that John's straying—and word of his straying—go no further than absolutely necessary.

Remember Noah's drunkenness (Gen. 9:18–27)? The Bible says Noah became drunk and "uncovered himself inside his tent" (v. 21), a biblical phrase for various kinds of immoral conduct. Noah's sin is not specified, but the text says he was naked.

As Noah lay in his drunken stupor, his son Ham came into the tent, saw his father in that humiliating condition, and reported it to his brothers Shem and Japheth. Ham spread the word about Noah instead of covering his father up and removing his shame. The implication is that a disrespectful Ham mocked his father in some way, possibly even leering at Noah's nakedness.

While Ham may have been nonchalant and even mocking about his father's sin, Shem and Japheth were not. They hurriedly got a garment and walked in backwards to cover their father so they would not even see his nakedness. Their behavior was a sharp contrast to Ham's. Ham acted out of the wrong motive, but Shem and Japheth covered Noah's sin rather than exposing it. Theirs was an act of love.

Now let me clarify that your acting in love to cover sin may mean pain for the sinning saint. We're not saying it won't hurt to open that wound of sin and clean it out: It most likely will. But that hurt is the kind of hurt that heals.

Paul told the Corinthians, "Though I caused you sorrow by my letter, I do not regret it" (2 Cor. 7:8). In fact, Paul rejoiced. Why? Because he had made the Corinthians "sorrowful to the point of repentance" (v. 9). Sometimes you have to make other Christians sorrowful so they will repent. You have to hurt them to help heal them.

So when we reach out in sacrificial love to restore a straying brother or sister our efforts may mean pain for them. But our efforts also shield or hide the sin, not giving it unnecessary exposure that can only hurt the straying person in the wrong way.

This kind of love for the wanderer that risks rejection and often causes pain reflects the perfect love our Father shows to us as He seeks to make us more like Christ.

A Blessing for You

I want to close this book by pointing out something else wonderful about renewing a defector and acting in love to cover the sin: The blessing comes back upon you.

When God uses you to cover another believer's sin, you become a candidate for God's mercy to cover your sin. James 2:13 says,

"Judgment will be merciless to one who has shown no mercy; mercy triumphs over judgment." That's a great principle.

I learned the truth of this in reverse one time when I was growing up. My brother did something wrong and, like a typical sibling, I said, "I'm going to tell Dad." So I went and dutifully reported my brother's sin to my father.

Dad went in and spanked my brother. Then he called me to the bedroom and wore my backside out.

I was really confused at this point. So I asked my father, "Papa, why did you spank me, too?"

"I spanked you because before you came running to me to tell on your brother, you could have helped him fix the problem so there wouldn't have been anything to tell."

My father was right, of course. I wasn't loving my brother. Instead I was exposing his actions more than they needed to be exposed.

Now I can't give you any all-purpose, hard-and-fast rules on this matter of restoring a straying saint. Your action, timing, and approach will depend on the individual situation.

My point is simply that when a believer acts out of selfless biblical love to restore a brother or sister, sins are covered—not excused, not ignored, not exposed, but dealt with. And this covering rebounds for good in the life of the person who has the courage to take a risk and act in perfect biblical love.

A Closing Word

A husband and wife were fussing one day, really going at it. The wife said, "Why don't we write our complaints on a piece of paper and express exactly how we feel?"

Her husband agreed, so they each took a pencil and a piece of paper and started writing. The wife looked up at her husband for a minute and then started writing again. Pretty soon the husband did the same. Every time they looked at each other, they got angrier.

Finally, the wife finished her list and put down her pencil. But her husband kept on writing, and she got madder every minute, waiting for him to finish so they could exchange papers.

Just as his wife began to clench her fists and feel tears of anger well up in her eyes, he said, "OK, I'm finished."

So they exchanged papers, but as soon as the wife began reading her husband's sheet, she said, "Give me my paper back."

The reason was that, in spite of his anger, her husband had written on every line things like, "I love you," "I'm angry, but I love you," and "I don't want to be here right now, but I love you."

When his wife saw that much love coming out of her husband, his love covered a multitude of sins that had prompted the argument in the first place.

When believers can love one another like that—when you and I can love our brothers and sisters in the Lord like that—we will start covering a multitude of sins and seeing some straying saints turned back to the truth. The perfect Christian won't settle for anything less.

Test Your Perfection I.Q.

- What are some of the rewards of restoring the straying believer to fellowship with God and the community of faith? Give yourself four points for each answer.

  1.

  2.

  3.

- Spiritual defection is an issue for all Christians as individuals and as a church body.

—Any believer can stray. Be careful, because pride goes before a fall. Are you in need of restoration to greater intimacy with God and closer fellowship with believers? See where you may be on this downward road that spiritual defectors walk. On this scale, "1" is flagrant rebellion; "2," spiritual drifting; "3," spiritual dullness; "5," spiritual insensitivity; "6," spiritual neglect; and "10," spiritual health.

1 2 3 4 5 6 7 8 9 10

—The Bible calls the spiritually healthy to turn spiritual wanderers back to the Lord. How willing are you to assume this responsibility of reaching out to restore a straying believer? On this scale, "1" is "I don't want to get my hands dirty. Besides, it might be contagious!" and "10" is "I'm supposed to do for others what I may need them to do for me one day! Nothing can stop me from helping!"

1 2 3 4 5 6 7 8 9 10

—Restoring straying believers calls for us to be filled with God's agape love and willing to act as Jesus Himself would act. The essence of such love is giving oneself for the person who is loved. Biblical love simply does not exist without sacrifice. On this scale, "1" is "Don't bug me! I have my own problems" and "10" is "My Lord laid down His life for me, and I'm willing to lay down mine for His straying sheep."

1 2 3 4 5 6 7 8 9 10

Total Points _____

The Perfect Christian: Are You There Yet?

• Add together the 15 numbers you've written in the blanks labeled "Total Points." Then see where you fall in the scale below:

630   Congratulations! You're the first Christian ever to achieve perfection this side of heaven!

629–500 You're in the running for an early halo! But, beware! Pride goes before a fall!

499–370 Keep on keepin' on! Your eyes are on the Lord, and He will continue to bless your efforts!

369–240 God's power is made perfect in weakness! Call out to Him and He will answer!

239–0   Good thing you read this book! Now it would be a good idea to get on your knees, get into God's Word, and get into fellowship with mature believers.

No matter what your score, here is some encouraging truth:

> He who began a good work in you will perfect it until the day of Christ Jesus. . . . Work out your salvation with fear and trembling; for it is God who is at work in you, both to will and to work for His good pleasure. (Phil. 1:6; 2:12–13)

Remember that the perfect God who sets the perfect standard does not leave us to our feeble human resources to meet that standard. In the indwelling Holy Spirit, God becomes the very means by which we not only understand what He expects, but achieve it as well. The Spirit provides us with all the teaching, training, and divine assistance we need to fulfill God's requirements. At the same time, God offers us forgiveness and restoration when we fall short of the mark. Yet as long as we keep God's perfection before us as our goal, we are assured of making progress. God will honor us for making His perfection our passion and our goal.

Conclusion

The story is told of an ant who was dragging a thin piece of straw along the ground. He came to a crevice that posed a rather substantial challenge for one so small. How could the ant get himself across without leaving behind his straw?

Finally the ant came up with an ingenious plan. He laid the straw across the crevice and walked across it as a bridge to the other side. The burden he was carrying was also the solution to his problem.

You might conclude after reading this book that God has given you too great a burden to carry by calling you to perfection. After all, God is so holy, and we are so sinful. He never fails, yet we fail regularly. His demands are great, and our determination is so weak. How can we ever rise to the perfection our uncompromising God expects?

May I suggest that the answer lies within the problem? The God who burdens us with the demand also provides the ability, strength, direction, and support we need to grow into greater conformity to His character.

As we pursue God with all our being, not negotiating His parameters or reducing His standards, He will turn the very struggles of our lives into the roads and bridges we can walk across to discover a life of greater ministry, faithfulness, and growth.

At that point, temptations will become opportunities to demonstrate the truth that "greater is He who is in you than he who is in the world" (1 John 4:4). Problems will become platforms for spiritual performance at the highest levels. Setbacks will become springboards to spiritual maturity. Even sins will become circumstances that God can use to give us a clearer picture of the truth that without Him we can indeed do nothing (John 15:5).

This ought to be good news! The perfect God who sets the perfect standard does not leave us to our feeble human resources to meet that standard. In the indwelling Person of the Holy Spirit, God becomes the very means by which we not only realize what He expects but achieve it as well.

The Spirit provides us with all the teaching, training, and divine assistance we need to enable us to fulfill God's requirements. At the same time, He offers us forgiveness and restoration when we fall short of the mark.

Any football coach will tell you that his plays are designed to score touchdowns. He places the Xs and Os in an attempt to ensure his team's success and frustrate his opponent's efforts. On paper or a chalkboard, football plays are designed to work perfectly every time.

Of course, the plays don't always work perfectly on the field. Human flaws and limitations keep touchdowns to a minimum most of the time. But even if the play doesn't result in a score, because it has been designed to work perfectly a team can still make important progress such as making first downs or gaining big yardage. But unless the team strives for the goal line, no progress will be made at all.

God has given us a goal: His perfection. Our flaws and fumbles keep us from achieving that goal in this life. Satan's defensive maneuvers often interfere with our forward progress.

Yet as long as we keep God's perfection before us as our goal, we are assured of making progress: five yards here, ten yards there, and some big gainers along the way. Each day of our lives should be scripted for perfection, with the comforting knowledge that when the game is over and the final whistle blows, God will honor us for making His perfection our passion and our goal.

So be encouraged as you persevere toward perfection. Hold on to the unshakable confidence that Jude expressed when he wrote:

Now to Him who is able to keep you from stumbling, and to make you stand in the presence of His glory blameless with great joy, to the only God our Savior, through Jesus Christ our Lord, be glory, majesty, dominion and authority, before all time and now and forever. Amen. (Jude 24–25)

Scripture Index

Subject Index